METALINGUISTIC AWARENESS AND SECOND LANGUAGE ACQUISITION

Metalinguistic Awareness and Second Language Acquisition is the first book to present an in-depth overview of metalinguistic awareness as it relates to SLA. In this volume, Roehr-Brackin discusses metalinguistic awareness in the context of both child and adult language learning, and outlines the various methods that can be used to measure metalinguistic awareness. The author presents different approaches to metalinguistic awareness, including a cognitive-developmental perspective that explains how the concept relates to literacy, and an applied linguistics perspective that understands metalinguistic awareness as explicit or conscious knowledge about language. Roehr-Brackin explores the role of metalinguistic awareness in language education aimed at young learners, as well as in instructed adult SLA. This book is an excellent resource for those researching or taking courses in second language acquisition, bi- and multilingualism, and language teaching.

Karen Roehr-Brackin is Senior Lecturer in the Department of Language and Linguistics at the University of Essex, UK. She works in the area of second language acquisition. Her research interests include explicit and implicit knowledge and learning, as well as the role of individual learner differences such as language learning aptitude, working memory and cognitive/learning style in adult and child second language learning.

COGNITIVE SCIENCE AND SECOND LANGUAGE ACQUISITION SERIES

Peter Robinson, Series Editor

The *Cognitive Science and Second Language Acquisition Series* is designed to provide systematic and accessible coverage of the links between basic concepts and findings in cognitive science and second language acquisition (SLA). Titles in the series summarize issues and research in areas of cognitive science which have relevance to SLA, and when read in combination, provide a comprehensive overview of the conceptual and methodological intersects between these two fields. The series is a valuable reference for scholars who want to increase their knowledge of theoretical and operational definitions in cognitive science, and their applications to SLA. Its titles are ideal for graduate students and researchers in SLA, applied linguistics, cognitive psychology, educational psychology, and language education, and can also serve as textbooks for advanced courses in these fields.

Speech Production and Second Language Acquisition
Kormos

Cognitive Bases of Second Language Fluency
Segalowitz

Lexical Processing and Second Language Acquisition
Tokowicz

Second Language Sentence Processing
Juffs and Rodríguez

Metalinguistic Awareness and Second Language Acquisition
Roehr-Brackin

METALINGUISTIC AWARENESS AND SECOND LANGUAGE ACQUISITION

Karen Roehr-Brackin

NEW YORK AND LONDON

First published 2018
by Routledge
711 Third Avenue, New York, NY 10017

and by Routledge
2 Park Square, Milton Park, Abingdon, Oxon OX14 4RN

Routledge is an imprint of the Taylor & Francis Group, an informa business

© 2018 Taylor & Francis

The right of Karen Roehr-Brackin to be identified as author of this work has been asserted by her in accordance with sections 77 and 78 of the Copyright, Designs and Patents Act 1988.

All rights reserved. No part of this book may be reprinted or reproduced or utilised in any form or by any electronic, mechanical, or other means, now known or hereafter invented, including photocopying and recording, or in any information storage or retrieval system, without permission in writing from the publishers.

Trademark notice: Product or corporate names may be trademarks or registered trademarks, and are used only for identification and explanation without intent to infringe.

Every effort has been made to contact copyright-holders. Please advise the publisher of any errors or omissions, and these will be corrected in subsequent editions.

Library of Congress Cataloging in Publication Data
Names: Roehr-Brackin, Karen, 1968-
Title: Metalinguistic awareness and second language acquisition /
Karen Roehr-Brackin.
Description: New York, NY : Routledge, [2018] | Includes bibliographical references and index.
Identifiers: LCCN 2017057500 | ISBN 9781138958869 (hardback) |
ISBN 9781138958876 (pbk.) | ISBN 9781317338819 (web pdf) |
ISBN 9781317338796 (mobi/kindle) | ISBN 9781315661001 (ebk.)
Subjects: LCSH: Language awareness. | Metalanguage--Social aspects. |
Multilingualism--Social aspects. | Language and culture. | Second language acquisition. | Anthropological linguistics.
Classification: LCC P120.L34 R64 2018 | DDC 410.1--dc23
LC record available at https://lccn.loc.gov/2017057500

ISBN: 978-1-138-95886-9 (hbk)
ISBN: 978-1-138-95887-6 (pbk)
ISBN: 978-1-315-66100-1 (ebk)

Typeset in Bembo
by Taylor & Francis Books

To my parents, Ingrid and Helmut

CONTENTS

Series Editor's Preface   *ix*

1 Introduction   **1**
  1.1 Terminology and Definitions 1
  1.2 Outline of the Book 3

2 A Cognitive-Developmental Perspective on Metalinguistic Awareness   **5**
  2.1 Metalinguistic Awareness in Development 5
  2.2 Metalinguistic Awareness and Literacy 13
  2.3 Bialystok's Framework of Analysis and Control 20
  2.4 'Bilingual Advantage' Research 22
  2.5 A 'Bilingual Advantage' for L2 Learners? 33

3 Metalinguistic Awareness in Language Education   **42**
  3.1 Multilingualism and the 'M-Factor' 42
  3.2 Language Awareness 44
  3.3 Metalinguistic Awareness in the Primary-School Classroom 53

4 Metalinguistic Awareness as Explicit Knowledge and Learning: Theoretical Premises   **62**
  4.1 The Interface of Explicit and Implicit Knowledge 62
  4.2 Attention, Awareness and Metalinguistic Understanding 73
  4.3 Learning Difficulty 82
  4.4 Metalinguistic Awareness and Language Learning Aptitude 86

viii Contents

5 Metalinguistic Awareness as Explicit Knowledge and Learning: Empirical Evidence   **89**

    5.1 Effects of Explicit Learning and Teaching on L2 Knowledge and Use 89

    5.2 Relating Explicit Knowledge, L2 Achievement and Use 100

    5.3 The Role of Learner and Input Variables 106

6 Measuring Metalinguistic Awareness   **114**

    6.1 Tests and Self-Report as Measures of Explicit Knowledge 114

    6.2 Metalinguistic Awareness in Children and Low-Educated Adults 127

    6.3 Measures of Executive Function 132

7 Concluding Remarks   **134**

    7.1 Two Theoretical Perspectives 134

    7.2 Directions for Future Research 135

References   *137*

Index   *151*

SERIES EDITOR'S PREFACE

The Cognitive Science and Second Language Acquisition (CS&SLA) series is designed to provide accessible, and comprehensive coverage of the links between basic concepts, and findings, in cognitive science (CS) and second language acquisition (SLA) in a systematic way. Taken together, books in the series should combine to provide a comprehensive overview of the conceptual and methodological intersects between these two fields. This means the books in the series can be read alone, or (more profitably) in combination. The field of SLA is related to, but distinct from, linguistics, applied linguistics, cognitive psychology, and education. However, while a great many published book series address the link between SLA and educational concerns, SLA and linguistics, and SLA and applied linguistics, currently no series exists which explores the relationship between SLA and cognitive science. Research findings and theoretical constructs from cognitive science have become increasingly influential upon SLA research in recent years. Consequently there is great reason to think that future SLA research, and research into its educational applications, will be increasingly influenced by concerns addressed in CS and its subdisciplines. The books in the CS&SLA series are intended to facilitate this interdisciplinary understanding, and are grouped into four domains: (1) Knowledge Representation; (2) Cognitive Processing; (3) Language Development; and (4) Individual Differences.

The role of awareness in second language acquisition has been a major theoretical and pedagogic issue for over thirty years, and increasingly sophisticated methodologies and instrumentation are being used to advance empirical investigation of the extent to which awareness, at a variety of levels, is necessary for SLA, in instructed and naturalistic settings, and across populations of learners differing in age. In her book *Metalinguistic Awareness and Second Language Acquisition*, Karen Roehr-Brackin distinguishes two theoretical perspectives on the construct of metalinguistic awareness during SLA; the cognitive-developmental approach, and the approach distinguishing implicit from explicit learning, memory and knowledge. Research adopting one or another perspective is reviewed, and methods for measuring metalinguistic awareness are described and compared. The measurement issues and theoretical constructs Karen Roehr-Brackin describes are fundamental to current and future research into SLA and its cognitive underpinnings, and her book is an important and very welcome contribution to the CS&SLA series.

Peter Robinson
Series Editor

1

INTRODUCTION

1.1 Terminology and Definitions

The present volume is concerned with the role of metalinguistic awareness in second language acquisition (SLA). In the SLA literature, the adjective *metalinguistic* not only appears in combination with the noun *awareness*, but also in combination with *knowledge, ability, capacity* and *skill*, among others. Therefore, it is important to be clear about the meanings of these terms right from the beginning. It is possible to treat some of the terms just listed as synonymous, and indeed it is often difficult to make distinctions in practice. From a theoretical angle, however, precise definitions are both desirable and helpful because they enable us to formulate explanatory accounts and specify suitable measures for the properties described, as we shall see in later chapters.

Taking *metalinguistics* on its own, it has been suggested that it is "concerned with linguistic activity which focuses on language" (Gombert, 1992, p. 2), in the sense that attention is focused on language *as an object in its own right*. Accordingly, *metalinguistic development* can be defined as a growing awareness of certain properties of language and the ability to analyse linguistic input, that is, "to make the language forms the objects of focal attention and to look *at* language rather than *through* it to the intended meaning" (Cummins, 1987, p. 57, emphasis added).

Bialystok (2001) discusses the terms metalinguistic knowledge, ability and awareness in an attempt to identify the commonalities and distinctions characterising these concepts. She equates *metalinguistic knowledge* with knowledge about language. Metalinguistic knowledge is distinguished from linguistic knowledge by means of its greater level of generality; metalinguistic knowledge is considered broad and abstract in that it includes knowledge of general principles applicable to more

2 Introduction

than one language. It is noted, however, that such abstract knowledge becomes accessible to a speaker/learner through their knowledge of a specific language.

Metalinguistic ability is defined as "the capacity to use knowledge about language as opposed to the capacity to use language" (Bialystok, 2001, p. 124), and it can thus be regarded as synonymous with *metalinguistic capacity* and *metalinguistic skill*. Bialystok argues convincingly that in order to be a meaningful concept, metalinguistic ability has to be both distinct from and related to linguistic ability. Hence, metalinguistic ability is regarded as sufficiently unique to be detectable and distinguishable from linguistic ability, while at the same time it is accepted that the two types of ability have a common origin and can be related to each other. Finally, *metalinguistic awareness* can be defined in terms of attentional focus, since the term "implies that attention is actively focused on the domain of knowledge that describes the explicit properties of language" (Bialystok 2001, p. 127). Importantly, Bialystok favours a process-oriented, continuous view over binary, categorical divisions between constructs, so linguistic/cognitive processes are characterised as more or less metalinguistic rather than as either linguistic or metalinguistic.

In applied linguistics research concerned with SLA in instructed learners, researchers tend to conceptualise metalinguistic awareness in terms of *explicit knowledge about language*. In this research tradition, a categorical distinction between explicit knowledge on the one hand and implicit knowledge on the other hand is favoured, although the limitations of such a dichotomous view have been highlighted (Hulstijn, 2015; Sanz & Morgan-Short, 2005). Nevertheless, it remains common practice in this paradigm to distinguish between explicit and implicit knowledge, explicit and implicit memory, and explicit and implicit learning. There is relative consensus, at least with regard to the theoretical definitions of these constructs. Explicit knowledge about language refers to "the conscious awareness of what a language or language in general consists of and/or of the roles that it plays in human life"; in other words, "explicit knowledge is knowledge *about* language and *about* the uses to which language can be put" (R. Ellis, 2004, p. 229, emphasis in original). Explicit knowledge is knowledge an individual is consciously aware of, and it is potentially available for verbal report (R. Ellis, 2004). Explicit knowledge is represented declaratively (Hulstijn, 2005), subject to controlled processing and is considered symbolic in nature (R. Ellis et al., 2009). Implicit language knowledge, on the other hand, has directly opposing characteristics. It is tacit, intuitive and non-conscious, reflecting the speaker/learner's sensitivity to the statistical structure of learned material; it is knowledge an individual makes use of via automatic processing, but it is not subject to awareness and cannot be articulated (R. Ellis, 2004; R. Ellis et al., 2009).

Along similar lines, explicit and implicit memory refer to "memory of a past event with or without conscious awareness, respectively" (Hulstijn, 2005, p. 130). Put slightly more technically, explicit memory refers to "situations where recall involves a conscious process of remembering a prior episodic experience", while implicit memory refers to situations "where there is facilitation of the processing of a stimulus as a function of a recent encounter with the same stimulus but where the subject at no point has to consciously recall the prior event" (N. C. Ellis, 1994, pp. 38–39). Explicit long-term memory includes declarative facts, episodes (i.e. memories of experiences), and semantic memory, including vocabulary knowledge (Hulstijn, 2005). Finally, explicit learning describes situations "when the learner has online awareness, formulating and testing conscious hypotheses in the course of learning", while implicit learning "describes when learning takes place without these processes; it is an unconscious process of induction resulting in intuitive knowledge that exceeds what can be expressed by learners" (N. C. Ellis, 1994, pp. 38–39). Put more simply, then, explicit learning is learning with conscious awareness, whereas implicit learning is learning without conscious awareness of what is being learned (DeKeyser, 2003).

Throughout this book, L1 is used to refer to a speaker's first language or, in more traditional terms, a speaker's native language, while L2 is used to refer to any additional language(s) beyond the L1. The terms L2 learning and SLA are used as synonyms. L3, L4, Lx are used only when it is necessary to make a distinction between various additional languages. No principled conceptual distinction between bilingualism and L2 learning or trilingualism/multilingualism and L3/L4/Lx learning is attempted. Instead, these terms are used in a way that reflects the sources that are being referred to. By the same token, it is acknowledged that speakers may have more than one L1 as defined here.

1.2 Outline of the Book

Chapters 2 and 3 focus on research that conceptualises metalinguistic awareness as situated on a continuum, with knowledge and abilities being considered more or less (meta)linguistic in nature. Chapter 2 is concerned with a cognitive-developmental perspective on metalinguistic awareness and takes the emergence of metalinguistic abilities in children learning their L1 as its starting point. The relationship between the development of metalinguistic awareness and literacy skills is explained, and Bialystok's influential theoretical framework of analysis of (linguistic) knowledge and control of (linguistic) processing is introduced. The chapter includes a review of research into bilinguals' metalinguistic awareness, and the issue of potential cognitive advantages arising out of long-term bilingualism is considered. In addition, the question of whether L2 learners can expect to gain similar advantages is addressed. Chapter 3 takes a language-educational perspective and discusses the concept of multilingualism and possible advantages arising out of knowing and being able to use three or more languages. School-based initiatives aimed at fostering children's language awareness are highlighted, and research into the role of metalinguistic awareness in children's language learning at primary level is considered.

Chapters 4 and 5 focus on applied linguistics research that conceptualises metalinguistic awareness in terms of explicit knowledge about language and relies on a categorical theoretical distinction between explicit and implicit knowledge, memory, learning and teaching. Chapter 4 explores the theoretical assumptions of this approach and includes a discussion of the interface between explicit and implicit knowledge and processes as well as the cognitive mechanism of attention and the construct of conscious awareness. Explicit knowledge and learning are then discussed in relation to learning difficulty in SLA. The chapter concludes with an exploration of the theoretical connections between metalinguistic awareness and language learning aptitude. Chapter 5 is concerned with empirical evidence. Findings from experimental research into the impact of explicit learning and teaching on SLA are reviewed, and the relationship between learners' metalinguistic knowledge and their success in L2 learning is taken into consideration. Finally, findings pertaining to the interplay between explicit knowledge and learning on the one hand and individual difference variables such as learner beliefs and language learning aptitude on the other hand are presented.

Chapter 6 focuses on the measurement of metalinguistic awareness. It begins with a review of measures used in research taking an applied linguistics approach and conceptualising metalinguistic awareness in terms of explicit knowledge about language. The focus then shifts to measures used by researchers working in a cognitive-developmental approach who conceptualise metalinguistic awareness as situated on a continuum of analysis of knowledge and control of processing. The chapter concludes with a brief look at non-linguistic measures of executive function as the general cognitive component underlying control of linguistic processing. Finally, Chapter 7 offers concluding remarks which summarise key theoretical work and empirical findings to date and put forward suggestions for future research on metalinguistic awareness and SLA.

2

A COGNITIVE-DEVELOPMENTAL PERSPECTIVE ON METALINGUISTIC AWARENESS

2.1 Metalinguistic Awareness in Development

A monograph by Gombert (1992) comprises one of the most thorough and perhaps also most widely cited discussions of the development of metalinguistic awareness in children. In his work, Gombert is above all concerned with the notion of metalinguistic awareness itself rather than any connection of metalinguistic awareness with bilingualism or L2 learning, so the focus is firmly on L1. Gombert considers conscious awareness as a defining criterion of the concept of meta-linguistic awareness, with metalinguistic activity referring to reflection on language, its nature and its functions. The notion further encompasses the intentional monitoring of the processes of attention and selection during language processing, e.g. stopping to search for a word, or shifting one's attention from the content of language to the properties of language. Gombert also makes a distinction between declarative and procedural aspects of metalinguistic activity. In particular, meta-linguistic knowledge is seen as a pre-condition for any metalinguistic activity, since we cannot use knowledge we do not have. Metalinguistic capacities are regarded as an integral part of metacognition, with metacognition defined as "all knowledge which has as its object, or regulates any aspect of, any cognitive task" (Gombert, 1992, pp. 5–6). In short, metacognition is cognition about cognition (see also N. J. Anderson, 2008; Dunlosky, 1998; Flavell, 1979; Hacker, 1998; Hunt & H. Ellis, 2004). Metacognition is characterized by introspective awareness of cognitive states and their operations as well as the individual's ability to control and plan their thought processes. According to Gombert (1992), the set of meta-abilities that is available to an individual includes metalinguistic ability, meta-learning, or knowledge and control of the learning process, meta-attention, or the ability to pay attention voluntarily, social metacognition, or knowledge of the

6 A Cognitive-Developmental Perspective

cognitive processes at work in other people and their behavioural implications, and meta-memory, or the ability to control one's own memory. In summary, then, meta-learning is cognition about learning, meta-attention is cognition about attention, etc., and metalinguistic ability is cognition about language.

If metalinguistic activities are by definition performed consciously, their emergence presupposes that a child has the capacity for reflection and intentional self-monitoring. As the capacity for conscious reflection develops slowly and gradually as the child matures, Gombert makes a qualitative distinction between spontaneous, non-conscious behaviour such as self-repair, which he considers to be *epilinguistic*, and conscious knowledge intentionally applied in the context of reflective activity, which is *metalinguistic*. Epilinguistic behaviour is typically situated in a rich communicative context, while metalinguistic behaviour is possible with decontextualized tasks. In developmental terms, epilinguistic abilities precede metalinguistic abilities. It is accepted that the failure on the part of an individual to provide an explanation for their behaviour does not necessarily imply the absence of consciousness, but verbalisation certainly implies the presence of consciousness.

The development from epilinguistic to metalinguistic behaviour can be observed in all linguistic domains, though epilinguistic and subsequently meta-linguistic abilities emerge earlier in some domains than others. Metaphonological activities, for instance, are in evidence even in quite young children. Thus, at around ages 2–3, children start experimenting spontaneously with the morpho-phonological characteristics of language, e.g. in speech games and with rhymes. They might play with alliterative sound patterns and manipulate morphemes to invent new compounds, e.g. 'rainbrella' for 'umbrella' (Birdsong, 1989, p. 16). Between ages 3 and 5, the first instances of phonological segmentation ability appear, i.e. words can be segmented into syllables. Gombert (1992) considers all this to be evidence of epiphonological behaviour, that is, behaviour which is based on intuition rather than reflection. However, such epiphonological behaviour, or phonological sensitivity (Geudens, 2006), is regarded as a necessary precursor of metaphonological behaviour. From ages 6–7 onwards, children are able to count and then to segment phonemes – the first evidence of metaphonological behaviour proper, which is important for and coincides with learning to read and write in children receiving school education in an alphabetic language (see also Birdsong, 1989). Metasyntactic development can also be observed relatively early (Gombert, 1992). Episyntactic behaviour is evident in children's first intuitions about acceptability and their early self-corrections. These instances of behaviour are situation-specific and tied to particular utterances and their contexts, however, so they are not yet abstract or generalizable. As in the case of metaphonological development, episyntactic ability is seen as preceding metasyntactic ability. The latter emerges at ages 6–7, when children are first able to make seemingly rule-based acceptability judgements. Metasyntactic behaviour becomes useful and necessary through school education, especially in the context of explicit instruction and exercises drawing on grammatical rules as well as reading comprehension tasks.

Gombert notes that ages 6–7 appear to mark a critical transitional phase in children's metalinguistic development, with true metalinguistic behaviour in the sense of a child being able to use decontextualized knowledge about language becoming possible. Once children are able to separate words from their referents (see also Karmiloff & Karmiloff-Smith, 2002), i.e. once they grasp that words are essentially arbitrary labels for objects, actions, etc., the first appreciation of synonymy and simple metaphor appears, thus indicating the beginnings of metalexical or metasemantic behaviour. Conceptual understanding of metaphor and a full understanding of concepts such as 'word' or 'sentence' do not develop until later at around ages 10–12, however.

Metapragmatic awareness refers to an understanding of the use of language in different contexts and the ability to monitor messages for their referential adequacy in different contexts. Children's early and incidental adaptation of language to different contexts is considered as epipragmatic because their behaviour is still situation-specific at this stage. From around ages 6–7, metapragmatic behaviour proper that is indicative of reflection and monitoring is beginning to emerge, though. Children become increasingly aware of referential ambiguities and can take into account the characteristics of their interlocutor. Metapragmatic behaviour is established only gradually, however, and its development continues into adolescence.

At the level of connected discourse, Gombert argues that it is difficult to identify epitextual behaviour, i.e. behaviour that is based on intuition rather than reflection. Early metatextual behaviour refers to the ability to distinguish text from non-text, to identify contradictions and to note violations of prior knowledge. Children aged 8–9 begin to accept that a text can be summarised, but it is not until the ages of 9–10 that they can detect ambiguous anaphora or identify sentences in a paragraph that are thematically misplaced. From ages 12–13 onwards, children can define the notion of 'paragraph', and it is even later that they appreciate the hierarchy of information in a text. These metatextual activities are closely linked to schooling and are not normally implemented spontaneously even by adults.

Gombert (1992) proposes a model of metalinguistic development that comprises four successive phases. The same developmental phases apply to each linguistic domain, but initially the various domains develop independently of each other and not necessarily at the same time. The four phases refer to (1) the acquisition of the first linguistic skills, (2) the acquisition of epilinguistic control, (3) the acquisition of metalinguistic awareness, and (4) the automatization of metaprocesses. In Phase (1), the child acquires their first linguistic skills on the basis of the input s/he is exposed to, with negative and positive feedback aiding development. Implicit or explicit negative feedback, e.g. as a consequence of a failure to communicate successfully in certain circumstances, trigger Phase (2), which involves

8 A Cognitive-Developmental Perspective

organising the implicit knowledge acquired during Phase (1). In terms of the mental representation of language, multifunctional forms substitute the initial accumulation of simple form-function pairings. Epilinguistic control over language activities involves the application of increasingly general rules that progressively constitute a system. This achievement leads to a stable system and marks the end of Phase (2).

In Phase (3), the system is brought under intentional control. Access to this higher level of functioning is optional, in the sense that not all individuals will progress to this or the subsequent stage of development. The individual becomes conscious only of those aspects of language which need to be reflected on because of the (meta)linguistic tasks s/he is required to perform, in particular literacy skills. As the acquisition of metalinguistic awareness at this level is determined by external rather than maturational factors, certain aspects of language may never become subject to metalinguistic control, at least in the case of some individuals. Declarative metalinguistic knowledge precedes metalinguistic control and the application of this knowledge, as mentioned above. Thus, eventually, in Phase (4), cognitively costly metalinguistic processes are gradually automatized. Linking the proposed developmental phases with chronological age, Gombert (1992) posits that stable epilinguistic control appears around ages 5–6, while meta-functions are first identified at around 6–7 years of age, with learning to read and write triggering the progression from epilinguistic to metalinguistic functioning.

The observation that ages 6–7 seemingly constitute a critical stage in the development of metalinguistic awareness has led researchers to look for a theoretical account that might help explain why fundamental changes in cognitive functioning should occur at this point rather than any other (Gombert, 1992; Hakes, 1980; Pinto, Titone, & Trusso, 1999). A theory that posits a critical developmental shift at exactly this age is Piaget's account of the development of operations in children (J. R. Anderson, 2000; Gruber & Vonèche, 1977; Piaget, 1929; Sternberg, Lautrey, & Lubart, 2003), so it is not surprising that researchers have turned to this work in their search for a general theoretical framework. In Piaget's theory, operations are defined as "actions which are internalizable, reversible, and coordinated into systems characterized by laws which apply to the system as a whole" (Gruber & Vonèche, 1977, p. 456). Operations are considered actions because they are carried out on objects before they are carried out on symbols. As they can be applied in thought, they are considered internalizable. Finally, operations are reversible, unlike concrete actions, which are irreversible. A prerequisite for the emergence of operational systems is the concept of conservation, that is, the idea of invariants. Piaget posited four stages in the development of operations: (1) the sensorimotor period, (2) a period of preoperational thought, (3) a period of concrete-operational thought, and finally (4) a stage characterised by propositional or formal-operational thought. Crucially, in Piaget's account, the transition from preoperational to concrete-operational thought occurs at around age 7.

In (1), the sensorimotor period (ages 0 to 2 years), very young children who have not yet acquired language can only perform motor actions (Gruber & Vonèche, 1977). These actions do not yet qualify as operations because it is argued that in the absence of internalised representations, they do not involve thought, though features of intelligent behaviour are in evidence. Certain invariants are beginning to be constructed, e.g. the notion of object permanence. This refers to the fact that already at a very young age, children realise that an object continues to exist even if it is no longer within their perceptual field. Moreover, the child's ability to coordinate his/her movements in the spatial field around him/her shows characteristics of a system. In terms of motor actions, the child is able to return to his/her starting point (reversibility) and to change the direction of his/her movements (associativity). The appearance of a symbolic function marks the start of (2), the period of preoperational thought (ages 2 to 7 years). Language, symbolic play, fictional invention and deferred imitation all appear. As a consequence, the internalization of actions in the form of mental representations, i.e. thought, becomes possible. Overall, reversible operations are still absent, however, and there are no concepts of conservation beyond the sensorimotor level yet (Gruber & Vonèche, 1977).

The beginning of (3), the stage of concrete operations (ages 7 to 11 years), is marked by the emergence of the first concrete operations carried out on objects, though not yet on verbal propositions. Operations become reversible, enabling the child to return to the starting point or original state. The coordination of the actions of combining, dissociating, ordering and the setting up of correspondences allows for logical operations to be carried out on objects. Classification (hierarchical ordering) is one of the earliest operational systems to be acquired, as is seriation (ordering objects by a property such as increasing length). Multiplicative systems begin to appear somewhat later. These logical operational systems enable the child to construct concepts of number, time, motion and space/geometry. At the present stage, the operations the child is capable of are not yet dissociated from concrete data or the specific field to which they apply, however, i.e. they are not yet fully abstract. The child constructs a number of invariants or concepts of conservation in a number of fields, but without being able to generalise to all fields. In this sense, concrete operations do not represent a formal logic because they have not yet been combined into a structured system. In Piaget's terms, this developmental pattern is referred to as *horizontal décalage*, that is, "unevenness of development" (Gruber & Vonèche, 1977, p. xxv). In other words, development is localised to begin with, since a concept may appear in one form or field, but may take years to be extended over its full range. In Piaget's theorising, the coexistence of more and less highly developed structures leads to conflict or a lack of equilibrium, with further development occurring to resolve this situation of conflict and achieve equilibrium.

The final period of development (4) is characterized by the emergence of propositional or formal operations (ages 11–12 to 14–15 years) and leads to adult

10 A Cognitive-Developmental Perspective

logic once equilibrium has been reached. In this final developmental stage, children become able to reason verbally and by hypothesis. Thought no longer proceeds from the actual to the theoretical, but can take a theory as its starting point in order to establish or verify the actual. Logic is concerned not only with objects, but also with propositions. Moreover, the child can discover new invariants that are beyond empirical verification. Operational schemas emerge, e.g. in the areas of combinatorial operations, proportions and mechanics (action and reaction). The logic of propositions is formal and general, i.e. it is independent of specific content, which allows for various logical operations to be combined into a single system (Gruber & Vonèche, 1977).

Although Piaget's work approaches its centenary, it is still seminal and arguably ground-breaking in its contribution to our understanding of human cognitive development. While the theoretical apparatus proposed by Piaget has been super-seded by concepts and terminology from modern cognitive science that have been coined as a consequence of theoretical advances and substantiated by increasingly sophisticated empirical work made possible by advanced technology, the essential claims and assumptions about the developmental trajectory remain true today. Thus, it is generally accepted that cognitive development is gradual, initially localised (see, e.g., Gombert, 1992), and involves the construction of increasingly sophisticated mental representations (see, e.g., Bialystok, 1994a, 2001; Bialystok & Ryan, 1985) Importantly, the idea that language is an integrated part of general cognition that develops from localised, item-based to more abstract and general representations is again very much at the forefront these days, with cognitive-linguistic, emergentist, usage-based approaches to language development now arguably mainstream, both in L1 acquisition (e.g. Dabrowska, 2004; MacWhinney, 2001; Tomasello, 2003, 2005) and L2 learning (e.g. Cadierno & Eskildsen, 2015; N. C. Ellis, 2001, 2003, 2007; Ortega, Tyler, Park, & Uno, 2016; Robinson & Ellis, 2008). Therefore, it seems very apt to continue to take Piaget's work into consideration.

An early study (Hakes, 1980) aimed at exploring the connection between the onset of concrete-operational thought and critical progress in the development of metalinguistic awareness in children aged around 7 years serves to illustrate this point. Hakes (1980) argues that there are theoretical reasons which can be cited in support of the proposal that metalinguistic development may be a reflection of concrete-operational thought. Specifically, both metalinguistic thinking and concrete-operational thought rely on reflection, and both are controlled activities that require the child "to mentally stand back from a situation in order to think about the relationships it involves" (Hakes 1980, p. 38). As the child develops, multiple approaches to the same problem become available, and s/he has to choose which approach to use. This increased cognitive flexibility is associated with an increase in control. As a consequence, children become able to think and act deliberately, especially if they place themselves at a distance from a situation and reflect on it. This, in turn, is indicative of metacognitive development, or the child's emerging ability to control his/her own thoughts.

A Cognitive-Developmental Perspective   **11**

In order to seek empirical evidence for the proposed link between the onset of concrete-operational thought and metalinguistic development, Hakes (1980) conducted an empirical study involving 100 children in total, 20 each aged 4, 5, 6, 7, and 8 years, all monolingual speakers of American English. The younger children attended private nursery schools, the older ones kindergarten or elementary school. The location of the schools was in a predominantly white, middle-class area. Three tasks were administered to the children to assess their metalinguistic ability (synonymy judgements, acceptability judgements and phonemic segmentation), one task to prepare the ground for the synonymy judgements (comprehension), and one task to assess concrete-operational abilities (conservation). The conservation task comprised six situations: two-dimensional space, number, substance, continuous quantity, weight and discontinuous quantity. In each situation, the researcher created two arrays that were equal in the targeted property; one array was then altered for an irrelevant property. Standardised materials were used, and children's responses and their explanations were scored.

The synonymy judgement task comprised five types of sentences presented in pairs; different syntactic structures were represented, including active-passive-cleft sentences (*The nurse was called by the doctor. It was the nurse that the doctor called.*), existentials (*There is an apple on the table. The table has an apple on it.*), temporal relations (*The little boy fed the dog before he watched television. After the little boy fed the dog, he watched television.*), spatial relations (*The old lady is in front of the boy. The boy is behind the old lady.*), and size-amount sentences (*There is more cake than ice-cream. There is less ice-cream than cake.*) (Hakes, 1980, p. 43). The comprehension task assessed children's understanding of these sentence types; if a child failed on a particular sentence type in terms of comprehension, this type was not used in the synonymy task and instead replaced by additional items from the remaining types which they could comprehend. This was necessary for some of the younger children. The acceptability judgement task comprised deviant and non-deviant sentences that were manipulated in terms of word order, subcategorization, selectional restriction, use of *some* vs. *any*, and inalienable possession. In order to create the items, the researcher started out with well-formed sentences of the chosen types and then produced deviant versions. Finally, the phonemic segmentation task required children to segment words of different lengths into phonemes.

The conservation task was scored qualitatively in that children were assigned to one of three categories based on their overall performance: pre-conserving, transitional, and conserving. Performance on the task improved significantly with increasing age, as expected. On the comprehension task, performance also increased significantly with age. The youngest children had problems understanding some of the sentences, as anticipated, and the synonymy judgement task was adjusted accordingly for these children. The synonymy judgement task also showed a significant age effect, with performance improving with increasing age. Overall the children did consistently worse on synonymous than non-synonymous pairs of

12 A Cognitive-Developmental Perspective

sentences, and some sentence types were easier than others. Hakes argues that the synonymy task made greater demands on comprehension and memory than the comprehension task because the synonymy task required children to form representations of two sentences and to retain these in memory before carrying out a comparison.

An analysis of the performance patterns of the younger children on synonymous pairs showed that they did significantly worse than chance, suggesting that they did something systematically wrong. The researcher suggests that the younger children relied above all on a comparison of form rather than a comparison of meaning, since the former was less demanding, requiring them only to notice a different word or word order. Such a strategy would boost performance on non-synonymous pairs and depress it on synonymous pairs, which is the pattern that was obtained. Thus, it appears that changes in performance on synonymous pairs best reflect development, since they show how children increasingly rely on meaning, or both form and meaning, rather than on form alone as a criterion for their judgements. Hakes also suggests that comparing two sentences may be comparable to comparing two arrays in the conservation task before and after a transformation has been applied to the display.

As with the other tasks, children's performance on the acceptability judgement improved significantly with age. Overall, the young participants were more likely to make incorrect judgements for deviant sentences than for acceptable ones, with a tendency to accept unacceptable sentences. It is possible that there may have been some response bias because children were asked to give reasons for negative judgements, though not for positive ones, and the younger children in particular disliked having to give explanations. Improved performance on deviant sentences with greater maturity is attributed to increasing L1 proficiency and an associated improved understanding of the linguistic constraints of English. An analysis of the reasons given for judging sentences to be unacceptable shows that the younger children primarily focused on the meaning of the sentences, i.e. on what they asserted, rather than on their form. Assertions that were outside their experience, that were judged to exemplify 'bad' behaviour or that were thought to entail negative consequences could prompt the younger children to judge a sentence unacceptable. Children aged 7–8, by contrast, no longer provided content-related reasons. Instead, they focused on linguistic considerations. Thus, the pattern of results indicates that children gradually change the judgement criteria they rely on. It appears to be the case that very young children draw on whether they understand a sentence or not when making a judgement; 4- to 5-year-olds additionally draw on content, thus seemingly adding another criterion; older children (7–8 years) further add linguistic considerations, thus approaching adult criteria. It appears, then, that there is an increasing range of criteria that children have at their disposal to make acceptability judgements as they grow older.

The phonemic segmentation task shows the same effect for age as the other tasks, with significant improvement in evidence as children mature. Most of the younger children were unable to segment syllables phonemically, and instruction and feedback did not enable them to learn on task how to segment by phoneme. Conversely, the older children required only minimal instruction and practice to work out the underlying principle of the task and successfully segment words by phonemes.

A correlational analysis performed on the three metalinguistic tasks reveals that they correlate significantly at a medium level of strength, suggesting common underlying variance. The common factor of all the tasks appears to be the need to focus on language and reflect on its properties. In order to include the conservation task in the analysis, data from the metalinguistic tasks are converted into ordered categories. The results based on contingency coefficients show that the metalinguistic tasks all correlate with the conservation task. Hakes (1980) argues that the common source of variance here is the requirement for controlled processing rather than the automatic processing needed for language comprehension and production. Children become increasingly able to focus on and reflect upon the properties of language, and they can take a deliberate approach to problem-solving, linguistic or otherwise. They can comment on linguistic properties on request rather than doing so spontaneously but sporadically, in keeping with Gombert's (1992) distinction of epilinguistic vs. metalinguistic behaviour. Thus, as children mature, their metalinguistic performance becomes more systematic and wide-ranging in its application.

In sum, the findings arising from Hakes' (1980) study support the proposal that critical progress in metalinguistic awareness is associated with the onset of concrete-operational thought. There is, however, another important developmental step that children take at around the same age: learning to read and write.

2.2 Metalinguistic Awareness and Literacy

Over the years, researchers have highlighted the apparent link between the development of metalinguistic awareness and the onset of literacy in children who have the opportunity to go to school and learn to read and write (Bialystok, 2001; Bialystok & Ryan, 1985; Birdsong, 1989; Gombert, 1992; Yelland, Pollard, & Mercuri, 1993). Gombert (1992), for instance, notes the strong indications for a relationship between certain metalinguistic functions and learning to read, though he believes that positing a unidirectional causal link would not do justice to the complexity of the facts. In other words, while certain metalinguistic abilities first manifest themselves at around 6 to 7 years of age and thus coincide with school learning, and in particular learning to read, it is not obvious whether the development of metalinguistic awareness triggers the onset of literacy or vice versa, or whether the two abilities mutually influence each other and thus grow in a cyclical nature.

Bialystok (2001) describes learning to read as the central purpose of young children's school education. This is unsurprising, since in many societies a

14 A Cognitive-Developmental Perspective

functional level of literacy is crucial for social and economic success. The acquisition of literacy may be conceptualised in terms of three stages, which Bialystok labels pre-literacy, early reading, and fluent reading. At the pre-literate stage, children develop concepts of symbolic representation and learn about the writing system. Bialystok (2001) distinguishes two approaches to the teaching of literacy. In the emergent literacy approach, learning to read is seen as a natural consequence of language development rather than as a specialist skill. This approach is a minority view, however, with most researchers assuming that learning to read requires specialised knowledge and instruction. In this sense, reading is not a natural extension of speaking.

There are two broad methods of teaching reading, i.e. the whole-language approach and the phonics approach. The whole-language approach focuses on the meanings of written texts from which children are not to be distracted. By contrast, the phonics approach focuses on the decoding of sound-symbol relations (in alphabetic languages), and it assumes that meanings will subsequently arise from there. A number of prerequisite skills are posited for learning to read, including verbal, spatial and analytical abilities. Linguistic skills in the language in which literacy is to be achieved are also required, of course.

Bialystok argues that learning to speak and learning to read are both social activities. Reading aloud to young children enables them to access the conventions and language style used in stories, i.e. a literate register. Thus, reading stories to children not only introduces them to literacy in general, but also to language-specific competencies. As written text is a symbolic system for recording spoken language, learning to read requires an understanding of symbolic representation. Written text is a higher-order symbol system that is an indirect, opaque rather than a direct representation of meaning. In other words, it is not iconic, such as a drawing of a dog which directly represents the meaning 'dog'. Children must grasp this separation between a word and its referent in order to be able to learn to read. Put differently, they must acquire a certain level of metalexical/metasemantic knowledge.

Children at a pre-literate stage still have difficulty with word-referent differentiation, even though they may be able to print their own names, identify familiar signs with company names, or name the letters of the alphabet. Pre-literate children typically look for aspects of meaning in the visual properties of the printed word, e.g. they would expect big words to be written with big letters, or many objects to be represented by repeated letters or words. They have not yet understood that "print is symbolic; the letters are the code" (Bialystok, 2001, p. 161). In order to achieve this level of understanding, children must be able to separate form and meaning, or a word and its referent.

In the early reading stage, children learn the rules of how to decode the written system. In alphabetic languages, the key achievement needed for this is phonological awareness, that is, insight into how spoken words are structured and consist of individual phonemes and combinations of phonemes (Geudens, 2006).

Phonological awareness includes components attributable to general cognitive ability, verbal memory and speech perception. Learning to read in alphabetic languages not only requires the segmentation of words into sounds, but also learning the correspondences between letters and those sounds. Different writing systems pose different challenges to budding readers. Writing systems can be distinguished in terms of the use of different linguistic structures, such as phonemes in alphabetic systems and morphemes in character systems. In addition, we can distinguish different notational forms or scripts, e.g. Roman, Cyrillic and Greek alphabets. Different languages using the same writing system can show different levels of transparency in their phoneme–grapheme relationships. More transparent relationships in which the phonology can be generated directly from the printed word are referred to as a shallow orthography, less transparent ones as a deep orthography (Bialystok, 2001), with the latter posing greater challenges to children (and adults) than the former.

In the fluent reading stage, a number of cognitive skills are implicated, and knowledge from a number of domains is integrated. A fluent reader can interpret written symbols, use knowledge of genre conventions and appropriate reading strategies, access linguistic knowledge and incorporate prior subject knowledge relating to the meaning of a text. Decoding skills are typically referred to as bottom-up processes that draw on pattern recognition, letter identification and lexical access. Conceptual skills, by contrast, are top-down in nature (Bialystok, 2001).

The link between the development of metalinguistic awareness and literacy has been explored empirically in a fascinating study conducted in the Netherlands, which involved illiterate adults, literate but low-educated adults, and pre-literate children (Kurvers, van Hout, & Vallen, 2006). Importantly, the study offers insight into the question of cause and consequence, i.e. the issue of whether the development of metalinguistic awareness triggers literacy acquisition, or vice versa. Following Gombert (1992), Kurvers et al. (2006) define metalinguistic awareness as conscious reflection on different aspects of language, and metalinguistic ability as the analysis and control of different aspects of language. They highlight the fact that metalinguistic skills can be applied to a broad range of linguistic domains, including phonology, morphology, semantics, syntax and connected discourse, with metalinguistic awareness in the latter domain referring to the explication of meaning relations between sentences.

Kurvers et al. (2006) point out that only very little is known about adult illiterates' metalinguistic abilities. The only area that has been studied to some extent is phonological awareness, with findings showing that illiterate adults have difficulty segmenting words into phonemes, similar to pre-literate children. Research with young children has identified a boost in metalinguistic development in 'middle childhood', that is, between the ages of about 5 and 8. Different explanations have been put forward for this finding, emphasising either maturation or literacy. The maturation hypothesis argues that the linguistic and cognitive development

16 A Cognitive-Developmental Perspective

which occurs during 'middle childhood' is responsible for the observed progress in metalinguistic abilities. Conversely, the literacy hypothesis argues that the onset of literacy at the same age can explain the observed metalinguistic progress. Kurvers et al. aim to put these hypotheses to the test by comparing (a) readers (adults) with non-readers (adults and children), and (b) children (non-readers) with adults (readers and non-readers). Accordingly, their research question asked what illiterate adults know about the structural features of the language they understand and speak, compared with pre-literate children and low-educated literate adults. The maturation hypothesis would predict differences between children and adults, regardless of literacy, while the literacy hypothesis would predict differences between readers and non-readers, regardless of age.

The participants were selected for their similar social and ethnic backgrounds. There were 24 children at pre-school level (mean age 6.4 years), 23 low-educated but literate adults (mean age 34 years) who had had no more than six years of primary education (mean 4 years), and 25 illiterate adults (mean age 38 years) who had begun literacy classes, but were not yet able to decode. Most of the illiterate adults had never attended school, while a few had been to school in their home countries for less than two years. The participants were from migrant backgrounds, with most being of Moroccan, Turkish or Somali origin. Measures were administered either in Dutch or in the participants' L1, depending on participants' individual preferences. Almost all the illiterate adults were aware of the functions and uses of literacy and had at least one reader/writer in their direct environment, typically a partner or child/children. They understood the purpose of a newspaper, the workings of a calendar and telephone directory, the uses of bills and advertising, etc. Most could write their first names, and some their surnames and addresses as well. They appreciated the differences between looking at something and reading it, in the sense that they knew they could look at a newspaper, but could not work out what it said, for instance.

Participants' metalinguistic awareness was assessed by means of seven tests providing three measures of phonological awareness (rhyme production, rhyme judgement, word segmentation), four measures of lexical/semantic awareness (sentence segmentation, word-referent differentiation, word length judgement, word judgement), and one measure of textual awareness (syllogisms). More specifically, rhyme production required the participants to respond to a given word with a rhyming word. Rhyme judgement asked them to decide whether two words that were presented to them rhymed or not. A progressive segmentation task asked participants to break sentences and then phrases down into pieces (sentence segmentation), and then to further break down multisyllabic and monosyllabic words into even smaller pieces, i.e. syllables or phonemes (word segmentation).

The word-referent differentiation task involved swapping the names of 'cat' and 'dog' for associated pictures and requiring the participants to answer questions about the animals under their new names, e.g. "What noise does the animal make that is called 'dog' now?". The word length judgement required participants to choose the longer word from a pair of words. The task included congruent, incongruent and neutral pairs. In the case of congruent pairs, word length and real-world size of the referent were matched (e.g. *goat – elephant*), whereas in the case of incongruent pairs, they were mismatched, with small referents having long names and vice versa. Neutral items were based on words and referents of roughly equal size. The word judgement task required participants to judge whether a given utterance was a word or not. Stimuli included content words, function words, groups of words and sentences. Finally, the syllogism task asked participants to solve simple syllogisms and explain their answers, e.g. "All stones on the moon are blue. A man goes to the moon and takes a stone. What colour is that stone?" (Kurvers et al., 2006, p. 76).

The results reveal significant main effects for participant group for all tasks except rhyme judgement. In summary, the illiterate adults differed significantly from the literate adults on all the tasks that showed a group effect. The children differed from the literate adults on most lexical/semantic tasks and one phonological task. Analyses by task show that for rhyme production, the children and the literate adults performed equally well, and both groups did significantly better than the illiterate adults. The same pattern of results applies to the word segmentation task. When segmentation strategies are scrutinised, however, it becomes clear that the adult literates mostly segmented by phoneme, while the children mostly segmented by syllable. The illiterates did not normally segment into sub-lexical units at all, but when they did, they also segmented by syllable. In other words, phonemic segmentation is used by readers, while the syllable appears to be the natural unit of sub-lexical segmentation for non-readers.

On the word-referent differentiation task, the children and literate adults did not differ significantly from each other, but both groups did differ significantly from the illiterate adults. About half of the children and half of the literate adults were able to play the game, while the illiterate adults were not. The adults tended to question the idea of changing names, while the children did not argue. Although the adults could distinguish word and referent when discussing the fact that their L1 and L2 (Dutch) had different words for the same concept, they could not transfer this awareness to the cat/dog task. On the word length task, the non-readers differed significantly from the readers, but not from each other. The literate adults took an analytic approach to making judgments, while some of the children and the illiterate adults used referent size as the basis for their judgements. Some children counted syllables, while some illiterates made holistic judgements on the basis of word sound.

On the word judgement task, the non-readers again differed significantly from the readers, but not from each other. Differences in performance were mostly found with regard to function words and multi-word sequences, but not with regard to content words. The readers based their answers on linguistic units, while the non-readers tended to judge clauses and sentences as words and did not

18 A Cognitive-Developmental Perspective

readily accord word status to function words. The sentence segmentation task showed the same pattern of results, with the non-readers differing significantly from the readers, but not from each other. The literate adults segmented along word boundaries, while the non-readers segmented by content or clause.

On the syllogism task, a response was considered correct if it included the correct answer as well as a suitable explanation. Yet again, the readers differed significantly from the non-readers, who did not differ from each other. The readers tended to use deductive reasoning based on the premises, as intended, while the non-readers tended to draw on their personal experiences or, in the case of some children, gave no explanations at all. In addition, some adult non-readers questioned the premises, arguing that they were unreasonable or nonsensical. Example answers for the following syllogism are shown below: "All stones on the moon are blue. A man goes to the moon and finds a stone. What colour is that stone?" (Kurvers et al., 2006, p. 83):

- Yellow, because the moon is yellow as well (child)
- White, I once saw white stones (child)
- Green with black, I've seen that in Turkey (child)
- Black, because it's very hot there (illiterate adult)
- Surely there are no stones on the moon (illiterate adult)
- I have to see it first (illiterate adult)
- Blue, all stones are blue there (literate adult)
- If he really was there, and all stones there are blue, then it must have been blue (literate adult)
- All stones there are blue, so that one too (literate adult)

The authors argue that their findings support the literacy hypothesis rather than the maturation hypothesis, since there were more differences between readers and non-readers than between children and adults. Readers and non-readers differed quite consistently on the lexical/semantic tasks and the syllogisms, while the phonological tasks exhibited a more complex picture. Non-readers were unable to segment by phoneme, but the children were quite good at rhyming, while the adult illiterates were not. The illiterate adults and the children tended to react to content or meaning on the lexical/semantic tasks. When the illiterate adults did take language form into account, they used holistic strategies rather than the analytic formal approach exhibited by the literate adults. Solving the syllogisms requires decontextualized thinking that ignores personal experiences – something the non-readers could not accomplish. As literacy instruction is likely to help individuals focus exclusively on in-text relations and thus cope with decontextualized language use, imagined realities can be separated from real-world experiences. Hence, Kurvers et al. (2006) conclude that learning to read and write fosters metalinguistic awareness. For illiterate adults, language is a medium of communication, and not an object that is accessible to deliberate reflection and

A Cognitive-Developmental Perspective **19**

analysis. Illiterates can reflect on content, an utterance as a whole, or, in holistic terms, on the way something is said. However, they cannot take formal aspects of language into account, seemingly because they have not received literacy training.

Although the researchers in this study favour the literacy hypothesis over the maturation hypothesis, it is worth bearing in mind that the two approaches are not necessarily mutually exclusive. It is perfectly conceivable that a certain level of metalinguistic development is required for an individual to learn to read and write, and that the onset of literacy in a formal educational context then triggers further metalinguistic development, and so forth. In other words, a cyclical developmental path is possible and, arguably, likely. As already discussed, meta-linguistic abilities develop at different points in different linguistic domains, with metaphonological and some metalexical knowledge appearing relatively early and at around the same time as literacy instruction typically begins, while more advanced metasemantic, metapragmatic and metatextual knowledge emerges years later, in association with more fluent reading and writing skills and more advanced schooling in other subjects as well. By the same token, cognitive development in Piagetian terms does not stop at the concrete-operational stage, but continues into the stage of formal operations, which is in keeping with the abstract thought required for advanced metalinguistic abilities as well as secondary levels of education in language, science, etc.

Up to this point, the discussion has focused on the development of meta-linguistic awareness and the associated development of literacy. Let us now turn to the question of how these concepts relate to the phenomenon of bilingualism, i.e. a situation in which children (or adults) have command of more than one language. With regard to literacy development, is it the case that bilingual children are at an advantage? Bialystok (2001) argues that this may be the case at the pre-literate stage, and it may still be the case, though to a much lesser extent, at the early reading stage, but it is probably no longer the case at the fluent reading stage. As detailed below, it has been shown that bilingual children are typically able to understand the separation of language forms and their meanings at an earlier age than monolinguals because they have experienced the association of two different forms in two different languages with a single referent. By contrast, the development of phonological awareness, and especially the ability to segment words into phonemes which is so important for learning to read in alphabetic languages, seems to be minimally affected by bilingualism. In the fluent reading stage, reading in a weaker language (L2) may always remain slower and draw on strategy transfer from L1 rather than language-specific strategies, thus putting bilinguals with unbalanced linguistic skills at a potential disadvantage compared with monolingual readers (Bialystok, 2001). Literacy skills aside, however, bilinguals may enjoy other advantages over monolinguals. Before these potential advantages are discussed in depth, a current theoretical framework for researching linguistic, metalinguistic and general cognitive development in both monolinguals and bi- or multilinguals is presented.

2.3 Bialystok's Framework of Analysis and Control

Arguably the most widely used conceptualisation in the cognitive-developmental perspective on metalinguistic awareness, as exemplified primarily, though certainly not exclusively, in research with bilingual children, is the framework of analysis and control (Bialystok, 1988, 1994a, 1994b, 2001; Bialystok & Ryan, 1985), which outlines a key set of cognitive mechanisms that account for language acquisition and use. In fact, the framework is not restricted to the linguistic domain, but has a broad application to cognitive development more generally. In the context of language acquisition, whether L1, L2 or Lx, the framework is meant to be used in conjunction with other theories aimed at addressing linguistic, social and cultural factors as well as individual learner differences, so there is no claim that the two key mechanisms it posits can offer an exhaustive explanation of a phenomenon as complex as language learning (Bialystok, 1994a). A clear strength of the proposed framework lies in its wide-ranging applicability, offering a coherent account of both linguistic and metalinguistic knowledge, ability and awareness, as detailed in the following.

The two basic theoretical concepts that make up the framework are the processes of *analysis of knowledge* and *control of processing*, which are responsible for the development of and accessibility to mental representations – the essence of learning. Analysis of knowledge refers to the ability to mentally represent increasingly explicit, complex and abstract structures in an increasingly systematic way (Bialystok, 2001). It is worth noting here that explicitness is not directly equated with consciousness; instead, an explicit representation is

> something that has been stated exactly, leaving nothing to interpretation or implication. Explicit knowledge is knowledge that includes precise boundaries and is organised in known systems. Explicit knowledge may be conscious or not, and it may be accessed automatically or not. It is different from implicit knowledge in the clarity with which it is represented.
>
> *Bialystok, 1994b, pp. 565–566*

Bialystok (1994a) identifies three levels of analysis ranging from conceptual via formal to symbolic representation. The conceptual level of representation is the most basic one, e.g. the words 'dog' and 'bone' are connected through meaning only. At the formal level, representations are based on taxonomical associations, e.g. 'dog' and 'cat' are connected because they belong to the same basic-level category 'pet' and the super-ordinate category 'animal'. Eventually, symbolic representations are organised around systems of abstract-level categories, e.g. 'dog', 'cat' and 'bone' are associated by virtue of being nouns (Bialystok, 1994a). The more analysed a speaker's knowledge representations are, the more readily they can be applied to a full range of purposes. Control of processing refers to the ability to selectively allocate attention to specific, task-relevant aspects of a mental

A Cognitive-Developmental Perspective **21**

representation in real time and to simultaneous inhibit aspects that are task-irrelevant (Bialystok, 1994a, 2001). As with analysis of knowledge, control of processing is required to a greater extent for some language uses than others (Bialystok, 1994a).

Accordingly, the framework of analysis and control can be used to provide a contextualized account of the development of (meta)linguistic proficiency. In the most general terms, different levels of analysis and control are required for oral, literate and metalinguistic language use, with the latter drawing on the highest levels of both components (Bialystok, 2001). As metalinguistic knowledge is defined by its abstract, general and decontextualized nature, activities or tasks drawing on such knowledge by definition require highly analysed and structured knowledge representations. Along similar lines, as metalinguistic ability is defined as the capacity to use knowledge about language by focusing on language form rather than the meaning being expressed, activities or tasks drawing on such abilities by definition require a high level of attentional control and inhibition (Bialystok & Ryan, 1985).

Furthermore, individual oral, literate and metalinguistic tasks can be described in terms of the relative levels of analysis and control required for their successful completion. To exemplify, conducting an informal conversation will require relatively low levels of either component, whereas engaging in simultaneous interpreting will require very high levels of both components. Skimming while reading is likely to require high levels of control, but not necessarily high levels of analysis, but writing poetry will draw on high levels of both components. By the same token, although all metalinguistic tasks are relatively more demanding than oral or literate language use in terms of the levels of analysis and control required, individual tasks differ in their specific requirements. Thus, judging correct sentences, detecting errors, identifying rhyme or synonymy, segmenting text and counting words in sentences require increasingly high levels of both analysis and control. By contrast, correcting sentences draws on high levels of analysis while requiring relatively little control, whereas judging semantic anomalies requires high levels of control but relatively little analysis of knowledge (Bialystok, 2001; Bialystok & Ryan, 1985).

In general developmental terms, increases in levels of analysis are thought to precede increases in levels of control, with the latter seen as a response to improvements in analysis. Correspondingly, a developmental trajectory from metalinguistic knowledge to metalinguistic ability to metalinguistic awareness is predicted (Bialystok, 2001). While the framework can thus be applied broadly to the acquisition of any language(s) (L1, L2, Lx), it is accepted that exposure to language instruction may alter the rate of learning. Depending on the focus of instruction, a learner may primarily develop his/her level of analysis of knowledge or his/her level of control of processing, for instance. A teaching methodology that relies on both form-focused and meaning-focused input should lead to a balanced development of both processes (Bialystok, 1994a).

The framework of analysis and control appears to be reflected in the argument that (meta)linguistic proficiency can be conceptualized along two continua that specify the range of contextual support available for expressing and comprehending meaning, and the degree of active cognitive involvement on the part of the speaker/learner (Cummins, 1987). Context-embedded communication is exemplified in everyday communication, while context-reduced communication is often typical of the language classroom. Along similar lines, cognitively undemanding tasks are communicative activities which draw on automatized language use, whereas cognitively demanding tasks require active, effortful and controlled involvement on the part of the speaker/learner. By definition, metalinguistic tasks are context-reduced and require controlled language use, although the latter depends to some extent on the speaker/learner's level of development and experience with such tasks. Metalinguistic skills as well as related academic skills such as proficient reading and verbal ability are expected to transfer across languages (Cummins, 1987). The argument that metalinguistic abilities are closely related to and may interact with more general cognitive abilities not only sits well with the theoretical conceptualisation of metalinguistic development presented here, but is also linked to a line of empirical work that is of direct interest to the field of L2 learning, namely, research into the so-called bilingual advantage.

2.4 'Bilingual Advantage' Research

Research conducted under this heading is concerned with the question of whether learning and using more than one language can convey general cognitive advantages. Under this rather broad theme, a number of more differentiated issues has been investigated over the past decades, including the question of whether a certain length and/or quality of bilingual experience is required for potential advantages to arise, the question in which age range(s) bilingualism may be of particular benefit or otherwise, the question of whether trilingualism differs from bilingualism in relation to general cognitive abilities, and the question of precisely which cognitive processes might be influenced by prolonged bilingual experience. In a review of research into the effects of bilingualism on the mind and brain, Bialystok, Craik and Luk (2012) justify the focus on bilingualism by the fact that more than half of the population of the world is bilingual. Importantly, however, bilinguals often do not choose to learn more than one language; the need is rather brought about by external circumstances such as place of birth or migration history. In the broadest terms, cumulative research findings to date suggest that the development, efficiency and decline of certain cognitive abilities over the lifespan are different for bilinguals than for monolinguals. The researchers argue that functional neuroplasticity underlies these abilities, i.e. the modification of brain structure and brain function by prolonged experience.

Existing research findings suggest that compared with monolingual children, bilingual children show enhanced metalinguistic abilities, in the sense that they are better able to separate linguistic form from meaning, and they are also superior in solving non-verbal problems that require them to ignore misleading information (Bialystok et al., 2012). At the same time, as shown primarily by research with adults, bilinguals have generally weaker linguistic abilities in each of their languages than monolinguals, if their skills are measured by means of vocabulary knowledge and lexical access tasks (Bialystok & Craik, 2010; Bialystok et al., 2012). However, bilinguals have better executive control, i.e. they exhibit superior performance on measures tapping "the set of cognitive skills based on limited cognitive resources for such functions as inhibition, switching attention, and working memory" (Bialystok et al., 2012, p. 241). Executive control is a cognitive mechanism that develops in early childhood and declines in ageing adults; it supports activities such as high-level thought, multi-tasking and sustained attention. Interestingly, the bilingual advantage in executive control not only comes to the fore in young children, but also appears to last into older age and protect against cognitive decline – a phenomenon referred to as cognitive reserve (Bialystok & Craik, 2010; Bialystok et al., 2012).

The reason for a bilingual advantage in executive function is attributed to the fact that bilinguals activate their two languages jointly, with some interaction between the two linguistic systems in evidence at all times, even when only one of the languages is needed for a task. This joint activation can help explain the consequences of bilingualism for linguistic and non-linguistic processing: Bilinguals must select the correct language, which makes linguistic processing more effortful than in a monolingual scenario. It has been suggested that successful language selection is achieved through inhibition of the language that is not relevant in a given context. Here researchers distinguish between global and local inhibition. Global inhibition is proactive and refers to the suppression of an entire language system, while, by contrast, local inhibition is typically reactive and refers to the inhibition of specific competing representations, such as the translation equivalent of a particular word. Both processes are used in bilingual language processing, but local inhibition primarily affects linguistic performance, while global inhibition affects both linguistic and more general cognitive performance. In addition to inhibition, activation of the required language or concept is needed, that is, a selection bias towards the target language. It is argued that the outcome of these needs in bilingual language processing is enhanced attentional control (Baum & Titone, 2014; Bialystok et al., 2012).

Early research into the bilingual advantage carried out in the 1970s to 1980s was typically based on the assumption that effects of linguistic experience would be most readily apparent in the domain of linguistic competence rather than general cognitive abilities, so there was a focus on the development of meta-linguistic awareness in bilingual children compared with monolingual children. Studies using grammaticality judgement tasks found that bilingual children outperformed monolingual children on semantically anomalous sentences, but not on meaningful sentences, which suggests that bilingual children were better able

24 A Cognitive-Developmental Perspective

to ignore the misleading meaning component and focus on relevant formal information instead. One can infer from this that bilinguals do not necessarily show advantages in terms of better metalinguistic *knowledge* (analysis), but in better *access* to that knowledge (control). In other words, the bilingual advantage seems to lie primarily in advantages in selection and inhibition, that is, components of executive function (Bialystok & Craik, 2010). Therefore, later research carried out from the 1990s onwards was more specifically aimed at examining control of processing rather than analysis of knowledge. In addition, more recent work has asked much more fine-grained questions, in accordance with researchers' increasingly differentiated understanding of the specific cognitive mechanisms involved in control of processing, especially executive function and its component processes of attention and inhibition.

The two pieces of research described in what follows exemplify the shift from a focus on metalinguistic awareness conceptualised in terms of analysis and control (Bialystok, 1988) to the more recent interest in executive function in particular (Bialystok & Martin, 2004); they also give an indication of the increasingly sophisticated experimental manipulations that are in use, thus illustrating the direction taken in bilingual advantage research more generally.

The work reported in Bialystok (1988) examined the relationship of degree and type of bilingualism with metalinguistic awareness, conceptualised in terms of levels of analysis of knowledge and control of processing. Two theoretical positions on degree and type of bilingualism are contrasted: the threshold hypothesis (Cummins, 1979), which is concerned with absolute levels of L1 and L2 knowledge, and a position that emphasises the degree of balance between two languages in terms of relative levels of L1 and L2 knowledge (Hakuta & Diaz, 1985). Analysis of linguistic knowledge is linked with crystallised ability, if it is to be expressed in information processing terms. Development in this domain can be conceptualised as the gradual organisation of mental representations into networks, schemas or systems whereby holistic and implicitly stored representations become increasingly explicit in terms of structure. Control of linguistic processing is conceptualised in terms of executive function, the direction of attention, and the selection and integration of information, and it is thus linked with fluid ability, if expressed in information processing terms.

As already noted, metalinguistic tasks typically require high levels of both analysis and control, but specific tasks differ in terms of which component is most relevant for their resolution. Bialystok (1988) points out that tasks requiring the detection, extraction or articulation of linguistic properties or structures draw primarily on analysis of linguistic knowledge. They include tasks tapping awareness of syntax, awareness of the concept of word, error correction, providing definitions, paraphrase and judgements of ambiguity. Conversely, tasks involving misleading cues and requiring a focus away from meaning draw primarily on control, i.e. their solution depends on the appropriate selection and integration of information. Such tasks include the sun/moon problem (Piaget, 1929), sentence

A Cognitive-Developmental Perspective **25**

segmentation, symbol substitution and repetition of deviant sentences. It is hypothesised that bilingual children at any level will have advantages in control of processing, while fully bilingual children will have advantages in analysis of knowledge.

Study 1 looked at two groups of children who differed in terms of type and level of bilingual experience; they were compared with a group of monolingual children. The 57 participants were Canadian children in Grade 1 of elementary school (ages 6–7 years). There were 20 English monolinguals, 20 partially French-English bilinguals who had been exposed to French for two years via immersion education, and 17 fluent French-English bilinguals who were educated in French and had a French parent and/or other French-speaking relatives. All children were from middle-class backgrounds. Language proficiency was assessed by means of the Peabody Picture Vocabulary Test (PPVT) in English and a French translation of the test. The children also completed an IQ test and a digit span test as a measure of their general cognitive abilities. There were no significant differences between the groups on the general ability measures.

In order to address the research issue, the children completed three metalinguistic tasks in English. The first task assessed their understanding of the arbitrariness of linguistic form-meaning mappings. It made use of (a) Piaget's sun/moon problem (see Chapter 6 for details) and (b) a matched condition employing pictures of a cat/dog (see also Kurvers et al., 2006). This task tapped control of processing (Bialystok, 1988). The second task was a concept-of-word task requiring the children to (a) judge whether certain words and phrases were words and (b) provide a definition of the concept 'word'. The final task was a syntax correction task which asked the young participants to correctly repeat orally presented sentences that contained a grammatical error. These latter two tasks tapped analysis of knowledge.

The results show that, as expected, the monolingual children outperformed both bilingual groups on the English PPVT. As discussed below, this did not translate into advantages on any of the metalinguistic tasks, however. The fully bilingual group outperformed the partially bilingual group on the French version of the PPVT, again as expected. With regard to the metalinguistic tasks, the bilingual groups outperformed the monolingual group on the sun/moon task, while there were no differences on the cat/dog version of the task. The result for the sun/moon task confirms the hypothesis that any level of bilingualism will be advantageous for control of processing. However, this was not replicated in the cat/dog condition. Bialystok suggests that a possible reason for this could be the greater concreteness of the cat/dog version, which draws on familiar properties of concrete objects. Given the different patterns of results, the cat/dog condition may not be equivalent to the sun/moon condition.

On the concept-of-word task, the fully bilingual group outperformed the monolingual group on the definition part, but there were no between-group differences on the judgement part. On the syntax correction task, the fully

26 A Cognitive-Developmental Perspective

bilingual group outperformed both the partial bilinguals and the monolinguals. Thus, the hypothesis that the fully bilingual group would score more highly than the other two groups on tasks tapping analysis of knowledge was supported in part. It is suggested that a possible reason for this might be that analysis of knowledge develops gradually, with different representations in different children occupying different positions along a continuum of increasing structure and systematicity.

In summary, the results of Study 1 show that the fully bilingual group did best throughout on the metalinguistic tasks, while the monolingual group scored lowest. In terms of control, the partially bilingual group was closer to the fully bilingual group, whereas in terms of analysis, the partially bilingual group was closer to the monolingual group.

Study 2 used a within-groups design with bilingual participants only in order to allow for children's individual levels of bilingualism to be included in the analysis. The hypotheses tested were the same as for Study 1, i.e. control of processing was not expected to differ between groups, while more proficient bilinguals were expected to show greater analysis of knowledge than less proficient bilinguals. The study included 41 Italian-English bilingual children in Grade 1 (ages 6–7 years) from two different Canadian schools. The participating children had different experiences of speaking Italian, based on their home background. Schooling was in English, and the children had learned to read in English. The socio-economic background of the families the children came from is described as working class. In this study, the children completed the English PPVT and an Italian version of the test.

The metalinguistic tasks used were similar to those in Study 1, except that the cat/dog condition of the arbitrariness-of-language task and the syntax correction task were left out. Instead, a grammaticality judgement task was used, which was administered in both English and Italian. The children had to judge sentences that were read out to them. Items covered four conditions: (a) grammatically and semantically correct sentences, (b) grammatically incorrect and semantically correct sentences (labelled 'incorrect', e.g. *Why the dog is barking so loudly?*), (c) grammatically correct but anomalous sentences (labelled 'anomalous', e.g. *Why is the cat barking so loudly?*), and (d) grammatically and semantically incorrect sentences. The critical conditions were (b) and (c), which were intended to tap analysis of knowledge (b) and control of processing (c).

The PPVT results from the English and Italian versions showed that the children were more proficient in English than in Italian. As the scores on the two measures were not correlated, it can be argued that the Italian version of the test provided a measure of the children's level of bilingualism. As scores did not differ on the English and Italian versions of the grammaticality judgement task, they were combined into a single score. The results from the main data analyses reveal significant correlations between level of bilingualism as assessed by the Italian PPVT score and the two measures aimed at assessing analysis of knowledge, that is,

A Cognitive-Developmental Perspective **27**

judgement of 'incorrect' sentences on the grammaticality judgement task and performance on the concept-of-word task. Bialystok argues that this constitutes evidence in support of the hypothesis that a higher level of bilingualism would be associated with greater analysis of knowledge. Based on their Italian PPVT scores, the children were then divided into two groups, a high-bilingual and a low-bilingual group. An ANOVA confirmed the hypothesised pattern of results: There were significant differences between the two groups on the tasks aimed at measuring analysis of knowledge, but not on the tasks aimed at measuring control of processing. In other words, level of bilingualism did not matter with regard to control of processing; the mere presence of another language was sufficient to have an effect in this area.

Bialystok (1988) concludes that the overall findings from Study 1 and Study 2 are consistent with the argument that different metalinguistic tasks have different processing requirements, and that performance on these tasks is differentially affected by a child's level of bilingualism. Bilingual children have more highly developed control of processing at an earlier age than monolinguals, and more proficient bilinguals have more analysed knowledge representations than less proficient bilinguals or monolinguals.

The second piece of research to be considered here illustrates the more recent interest of bilingual advantage researchers in executive function specifically. Bialystok and Martin (2004) used a Dimensional Change Card Sort (DCCS) task to investigate cognitive processes in bilingual children. As before, the two processes in focus are analysis of knowledge representations and control of attention in processing. As already discussed, analysis of representations refers to the organisation of knowledge around abstract categories as well as the ability to retrieve details independently of their context. Control refers to the ability to selectively attend to specific aspects of a representation and to inhibit attention to irrelevant or misleading aspects. This is particularly difficult when a salient or habitual response must be overcome because it is inappropriate in the context of a particular task. Bialystok and Martin (2004) point out that attention comprises two independent components: one dedicated to selection, and another to inhibition. As bilingual language management requires selection and inhibition on a regular basis, long-term experience with exercising these functions in the context of language selection and/or inhibition may carry over to general cognitive tasks. Indeed, the cumulative findings from empirical research to date suggest that any bilingual advantage appears to be attributable above all to the more efficient development of control of attention.

The DCCS task requires test takers to sort cards by one dimension and then to re-sort them by a different dimension. Typically, young children are able to do this from around age 4 or 5; younger children are unable to switch to new rules for re-sorting the cards. The DCCS task places high demands on both knowledge representations and attentional control. Children need to conceptualise the stimuli and the rules of the task, i.e. they need to construct mental representations

28 A Cognitive-Developmental Perspective

accordingly. In addition, they need to inhibit the response that was set up in the pre-switch part of the task when performing the post-switch part with a new sorting rule. Two types of inhibition can be distinguished here, that is, response inhibition and conceptual inhibition. Response inhibition refers to inhibiting a pre-potent motor response, in this case the familiar motor action of sorting according to the default or pre-switch rule. Conceptual inhibition refers to the inhibition of a pre-potent mental representation. It is necessary to inhibit a previously relevant feature for sorting, e.g. colour, in favour of a newly relevant feature, e.g. shape, in accordance with changed sorting rules post-switch. Thus, conceptual inhibition is partially dependent on the construction and manipulation of mental representations of the task stimuli. Bialystok and Martin's (2004) work aimed to disentangle the three processes involved in the DCCS task, i.e. representation (encoding rules and representing relevant stimulus features), response inhibition (resisting previous motor patterns) and conceptual inhibition (inhibiting attention to previous mental descriptions).

In Study 1, the DCCS task was computer-administered. The representational demands of the sorting rules and the stimuli were varied by means of four experimental conditions. Specifically, representational demands were varied by manipulating the number of dimensions depicted in the stimulus and the semantic content of those dimensions (one perceptual feature, two dimensions of colour and shape, two dimensions of colour and object outlines, and semantic properties of objects). The stimuli became increasingly detailed, resulting in increased stimulus complexity. The type of information that needed to be ignored post-switch thus varied, so demands on conceptual inhibition varied between conditions as well. Response inhibition was identical across all conditions.

A total of 67 Canadian children participated in the study, including 36 English monolinguals (mean age 4 years and 9 months) and 31 Chinese-English bilinguals (mean age 4 years and 9 months). The children completed the Peabody Picture Vocabulary Test-Revised (PPVT-R) as a measure of their competence in English. They also completed a forward digit span task as an indication of their working memory capacity and Raven's Coloured Progressive Matrices as a measure of general intelligence. The computerised DCCS task included the following conditions, which were presented to the children as games: The colour game (1) employed red and blue squares as stimuli. The pre-switch rule was 'Press X for red square, O for blue square'; the post-switch rule was 'Press X for blue square, O for red square'. The colour-shape game (2) used red circles and blue squares as stimuli. Children were asked to sort cards into boxes which showed a picture of either a red square or a blue circle. The pre-switch rule was 'Put all blue pictures in the box with the blue picture and all red pictures in the box with the red picture'; the post-switch rule was 'Put squares in the box with the square and circles in the box with the circle'. The colour-object game (3) used red flowers and blue rabbits as stimuli. Children were asked to sort cards into boxes which showed a picture of either a red rabbit or a blue flower. The pre- and post-switch rules were

A Cognitive-Developmental Perspective **29**

analogous to those in (2). Finally, the function–location game (4) used as stimuli things to play with that go outside the house and things to wear that go inside the house. Children were asked to sort cards into boxes which showed a picture of either a teddy bear (play – inside) or a winter jacket (wear – outside). The pre-switch rule was 'Put all things to play with in the box with the teddy bear and all things to wear in the box with the jacket'; the post-switch rule was 'Put all things that go inside the house in the box with the teddy bear and all things that go outside the house in the box with the jacket'.

The results from the study reveal that the monolingual children outperformed the bilinguals on the PPVT-R, confirming the expected pattern. There were no differences between monolinguals and bilinguals on the forward digit span task and Raven's scores, suggesting equivalence of the two groups in terms of working memory capacity and general intelligence. With regard to the DCCS task, an ANOVA showed main effects of game and group, indicating better performance on pre-switch trials and by the bilinguals, who had an advantage on the colour-shape game (2) and the colour-object game (3). A chi-square analysis comparing children who passed the post-switch phase by scoring at least 8 out of 10 correct responses showed a bilingual advantage for the colour-shape game (2) only. Bialystok and Martin argue that this pattern of results suggests a bilingual advantage in conceptual inhibition, although there were no differences between groups on the function-location game (4). The researchers further posit that the function-location game (4) was more demanding in terms of representation than the other games which relied on purely perceptual features without any need for interpretation. Put differently, the stimuli in the function-location game (4) required the encoding of semantic features, so there was a need for interpretation of the stimuli.

Study 2 was aimed specifically at comparing the colour-shape game (2) and the function-location game (4) because these two conditions differed in terms of their reliance on perceptual as opposed to semantic features. Instead of using a computer, the DCCS task was administered manually in this study in order to increase the need for inhibition. The participants were 15 English monolingual children (mean age 5 years and 1 month) and 15 French-English bilingual children (mean age 4 years and 6 months). The children completed the PPVT-R and the forward digit span test; the bilinguals additionally completed the EVIP, the French version of the English Peabody. The results showed no differences in terms of forward digit span, but as before and as expected, the monolinguals outperformed the bilinguals on the PPVT-R. With regard to the DCCS task, an ANOVA revealed that the bilinguals outperformed the monolinguals on both DCCS task conditions (2) and (4) in the post-switch phase. A chi-square analysis based on children passing the post-switch phase showed a bilingual advantage on the colour-shape game (2) but not the function-location game (4). Thus, the findings of Study 1 were mostly replicated in Study 2. This leads Bialystok and Martin (2004) to conclude that there is a clear bilingual advantage on the colour-shape

30 A Cognitive-Developmental Perspective

game (2) and a more sporadic one on the function-location game (4). As the difference between the two conditions lies in whether classification of stimuli is based on perceptual or semantic properties, this issue was investigated further in Study 3 by extending the two conditions.

In Study 3, the DCCS task was administered manually in four conditions, with two conditions each requiring the inhibition of attention to representations of either perceptual or semantic information. The perceptual conditions were the colour-shape game (2) and the colour-object game (3) from Study 1. The semantic conditions were the function-location game (4) from Study 1 and a new kind-place game (5). The kind-place game (5) used as stimuli animals that go in the water and vehicles (things to ride in) that go on land. Children were asked to sort cards into boxes which showed a picture of either a sailing boat (water vehicle) or a squirrel (land animal). The stimuli in each category of the kind-place game (5) resembled each other in that fish-like creatures and car-like objects were used throughout. In this sense, (5) was closer to the perceptual conditions (2) and (3) than the function-location game (4), where the stimuli were completely different objects.

The participants in Study 3 were 27 English monolingual children (mean age 4 years and 2 months) and 26 Chinese-English bilingual children (mean age 4 years and 4 months). The children completed the PPVT-R, with the monolinguals out performing the bilinguals, as before. With regard to the DCCS task, an ANOVA showed a main effect of condition and phase, suggesting better scores in the pre-switch phase. The two perceptual conditions (2) and (3) were easier than the two semantic conditions (4) and (5), with no differences within these pairs. The bilingual children did better than the monolingual children in the post-switch phase of the perceptual conditions, but there were no differences between the groups in the semantic conditions. A chi-square analysis based on children passing the post-switch phase indicated a bilingual advantage in the perceptual conditions, i.e. the colour-shape game (2) and the colour-object game (3). Bialystok and Martin conclude that Study 3 both replicates and extends the findings from Study 2 by demonstrating a reliable bilingual advantage on the perceptual conditions and equivalence between groups on the semantic conditions.

Taken together, the studies reported by Bialystok and Martin (2004) show that different groups of young bilingual children achieved greater success on the DCCS task than comparable groups of young monolingual children when the sorting dimension was a perceptual stimulus feature. Conversely, when the sorting dimension was a semantic stimulus feature, bilinguals and monolinguals tended to perform similarly. In theoretical terms, Bialystok and Martin attribute the observed bilingual advantage to enhanced conceptual inhibition rather than enhanced response inhibition or any enhanced ability to represent the stimuli. It seems that the burden of representation was a challenge for all children, as indicated by the equivalent and overall less successful performance of all groups on the semantic conditions, where the stimuli were more complex because they required interpretation. The inherent difficulty of the DCCS task appears to lie in the conceptual inhibition that is required, and this is where the bilingual children performed better:

> Our interpretation is that the crucial step is in the ability to reinterpret the target stimulus for the post-switch phase, an achievement that requires ignoring its perceptual properties that had just been critical to the pre-switch phase. The lure of misleading information is most salient in the perceptual conditions, and it was in these that the bilinguals asserted an advantage
>
> *Bialystok & Martin, 2004, p. 338*

In summary, the findings are consistent with the argument that bilingualism may foster the development of inhibitory control because bilingual children must constantly inhibit a non-relevant language. By contrast, there appears to be little influence of bilingualism on the development of analysis of representations. It is control in the sense of attention and inhibition that is crucial.

Having presented two pieces of research from the bilingual advantage field in some detail, it is important to point out that this research strand has been subject to criticism, especially in recent years. Equally importantly, many of the issues raised by critical commentators are not only perfectly valid, but also constructive and forward-looking. Early criticism focused on the possibility that the superior performance of bilinguals as opposed to monolinguals may be due to factors other than their bilingualism (Morton, 2014; Morton & Harper, 2007). For instance, Morton and Harper (2007) posit that differences in children's performance may at least in part be due to differences in ethnicity and/or socioeconomic background. They argue that parental emotional support as well as the provision of cognitive stimulation in terms of joint attention, direct teaching, bedtime reading, explaining events etc. is likely to contribute to the development of attentional control. Thus, children who have experienced such an upbringing to a greater extent than others may show enhanced performance on tasks measuring executive function, including tasks requiring attentional selection, inhibition and conflict resolution. In a number of bilingual advantage studies, ethnicity and socioeconomic status are not adequately controlled, in the sense that the bilingual children tend to come from different and potentially more advantaged backgrounds than the monolingual comparison groups.

In a perceptive and very thorough review of research concerned with a potential bilingual advantage across the lifespan, Baum and Titone (2014) focus on the factor of age, with normal ageing described as "an inevitable race between increasing knowledge and decreasing cognitive capacity" (p. 857). According to the authors, this description applies to language as well, where older individuals have both advantages and disadvantages. Advantages lie in the fact that older adults have better world knowledge and can make greater use of context. Disadvantages include reduced perceptual acuity and executive control functions, with the latter

32 A Cognitive-Developmental Perspective

including working memory and inhibition. Research into the bilingual advantage suggests that life-long bilingualism may offer some protection against age-related decline in executive function. This has been termed cognitive reserve (see, e.g., Bialystok & Craik, 2010; Bialystok et al., 2012) and is attributed to bilinguals' ample experience with using executive control to manage the processing and use of two languages.

However, the hypothesis of a bilingual advantage is not uncontroversial. Baum and Titone (2014) mention the fact that many studies in the field have relied on broad comparisons of bilinguals and monolinguals that do not take into account the considerable inter-individual variation within these groups. The authors argue that future research should embrace individual differences both within and across groups, including neurocognitive capacities and sociocultural factors. Moreover, while many studies have produced evidence for a bilingual advantage in various groups, especially young children and older adults, there are also studies that have failed to find such an effect. A null effect is particularly common in studies with young adult participants (see, e.g., Samuel, 2015). Baum and Titone (2014) believe that there are at least two potential reasons for this variability in findings, namely the various kinds of tasks used and the kinds of bilinguals tested, i.e. their qualitative and quantitative differences.

It is also pointed out that research drawing on neuroimaging methods is still in short supply. In the context of ageing and associated changes in brain structure and function, researchers are still trying to establish exactly how neural changes map onto cognitive performance and vice versa. Existing work suggests that ageing is associated with decreased processing speed, reduced sensory acuity and reduced working memory and other executive control functions, and any language processes relying on these functions will be affected accordingly. However, it is worth noting that there are individual differences in patterns of cognitive decline or resilience, as well as in changes across cognitive and linguistic domains. Biological and environmental factors are believed to play a role in this heterogeneity. Bilingualism could be seen as an advanced language ability which contributes to cognitive reserve. But, alternatively, it is also possible that individuals who are better at language and thus become bilingual may have inherent differences in their brains (Baum & Titone, 2014).

In view of the argument that bilingualism may be associated with increased cognitive reserve, researchers have investigated the potential clinical significance of bilingualism in the context of dementia. Findings reported by some researchers suggest that while bilingualism does not alter pathological brain processes, it may lead to a greater tolerance of dementia (Bialystok & Craik, 2010; Bialystok et al., 2012). Put differently, bilingualism cannot delay the onset of dementia, but it may delay the appearance of actual behavioural symptoms. Other researchers have not found such an effect, but have argued that multilingualism may confer some measure of cognitive reserve. Yet others have suggested that bilingualism may only increase cognitive reserve in individuals who have not achieved their maximum potential already as a result of other factors such as education or socioeconomic status (Baum & Titone, 2014).

Bearing in mind the mixed findings to date, Baum and Titone (2014) set out a research agenda that is guided by three themes. The first theme focuses on individual differences among bilinguals. Future research should explore the language learning characteristics and language proficiency of bilingual participants more fully. Specifically, it is argued that individual bilinguals can be expected to differ according to their behavioural ecology. Depending on context, high language integration and frequent code-switching may be normative for some, while using one language exclusively in the work place vs. the home may be normative for others, for instance. Other differences include differing proficiency levels in terms of oral vs. written skills, intentional vs. unintentional code-mixing, and knowledge of an L3 or even an L4. Clearly, these qualitative and quantitative differences can have implications for executive control. It is also important to understand within-group variability in monolinguals, of course.

The second theme is concerned with the question of cause and consequence, or, put differently, with the question as to whether bilinguals show advantages because they had them to begin with. It is often argued that bilinguals do not generally choose their bilingualism, which suggests bilingualism may be a cause rather than a consequence of any observed cognitive advantages. However, it is also possible that small, local social decisions have the cumulative effect of producing 'better' bilinguals who were more cognitively flexible to begin with. In order to address this conundrum, longitudinal studies would be needed, as well as studies focusing on the effects of L2 learning on cognition (Baum & Titone, 2014). The latter point is beginning to be addressed, as we shall see below.

The third and final theme focuses on the relative importance of a bilingual advantage as opposed to improved life-long neuroplasticity. Here the authors argue for more sophisticated questions to be asked about bilingualism, so researchers can arrive at more informative findings. Baum and Titone would like to move beyond yes/no questions ('Is there a bilingual advantage?') towards deeper insights into "the specific points of contact within and across language and general executive control domains" (2014, p. 882). Eventually, this may enable the research community to recommend social policies, e.g. that every older adult should learn a language, or that multiple languages be taught from the earliest possible age.

2.5 A 'Bilingual Advantage' for L2 Learners?

While there is ample research investigating a potential bilingual advantage in children who have either been exposed to two languages from birth or have experienced bilingual immersion education from an early age in an environment where the L2 is also spoken outside the classroom (e.g. Canada), there is as yet relatively little work that has examined potential benefits for general cognitive

34 A Cognitive-Developmental Perspective

functioning in multilinguals, partial bilinguals, or children learning an L2 in a limited-input classroom setting. A small number of recent studies has begun to probe the boundaries of a possible bilingual advantage, addressing questions such as whether learning three languages instead of just two might convey additional benefits (Poarch & van Hell, 2012), whether L2 learning in the classroom over different lengths of time would have any impact on general cognition (Bialystok, Peets, & Moreno, 2014; Nicolay & Poncelet, 2013), and, in earlier research, even whether minimal L2 input can have an effect on metalinguistic awareness (Yelland et al., 1993).

In an attempt to answer the question of whether there might be a trilingual advantage over and above a bilingual advantage (Bialystok & Craik, 2010), Poarch and van Hell (2012) investigated whether advantages in executive control that have been identified in studies with bilingual children would extend to L2 learners and trilinguals. The former group are seen as being situated between monolinguals and bilinguals in terms of a hypothesised language development continuum, while the latter group is situated beyond bilinguals, since there is a potentially greater need to exercise monitoring and control functions when speaking three languages rather than just two. The study that is reported compared non-linguistic effects of language control in early L2 learners, bilinguals and trilinguals with the performance of monolinguals. All children except the mono-linguals had extensive contact with at least two languages in an immersion environment, that is, home and/or kindergarten or school. The children completed two tasks – the Simon task (see Chapter 6 for details) and an Attentional Network task (ANT) (see below for details) – aimed at assessing the attentional control component of executive function, specifically conflict monitoring and conflict resolution, in that participants were required to choose between two competing responses. Conflict monitoring includes conflict detection and the preparation of subsequent action, while conflict resolution includes inhibition, planning and rule representation. The two chosen tasks are considered particularly suitable for assessing cognitive differences arising from multilingualism because their reliance on language and language-related processes is minimal.

Study 1 focused on the Simon task, which was administered to 75 children in Frankfurt, Germany. The L2 learners, bilinguals and trilinguals all attended a German-English immersion kindergarten and primary school, while the mono-linguals attended a German-only primary school. The 19 participating L2 learners had a mean age of 6.9 years and had been immersed in English for an average of 1.3 years at school. The 18 bilinguals had a mean age of 6.8 years and had been immersed for an average of 2.8 years. They each had one English-speaking and one German-speaking parent. The 18 trilinguals had a mean age of 6.8 years and had been immersed for an average of 2.4 years. They spoke German and another language at home and learned L3 English, or they spoke English and another language at home and learned L3 German. The 20 participating L1 German monolinguals had a mean age of 7.1 years and had not learned any L2s. Children's proficiency in German and English was measured by means of receptive grammar tests in English and German. The children did not differ significantly in German, and only the bilinguals performed to the same level on the measures in the two languages, as expected. All other groups were stronger in German than in English. Socioeconomic status was estimated by means of parental education level; there were no significant differences between the groups in this regard.

The children completed the Simon task, and data were analysed for response times and accuracy. The response time analysis resulted in a main effect of stimulus type and an interaction between stimulus type and group, indicating a difference in the Simon effect between groups, with monolinguals showing a significantly greater effect than trilinguals and a marginally greater effect than bilinguals. The error data analysis showed a main effect of stimulus type, suggesting different error rates for incongruent and congruent trials, but there were no between-group differences. Taken together, the results show that the trilinguals, and marginally the bilinguals, exhibited superior conflict resolution compared with the monolinguals. The L2 learners were situated in between, showing no significant differences from either the monolinguals or the multilinguals. The researchers argue that the L2 learners' experience was not (yet) sufficient to result in advantages in conflict resolution. As there were no global response time differences, none of the groups displayed any advantages in monitoring (Poarch & van Hell, 2012).

Study 2 focused on a child version of the ANT. The participants were the same as in Study 1, except for the monolingual group, who were no longer included, and an additional bilingual child. The study was carried out 6–8 months after Study 1, so the children's mean age was accordingly higher. The ANT is designed to assess three attentional networks, namely alerting (attainment and maintenance of an alert state), orienting (selection of information from sensory input) and executive control (monitoring and conflict resolution). Executive control is measured by a flanker task, where the target stimulus is a central fish surrounded by four other fish that 'swim' either in the same (congruent) or a different direction (incongruent). On neutral trials, the target fish appears on its own. Alerting is explored through the display of a double cue or no cue before the target stimulus, and orienting is explored through the display of a spatial (informative) cue or a central (uninformative) cue.

The ANT data were likewise analysed for response times and accuracy. The response time analysis resulted in a main effect of cue type, but no main effect of language group. The accuracy analysis yielded a main effect of cue type as well. Thus, the overall performance of the children did not show any differences between groups. Subsequent analyses focused on the attentional networks of executive control, alerting and orienting. The results demonstrate that all groups showed alerting, orienting and conflict effects, but with the orienting and the conflict effects differing between groups. Specifically, the bilinguals and trilinguals had an advantage over the L2 learners in benefiting from the orienting cue, and they also experienced less interference from incongruent flankers. There was no

36 A Cognitive-Developmental Perspective

global response time advantage and thus no indication of enhanced monitoring for any of the groups.

According to Poarch and van Hell (2012), the findings from the two studies taken together suggest that the bilinguals and trilinguals had superior attentional control, as indicated by the significantly smaller Simon effect. By contrast, the L2 learners seemed to exhibit an emerging enhancement of attentional control, but presumably had not yet had sufficient experience with language management to reach the level of the bilinguals or trilinguals. In other words, a critical threshold in exposure and usage had not been crossed yet. The bilinguals and trilinguals also showed enhanced conflict resolution on the ANT, as well as enhanced orienting. However, trilingualism did not confer any additional advantages over bilingualism on any of the tasks. This indicates that managing three languages instead of two does not lead to any additional improvements in attentional control.

The issue of a critical threshold in bilingual experience was examined further by Bialystok, Peets and Moreno (2014), who investigated whether differing levels of immersion education can convey the same advantages in terms of cognitive and linguistic processing that have been identified in fully bilingual children. Existing research has demonstrated that bilingualism does not benefit linguistic knowledge per se, but rather access to that knowledge. This is illustrated by means of acceptability judgements of grammatically incorrect and semantically appropriate sentences (e.g. *Apples growed on trees*) vs. grammatically correct but semantically inappropriate sentences (e.g. *Apples grow on noses*) (see Bialystok, 1988). Bilingual and monolingual children perform equivalently on the former type of sentences, but bilinguals outperform monolinguals on the latter type. This appears to be due to their enhanced ability to selectively attend to relevant information (form) and inhibit misleading information (meaning). By contrast, monolingual children tend to score more highly than bilingual children on language proficiency measures such as tests of receptive vocabulary knowledge. Therefore, it is possible that bilinguals' performance on metalinguistic tasks is improved through better executive function, but actually hindered by restricted linguistic knowledge. Bialystok et al. (2014) argue that this issue can be disentangled by using two versions of a verbal fluency task, that is, a category fluency and a letter fluency condition (see below and Chapter 6 for details). The category fluency condition is in keeping with the structure of representations in semantic memory; it draws on knowledge representations and lexical access. The letter fluency condition does not reflect the structure of any memory representations and thus makes greater demands on monitoring, attention and selection. In summary, the researchers argue that judging grammaticality and generating lexical items are above all linguistic tasks with limited demands on executive control. Conversely, the ability to judge semantically anomalous sentences for grammaticality and the letter fluency condition of the verbal fluency task require not only linguistic knowledge, but also high levels of executive control.

A Cognitive-Developmental Perspective   **37**

In Bialystok et al.'s (2014) study, children in Grade 2 and Grade 5 of Canadian public schools, i.e. children at different levels of immersion education, were compared with children in L1-only education in the same grades. The participants were 124 pupils from monolingual English-speaking families. One group was in a French immersion programme while the other group was not, as follows: Grade 2: N = 28 monolingual, N = 34 immersion, ages 7.0 to 8.4 years; Grade 5: N = 28 monolingual, N = 34 immersion, ages 9.9 to 11.5 years. Language background and socioeconomic status were assessed by means of a questionnaire, the PPVT-III was used to estimate receptive English vocabulary as an indicator of English proficiency, and Raven's Matrices was the chosen measure of non-verbal visuospatial reasoning. In addition, the children completed three measures of metalinguistic awareness: the classic 'wug' test of morphological awareness (Berko, 1958), which makes little demand on executive control as there is no misleading information; a sentence judgement task including grammatically correct sentences (e.g. *Where does a horse like to run?*), grammatically incorrect but semantically appropriate sentences (e.g. *Where does a horse like to runs?*) and grammatically correct and semantically anomalous sentences (e.g. *Where does a horse like to sail?*), which places greater demands on executive control as misleading information in semantically anomalous sentences has to be inhibited; and a verbal fluency task in both the category fluency and letter fluency conditions, with higher demands on executive control in the letter fluency condition since monitoring, attention and selection are required, in addition to a certain dependence on literacy. The 'wug' test was scored for accuracy, while the researchers measured both response times and accuracy for the sentence judgement task. In the verbal fluency task, the children were required to produce as many items as they could within one minute that belonged to the categories 'clothing items' and 'girls' names' (category condition), and words starting with the letters F, A and S (letter condition).

The background measures showed no significant differences between groups in terms of socioeconomic status, home language use or English vocabulary knowledge. However, Grade 2 children outperformed Grade 5 children on the Raven's test. Therefore, all subsequent analyses that included grade as a variable were run with Raven's scores as a covariate. As the response times on the sentence judgment task were too slow to be interpretable in terms of processing differences, this aspect of the data was not considered further.

The results based on the metalinguistic awareness measures reveal that the immersion children outperformed their monolingual peers on the 'wug' test. The researchers argue that this finding is indicative of a bilingual advantage emerging after only two years of immersion education. However, the advantage in question refers to metalinguistic knowledge rather than any advantages in executive function, since demands on control are low on the 'wug' test. It is considered to be comparable to an error correction task in that there is a primary focus on linguistic information. The children did not differ in their ability to judge semantically appropriate sentences grammatically correct or incorrect, and older children did

38 A Cognitive-Developmental Perspective

better than younger children. However, the Grade 5 immersion children were more accurate in judging the semantically anomalous sentences than the monolingual children. This pattern of results bears out previous findings, but it is worth noting that the advantage did not appear until Grade 5, i.e. either greater cognitive maturity and/or more time in the immersion programme were required for benefits in executive control to accrue.

In the category condition of the verbal fluency task, older children produced more words than younger children, as expected. In the letter condition, however, the Grade 2 immersion children actually produced fewer words than the monolingual children, i.e. there was a cost rather than a benefit to the bilinguals here. Bialystok et al. believe that this result may reflect children's limited literacy experience in English. The Grade 5 immersion children performed to the same level as their monolingual peers. Thus, they had made up for the disadvantage, but there was no advantage in evidence for the older children either. Taken together, the pattern of results suggests that five years of L2 immersion education are not sufficient to modify monitoring, attention and selection as measured by a verbal fluency task. Alternatively, it is also possible that this specific task is simply very difficult for children of the given age.

In summary, the findings of the study show emerging advantages in metalinguistic awareness after two years of immersion education and more robust advantages after five years. However, the immersion children did not exhibit the same profile as fully bilingual children. Hence, Bialystok et al. (2014) posit a continuum of bilingualism, with greater experience leading to greater benefits through a gradual modification of abilities. It is also worth bearing in mind that in addition to L2 immersion, maturity and task demands may play a role in children's performance.

Indeed, the point about the role of task demands seems to be borne out by the fact that another study conducted with L1 French immersion learners of L2 English aged 8 years did identify the beginnings of attentional and executive function benefits after only three years of immersion education, in comparison with a monolingual control group (Nicolay & Poncelet, 2013). In this study, the researchers measured a number of attentional and executive control skills, i.e. alerting, auditory selective attention, divided attention, mental flexibility, response inhibition and interference inhibition, by means of a very different set of tasks, namely the so-called Test for Attentional Performance in Children, the Attentional Network task (ANT; see also Poarch & van Hell, 2012) and a computerised Flanker task.

While the studies considered so far have all involved children who had had at least a year (and mostly several years) of relatively intensive exposure to an L2, an earlier study by Yelland, Pollard and Mercuri (1993) took a rather more radical approach in that it examined whether minimal contact with an L2 can lead to improvements in young children's metalinguistic awareness, particularly word and phonological awareness, which play an important role in the acquisition of literacy skills and specifically in learning to read an alphabetic language, as discussed previously. Word awareness is defined as "an awareness that the speech stream is composed of discrete units called words, and that words are the units of the language that carry meaning, and that the relationship between a word and its referent is an arbitrary one", whilst phonological awareness is defined as "the knowledge that the spoken word is composed of distinct units of sound at both the sub-syllabic and phonetic levels" (Yelland et al., 1993, pp. 423–424). As existing research suggests that partial bilingualism may lead to improved metalinguistic skills, Yelland et al. wonder whether the development of metalinguistic awareness really requires a threshold level of competence in the L2 relative to the L1. In order to put this issue to the test, the researchers pose two research questions: (1) Do metalinguistic benefits accrue even after very limited exposure to an L2? (2) And do metalinguistic benefits carry over to reading skill?

The study focuses on the development of word awareness in young children during the first two years of schooling, and the task employed was aimed at assessing children's understanding of the arbitrariness of the word-referent relationship as well as their phonological awareness. Specifically, Yelland et al. (1993) used picture stimuli and asked children to make a judgement about the size of the word labelling the stimulus (big word vs. little word). Half of the items were congruous, while the other half were incongruous in terms of word and object size, i.e. little words named big objects (e.g. *whale*), or big words named little objects (e.g. *caterpillar*). Little words were monosyllabic, while big words were multisyllabic, ranging from two to five syllables. The participants were four groups of 14 L1 English children each. Two groups were in the preparatory grade (aged approximately 5 years), and two groups were in Grade 1 (aged approximately 6 years). Two groups at each level were monolingual English, while the other two groups had been exposed to one hour of Italian per week from the beginning of their schooling. Italian classes focused on rhymes, stories, pictures, songs, games and some vocabulary learning; the children achieved no measurable level of competence in Italian, so proficiency tests were not used. The children who were exposed to Italian are referred to as the marginal bilingual group. All children went to school in the same suburb of Melbourne, Australia, and were recruited from three different schools. The children were matched for age, PPVT scores and English spoken language comprehension. The word awareness task was administered twice, once two months into the school year, and again seven months into the school year. Grade 1 children were tested for a third time at the end of the school year in order to establish whether there was any association between metalinguistic awareness and learning to read.

The development of metalinguistic awareness was investigated based on what the researchers call the congruity effect, i.e. the difference between correct judgements on congruous vs. incongruous items on the word awareness task: the smaller the congruity effect, the greater a child's word awareness. At the first testing time, preparatory grade children performed significantly better on

40 A Cognitive-Developmental Perspective

congruous than incongruous items, and congruity effects were similar across the monolingual and marginal bilingual group, with no significant differences in evidence. At this point, the marginal bilingual group had only had three hours of exposure to Italian, so the result is unsurprising. At the second testing time, the marginal bilinguals outperformed the monolinguals and showed a significantly smaller congruity effect. The source of this was a marked improvement of performance on incongruent items, suggesting that the marginal bilinguals were better able to use word size as the basis for their decisions. According to Yelland et al. (1993), this indicates a higher level of word awareness. At the first testing time, monolinguals and marginal bilinguals in Grade 1 exhibited equivalent congruity effects, suggesting that the former had caught up with the latter and were equally able to understand the arbitrary relationship between a word and its referent. At the second testing time, the initial gap in overall performance between marginal bilinguals and monolinguals had closed as well, with performance now approaching ceiling level for all Grade 1 children.

In order to achieve syllable segmentation to judge the size of the stimulus words, children had to have a certain level of phonological awareness. The congruity effect results indicate that this awareness was developing at the same time as word awareness began to emerge. While the study provides evidence that word awareness develops between the ages of 5 and 7, it cannot show whether this is a consequence of education or maturation or indeed both. The researchers further argue that their results also show that metalinguistic benefits could be derived from minimal L2 exposure, suggesting that there is no threshold level of L2 competence which a learner must reach for advantages to accrue. It should be noted, however, that the advantage in word awareness shown by the marginal bilinguals was relatively short-lived. It disappeared after a few months, with the monolinguals catching up fast. Therefore, level of L2 competence may determine the degree of benefit and/or the speed with which a benefit takes effect.

In order to gauge a potential impact of metalinguistic awareness on the acquisition of reading, children's early reading achievement was assessed by means of a written word recognition test at the end of their second year of schooling, i.e. at the end of Grade 1. The test required children to match one of three written words with a corresponding picture. Word recognition is described as an early and critical step on the way to literacy, though fluent reading requires other skills as well, of course. The marginal bilinguals significantly outperformed the monolinguals on the word recognition test. Yelland et al. (1993) argue that this finding constitutes evidence for a carry-over effect to reading acquisition of word awareness brought about by minimal exposure to an L2. Thus, there appears to be a cause-and-effect relationship between metalinguistic skill and a critical component of early reading achievement. This in turn indicates that minimal L2 exposure can potentially convey cognitive and educational benefits to young children, even if it does not lead to measurable L2 proficiency (see also Murphy,

Macaro, Alba, & Cipolla, 2014 on the effects of learning an L2 with transparent grapheme-phoneme mappings on L1 English literacy).

It is interesting to note here that Yelland et al.'s (1993) conclusion appears to be in direct opposition to the conclusion reached by Kurvers et al. (2006) in their research with adult illiterates. This arguably further substantiates the view that there is no simple, one-way cause-effect relationship between metalinguistic awareness and the acquisition of literacy, or vice versa. In view of the empirical evidence that has been considered up to this point, a more plausible argument would be to posit that early metalinguistic abilities such as basic word-referent separation and syllable segmentation arise in conjunction with key steps in cognitive development such as the emergence of concrete-operational thought. These early metalinguistic abilities facilitate the first steps of learning to read and write, which in turn lead to the development of more advanced metalinguistic abilities, such as phoneme segmentation and a more sophisticated level of word awareness. In this way, progress in literacy and progress in metalinguistic skills mutually reinforce each other, so the two sets of abilities have a bilateral or cyclical relationship. Bilingualism, or the knowledge of more than one language, can function as a catalyst in this relationship, with increasing levels of L2 knowledge potentially resulting in larger and more lasting effects on metalinguistic (and literacy) development.

3

METALINGUISTIC AWARENESS IN LANGUAGE EDUCATION

3.1 Multilingualism and the 'M-Factor'

In the context of L2 education, work by Ulrike and colleagues (Cenoz & Jessner, 2009; Herdina & Jessner, 2002; Jessner, 1999, 2003, 2006, 2008, 2014) which is specifically concerned with multilingual learners and learning has placed strong emphasis on the role of metalinguistic awareness. Multilingualism is defined as a speaker's use of two or more languages (Herdina & Jessner, 2002), so the concept includes bilingualism, but is not restricted to it. The key argument put forward by these researchers is that L2 learning on the one hand and L3/L4/Lx learning on the other hand not only differ in quantitative terms, but also, and crucially, in qualitative terms (Cenoz & Jessner, 2009; Jessner, 1999, 2006), as explicated by the so-called 'M-factor' (Cenoz & Jessner, 2009; Jessner, 2008, 2014), with 'M' standing for multilingualism.

Jessner and colleagues acknowledge that multilingualism and bilingualism share certain characteristics – a circumstance that is in evidence in similar potential advantages arising from speaking more than one language. Three aspects are highlighted in this regard, namely divergent thinking, communicative sensitivity, and most importantly, metalinguistic awareness (Baker, 1993; Jessner, 1999, 2006). Divergent thinking refers to creative, imaginative and open-ended thinking. Instead of converging on a single answer to a problem, divergent thinkers can provide a variety of answers, all of which may be valid. Divergent thinking can be investigated by means of questions such as 'How many uses can you think of for a brick?', 'How many uses can you think of for a car tyre?' etc. It is argued that knowledge of more than one language may increase flexibility, originality and elaboration of thought. In addition, speaking more than one language is also expected to confer advantages in terms of communicative sensitivity, that is, an "increased sensitivity to the social nature and communicative functions of language" (Baker, 1993, p. 125). This is attributed to bi/multilinguals' need to constantly monitor their language use in terms of which language to speak in which situation. As a consequence, bi/multilingual individuals may become more highly aware of the needs of their listeners. Finally, it is proposed that metalinguistic abilities that draw on cross-linguistic awareness, e.g. comparing and contrasting two or more languages, can account for findings which are indicative of a bi/multilingual advantage (Baker, 1993). In other words, in bi/multilinguals, meta-linguistic awareness includes cross-linguistic awareness, defined as "the learner's tacit and explicit awareness of the links between their language systems" (Cenoz & Jessner, 2009, p. 127).

Despite these commonalities between bilingual and multilingual learners, the prior language learning experiences of bilinguals and multilinguals are different, in the sense that bilingualism or L2 learning relates to a monolingual system as the norm, whereas multilingualism or L3 learning relates to a bilingual system as the norm (Jessner, 1999, 2006, 2008, 2014). This has prompted the proposal of a qualitative difference between bi- and multilingualism. In addition, multilingual learning is by definition more complex than bilingual learning (Cenoz & Jessner, 2009). A number of factors need to be taken into consideration in the context of multilingualism, including the age at which the learner has encountered their various languages, the social environment and, associated with this, the status of the various languages, e.g. minority language, English as a lingua franca, etc. In a school context, L3 learning builds on L2 learning and thus shares certain char-acteristics with it. However, L3 learning is also influenced by the degree of bilingualism the learner has already achieved – something that does not apply to L2 learning. In bilingualism, the two languages involved may either be learned simultaneously or consecutively. Conversely, in multilingualism there are more possibilities: Simultaneous trilingualism can be contrasted with consecutive learning of L1, L2 and L3, but also with simultaneous learning of L2 and L3 after L1, or with simultaneous acquisition of L1 and L2 prior to L3, for instance. The learning process of a specific language may also be temporarily interrupted when another language is added (Cenoz & Jessner, 2009).

Jessner (2008, p. 275) defines multilingual proficiency holistically as "the dynamic interaction among the various psycholinguistic systems (LS_1, LS_2, LS_3, LS_n) in which the individual languages (L1, L2, L3, Ln) are embedded, cross-linguistic interaction, and what is called the M(ultilingualism) factor". The M-factor comprises everything that distinguishes a multilingual from a monolingual system, i.e. qualities that develop in a multilingual speaker due to contact and experience with different languages. The M-factor is seen as an emerging property that can have a catalytic or accelerating effect in L3/L4/Lx learning. The key component of the M-factor is metalinguistic awareness, which is constructed on the basis of prior linguistic and metacognitive knowledge. The multilingual learner develops language learning, language management and language maintenance skills, and all of these skills are related to metalinguistic awareness in one way or another (Jessner, 2008, 2014). This view of multilingual proficiency is in keeping with the notion of multicompetence, which takes into account the fact that language systems are dynamically interrelated. Thus, when assessing multilingual proficiency, multilinguals should not simply be compared to monolinguals who speak the various languages that the multilingual has knowledge of (Cenoz & Jessner, 2009). Put differently, applying a monolingual norm in a multilingual context is deemed inappropriate.

In accordance with this view, Jessner and colleagues have put forward what they refer to as a dynamic model of multilingualism (Herdina & Jessner, 2002). Specifically, they argue that the complexities of multilingual development can be framed within dynamic systems or complexity theory (for work drawing on this theoretical framework, see, e.g., de Bot & Larsen-Freeman, 2011; de Bot, Lowie, & Verspoor, 2007; Howe & Lewis, 2005; Larsen-Freeman, 1997; Larsen-Freeman & Cameron, 2008; Roehr-Brackin, 2014, 2015). In order to explain multilingual development, a number of variables and their interplay need to be taken into account, including psychological individual difference factors, learners' physical traits, and any changes in the learner and the learning situation over time (Jessner, 2014). The language systems in a multilingual individual interact. Moreover, the phenomenon of language attrition demonstrates that language development is a reversible process, and indeed learning an L3 can counteract maintenance of L2 and/or L1. As the learner's resources are limited, access to knowledge may be lost, unless time and energy are expended on active language maintenance. The multilingual system is dynamic and adaptive, in the sense that there is continuous change, including non-linear positive and negative growth. The social setting surrounding the individual also affects the linguistic systems, with perceived communicative needs the driving force behind language learning and use (Jessner, 2008).

In summary, it would appear that the application of a dynamic systems-theoretic or complexity-theoretic framework to multilingualism is certainly appropriate. However, the notion of the so-called M-factor and the associated argument that multilingual learning differs qualitatively from bilingual learning are still awaiting empirical substantiation, as conceded by the main proponent of this idea herself (Jessner, 2008). Having said this, the notion of the M-factor and the key role ascribed to metalinguistic awareness in multilingual proficiency are arguably useful conceptual tools. As a matter of fact, they tie in well with the proposals of the language awareness movement in primary- and secondary-school education.

3.2 Language Awareness

The concept of language awareness is fundamentally concerned with language education in both L1 and L2, and the language awareness movement thus has above all educational aims rather than a research-oriented agenda. Language awareness is deemed important because language is central to human life; it is needed to build and maintain interpersonal relationships, to help us think and reflect, and to educate and be educated (van Lier, 1995). The concepts of meta-linguistic awareness and language awareness overlap in part, but the notion of language awareness is somewhat broader in outlook and therefore arguably less clear-cut: "Language awareness can be defined as explicit knowledge about language, and conscious perception and sensitivity in language learning, language teaching and language use" (Svalberg, 2007, p. 288, drawing on the website of the Association for Language Awareness). The concept of language awareness goes beyond the context of language learning and teaching in that it pertains to language use in the most general sense; it is thus assumed to have a value in itself – something that, strictly speaking, does not apply to metalinguistic awareness, which is typically associated with learning and development.

According to the introduction in James and Garrett's (1991) frequently cited volume on the topic of language awareness, one of the key goals of language awareness in school education is to bridge the gap between learners' L1 and L2, which can be achieved through programmes of study about language. In this regard, the objectives of language awareness programmes are to provide a meeting place and common vocabulary for different fields of language education, to facilitate discussion of linguistic diversity in order to prevent prejudice, to develop listening skills, which are considered a prerequisite for efficient L2 study, and to foster confidence in reading and motivation for writing. Accordingly, language awareness programmes are expected to help make learners' intuitive knowledge of their L1 explicit, strengthen language skills and increase communicative effectiveness in L1 and L2/L3/Lx. Language awareness requires the learner to come to terms with language through thinking about it as well as through learning to talk about it. Talk about language is likely to make use of "a common, acceptable and adequate metalanguage that is accessible to both teachers and learners", but it should not be confused with instruction in formal linguistics (James & Garrett, 1991, p. 7)

The concept of language awareness has cognitive, affective and social dimensions. The cognitive domain is exemplified by developing awareness of patterns in language and contrasts between languages, the functions of language, and the language-analytic demands of academic discourse. Increased awareness and conscious reflection about language may help learners improve their language use, although it is pointed out that language awareness does not need to be justified as a means to an end, since the study of language is regarded as "patently self-justifying" (James & Garrett, 1991, p. 18). The affective domain is exemplified by learners forming attitudes and developing sensitivity, curiosity and an aesthetic response to language. The social domain refers to learners' effectiveness as citizens and consumers. Through an improved understanding of language, it is believed that an appreciation of variety, intercultural and multicultural understanding and thus greater social harmony can be achieved. At the same time, language awareness can help learners develop the sensitivity required to detect the fact that language

46 Metalinguistic Awareness in Language Education

can be employed as a means of manipulation, e.g. in political discourse or advertising. In this way, learners can be empowered to make meaningful choices (James & Garrett, 1991; Svalberg, 2007). Finally, language awareness has a practical, instrumental purpose as well, since it is considered important in professions that require efficient and precise language use, e.g. teaching, law, sales and marketing, or journalism (van Lier, 1995).

The rather broad educational aims of language awareness programmes become apparent in proposals for their implementation as well as concrete projects that have sought to introduce the concept into the school curriculum. For instance, in the context of primary and secondary education in England, where L2 teaching and learning is perceived as being in crisis, Hawkins (2005) has proposed a two-stage approach. In the first stage (ages 5–14), language teaching would have an educational purpose, including the development of language awareness and strategies and skills as tools for L2 learning. This is referred to as a school foreign language apprenticeship. In the second stage (ages 14–19) when learners are old enough to make informed choices, language teaching and learning would have an instrumental purpose. The proposal is justified by the fact that in continental Europe, for example, the need for learning the 'global language' English is predictable from an early age onwards, and this can inform schools', learners' and parents' priorities and planning. In England and the UK more generally (as well as in other English-speaking countries, of course) the situation is different, however. Learners do not know until they are adolescents at the earliest what languages they may need later in life, e.g. for further study or for their careers, so it arguably does not make sense to require instrumental choices too early.

According to Hawkins' (2005) proposal, the educational stage, i.e. the foreign language apprenticeship, would be aimed at awakening children's minds to the power of language to both inform and mislead, e.g. in advertising, political propaganda or via hidden prejudices in texts, as mentioned above. Another aim would be to enable children to 'learn to listen', or to 'educate the ear'. This can be achieved through music and song, for instance. Between ages 7 and 11, schools should aim to develop a wide concept of language awareness by drawing on multilingual dimensions of the school itself, the community, town, nation and world, and children should be made aware of the existence of languages other than English. Children can be guided by the teacher – who does not need to be a specialist in any language – to look for patterns in languages or similarities and differences across languages; children's speaking, listening, reading and writing abilities should be fostered in preparation for future L2 learning. Links with other subjects such as literacy, citizenship and information technology are to be encouraged. As a final step in the educational stage between ages 11–14, children should be taught an apprenticeship language, which should be chosen by the school, depending on the availability of expertise and resources. By getting to grips with listening, speaking, reading and writing in the apprenticeship language, children are expected to 'learn how to learn'; having learned one L2 is expected to facilitate learning L3 (see the 'M-factor'). Schools may wish to adopt a community language as the apprenticeship language, so they can incorporate reciprocal teaching and learning of that language and English among their pupils. A further aim of the apprenticeship language would be to allow each pupil to better understand his/her own capacities and interests. Following on from the educational stage, the next step from age 14 onwards constitutes the instrumental stage, at which learners should be able to choose the language they wish to learn with a view to its later usefulness to them and to their future. The instrumental stage would include the opportunity for all learners to be immersed in the L2 for a period of time, e.g. via short intensive programmes (Hawkins, 2005).

While this rather ambitious proposal of a two-stage L2 education across England has not been realised and is perhaps unlikely to ever be implemented in full, the idea of incorporating a language awareness programme into the school curriculum has been put into practice in individual schools in both the UK and continental Europe in the context of a number of specific projects. In continental Europe, several projects aimed at raising cultural and linguistic awareness among school children have been conducted in recent years, e.g. EVLANG, a three-year project that has since turned into an organisation. This project involved teachers, children and researchers in several European countries, and it introduced over 40 languages into Grade 5 and Grade 6 classrooms (ages 10–12). The original initiative was aimed at awakening language awareness rather than teaching specific languages, so the tasks which children completed revolved around becoming aware of knowledge already held as well as misconceptions or lack of knowledge, creating new knowledge, and becoming aware of what knowledge had been gained and how. There was a focus on language structure, language and culture, language contact and variation, languages in a global context, bilingualism, and the status of languages (Svalberg, 2007). This was followed by the JA-LING project (Candelier, 2004), which included all primary and secondary grades and was implemented in a number of schools in 10 European countries.

A short overview of three school-based projects implemented in the UK – 'Thinking through languages', 'Discovering language' and 'Springboard to languages' – will serve to illustrate language awareness initiatives in an English-speaking context that have been informed by the idea of a language apprenticeship as put forward by Hawkins (2005). The 'Thinking through languages' project (Jones, Barnes, & Hunt, 2005) was aimed at raising language awareness through multilingual exposure, and the project was carried out in six primary schools in both suburban and inner-city areas in Coventry over the school year 2002–2003. Specific objectives included fostering notions of equality and acceptance of diversity, providing children with a sound basis for language learning, introducing language awareness activities that can bridge English, literacy and L2s, and the idea of exploiting new technologies. The internet was a central resource for developing teaching and learning materials, although some schools were able to additionally draw on the expertise of bilingual speakers already present. It is reported that

48 Metalinguistic Awareness in Language Education

Coventry pupils speak more than 50 different L1s, though of course not all of these were represented in the participating schools. A key aim of the language awareness activities was to challenge the misconception that "the English language represents absolute truth and the foreign language represents some kind of lesser confection of the teacher" (Jones et al., 2005, p. 65). Instead of taking the risk of children losing interest in language learning as soon as it gets harder, a further aim was to lay strong foundations for subsequent L2 learning by focusing on transferable strategies that are developed across a range of languages.

The project activities were intended to bring about curiosity about language and language learning. Year 3 pupils (ages 7–8) reflected on the variety of languages and people who speak them, they learned to identify languages, to look for similarities and differences across languages, and to consider different scripts and origins of words. Children engaged in copying words accurately in speech and writing, such as words in poems and songs. Essentially, pupils became "language investigators" (Jones et al., 2005, p. 66). The project also included a language encounter, that is, language taster sessions during which the pupils were taught by L2 teacher trainees who used the language they were studying to teach. Feedback from the teacher trainees and teachers in the participating primary schools is reported to have been very positive, and Jones et al. (2005) regard the project as a success.

The 'Discovering language' project (Barton, Bragg, & Serratrice, 2009) was undertaken in seven state primary schools in England, involving 374 children in Years 5 and 6 (ages 9–11). The participating schools represented different geographical areas and socioeconomic backgrounds, as measured by their locations (Derbyshire, Cambridgeshire and Northamptonshire, rural and urban), the proportions of pupils with special educational needs, with English as an additional language and with eligibility for free school meals. Like the 'Thinking through languages' project, the 'Discovering language' project introduced children to the basics of a number of languages rather than just a single language. The aims of the programme were to increase motivation among pupils to learn languages, to enhance their linguistic sensitivity to languages and make links with L1 literacy, and to improve intercultural awareness. This was to be achieved by means of a multilingual programme based on a total of five languages, including at least one non-European one with a non-alphabetic script. The project also wanted to offer a practical solution to the issue of non-specialist language teachers at primary level. The programme required the class teacher to learn the rudiments of a language alongside their pupils, with one hour per week (usually broken down into two or three shorter lessons) as the recommended teaching time. The project team provided teachers with all the necessary resources which were aimed at facilitating a cross-curricular approach, linking in with geography, history and citizenship. The linguistic syllabus itself was very basic: it included numbers, colours, animals, greetings, family, home and classroom objects, for instance. All four skills were practised, and metalinguistic elements were highlighted, not least to enable links with literacy lessons in English. The project exposed children to French, German, Spanish, Latin and Japanese. Another language, Punjabi, had been envisaged, but development of the materials took longer than expected and meant that the materials could not be used by the cohort of pupils in question.

The project underwent an evaluation conducted by researchers outside the project team itself (Barton et al., 2009), which made use of questionnaires for pupils and their parents and interviews with head teachers, teachers and a sub-sample of pupils. Out of the questionnaires provided to all pupils, 336 were returned. The questionnaire items were closed-ended and focused on children's views and attitudes. Out of the parent questionnaires, 148 were returned. In addition, the researchers conducted follow-up small-group interviews with some of the pupils, participating teachers and all seven head teachers. With regard to pupils' motivation to learn languages, both intrinsic and extrinsic motivation was assessed. According to the questionnaire data, 56% of pupils reported enjoyment of the 'Discovering language' lessons and thought that learning languages was fun. A total of 51% reported being keener than at the start of Year 5 to learn languages. Enjoyment and interest in continuing language study were significantly related. A total of 55% of the children stated that they had learned a lot from the programme, and 90% thought it was important to learn different languages, mostly for travelling abroad (70%). With regard to equipping children with the tools for successful L2 learning, 63% of the children thought that they understood how languages borrow words from each other, and 64% said they had learned to listen carefully when learning languages. A total of 46% claimed that they understood that grammar helped them with learning languages. Overall, the teachers had some difficulty in assessing the impact of the programme on children's metalinguistic skills, though.

In terms of intercultural awareness, the pupils who were interviewed generally expressed positive opinions about the existence of different cultures. It was not clear, however, whether these positive attitudes had arisen from the programme, or from the fact that the majority of children had travelled abroad (77%). Teachers were not certain whether the programme had broadened pupils' cultural understanding, but they were very much in favour of teaching languages within a cultural context. Most of the teachers and head teachers felt it was better to teach several languages rather than just one, although it must be borne in mind that the sample was self-selected, with participating schools most likely already in favour of a multilingual programme when they signed up for the project. Among the parents, 60% thought that a range of languages should be taught at primary school, while 40% thought a single language would be best.

None of the participating schools had had any formal language teaching on offer prior to participating in the programme, so they were enthusiastic about taking part. The teachers had been somewhat apprehensive about language teaching, but were greatly reassured by the quality of the resources they were provided with. Teachers and head teachers were in agreement that the programme really did not require specialist language teachers for its successful delivery. All except one of the project schools were set to continue with a modified version of 'Discovering language' at the end of the programme. Barton et al. (2009) concede that the evaluation was based on perceptual data only and that children's factual knowledge was not assessed. It is also not clear to what extent the programme was interpreted and implemented as a language awareness programme by the teachers rather than as a multilingual programme per se.

This assessment is very apt and points towards a seemingly consistent weakness in most of the language awareness projects that have been implemented so far: While language exposure of any kind can be expected to be more beneficial to children than no language exposure at all, it remains unclear whether the language awareness programmes that have been put into practice are in any way superior to other approaches to L2 instruction that do not involve a dedicated language awareness component and/or do not draw on the idea of a language apprenticeship. The final project to be considered here addresses this caveat to some extent because it underwent a more thorough (though by no means exhaustive) evaluation which involved comparisons of children participating in the project with children who were not exposed to the project programme.

Like its predecessors, the 'Springboard to languages' project (Tellier, 2012) was aimed at developing primary-school pupils' language awareness and, by extension, their subsequent L2 learning abilities. The programme was based on the hypothesis that the teaching and learning of Esperanto, a constructed language that is entirely regular and transparent in structure, in conjunction with targeted language awareness activities would enhance children's metalinguistic awareness, which, in turn, was expected to facilitate the subsequent acquisition of other languages. In addition, the project sought to foster children's global and cultural awareness via links between English schools and schools abroad that likewise offered the teaching and learning of Esperanto. Unlike its predecessors, the 'Springboard to languages' programme was accompanied by an ongoing evaluation by researchers from outside the project who produced a series of unpublished reports which were subsequently analysed and published in the form of a detailed digest (Roehr, 2012).

The 'Springboard to languages' project and its accompanying evaluation took place from 2006 to 2011, thus covering a period of five school years. The constitution and size of the participant sample varied between school years, although it always consisted of primary-school children and a small number of teachers. The focus was on pupils in Year 3 (ages 7–8), Year 4 (age 8–9), Year 5 (ages 9–10) and Year 6 (ages 10–11). A primary school on the outskirts of Cambridge participated for the entire project duration. In the first and fourth year of the project, two further primary schools were involved for purposes of comparison, one also on the outskirts of Cambridge and one in Lancashire. The languages taught were Esperanto, as mentioned above, as well as French and Spanish, which served as comparison languages. The evaluation combined quantitative and qualitative

Metalinguistic Awareness in Language Education **51**

methods, with emphasis on the latter. The main research instruments were questionnaires and interviews, supplemented by classroom observations. Data collection focused on children's attitudes, metacognition, metalinguistic awareness, and, in the first two years of the evaluation, knowledge of the L2(s) taught, as well as teachers' attitudes and views throughout the project.

Children's attitudes were examined in terms of their enjoyment of language lessons, whether they thought learning a language was fun, whether they felt they had learned a lot, whether they thought they were good at learning languages, whether they believed they needed to know other languages, whether they looked forward to learning other languages, and whether they enjoyed meeting people from other countries. Teachers' attitudes were investigated in terms of their views and perceptions of the project programme, i.e. whether or not they deemed it suitable for the pupils they were teaching, successful in achieving its stated objectives, and well-resourced. Children's metacognition was examined by asking them about their metalinguistic awareness, that is, whether they were able to spot patterns in languages and/or whether they understood how languages borrow from each other. Thus, the children were effectively asked to assess their own metalinguistic abilities. Children's self-reports were complemented by a number of tasks aimed at examining their actual metalinguistic awareness. Finally, the children completed a small number of language tasks based on the language(s) they were taught at the time. These tasks mostly focused on simple, discrete items of vocabulary and grammar and required, for instance, simple translation into English, plural formation, or answering basic reading comprehension questions.

Owing to practical constraints, the set-up of the project was complex, and, not unexpectedly, so were the results of the evaluation (for full details, see Roehr, 2012). The main findings can be summarised as follows. With regard to metalinguistic awareness, the pupils who were assessed over the five years of the project showed, on average, considerable facility when confronted with metalinguistic tasks requiring them to access unknown languages or to transfer knowledge between languages. Tasks targeting these skills included translation from different languages into English at word and sentence level, the identification of cognates in different languages, the matching of pairs of sentences in different languages for meaning, the identification of singular and plural nouns in different languages, and the identification of the adjective in adjective-noun pairings in different languages. When comparison groups were available, it was found that children who were participating in the 'Springboard' programme often performed as well as and on occasion even outperformed peers who were older, had more language learning experience, or had been exposed to a language taster programme. This finding suggests that the programme was successful in raising pupils' metalinguistic awareness, although it should be borne in mind that any comparisons with other groups of children must be interpreted with caution, since variables such as children's general ability, their home background, or the specific characteristics of the teaching context were not controlled. It should also be acknowledged that the research design that was employed did not allow for conclusions as to whether the teaching and learning of languages other than Esperanto, in conjunction with targeted language awareness activities, would have led to similar results.

Questions relying on children's metacognition, i.e. questions which effectively asked pupils to assess their own metalinguistic awareness often resulted in uncertainty, especially in the first three years of the project; it might be the case that slightly older children (age 10) are better able to make the required judgements. Nevertheless, the responses from the 'Springboard' cohorts in the last two years, though given by younger children (ages 8–9), were generally more positive. Children's knowledge of the language(s) taught was only assessed in the first two years, and to a very limited extent. On average, pupils performed well on the tasks they were given. However, based on the available data it is not possible to say whether participation in the 'Springboard' programme had any direct influence on pupils' performance.

With regard to the (limited) information available on children's cross-cultural awareness, it appears that pupils generally developed a positive attitude towards speakers of other languages, especially when the programme was combined with activities such as correspondence or exchanges with pupils in primary schools abroad. Children generally believed that they needed to know other languages and often reported that they enjoyed meeting people from other countries. With regard to children's attitudes more generally, an overall positive picture emerged over the five years of the project. More often than not, a majority of the children who had experienced the 'Springboard' programme reported enjoyment of their language lessons, thought that learning a language was fun, and looked forward to learning other languages. It is noteworthy, however, that there was some fluctuation in attitudes in evidence, both for 'Springboard' cohorts and pupils learning other languages. On occasion, a minority of pupils had positive attitudes, with a majority opting for a 'not sure' response instead. This was particularly the case with respect to the question of whether children felt that they had learned a lot in their language lessons. Reasons for this fluctuation in attitudes are not immediately apparent, although the quality of teaching and learning resources may have had a role to play, especially in the cohorts learning languages other than Esperanto.

The views and perceptions of the teachers and head teachers involved in the 'Springboard' programme were generally positive. Overall, the teachers interviewed felt that the programme was fulfilling its aims. They believed that the regularity of Esperanto helped with the development of children's literacy and even numeracy skills, they had the impression that lower-ability children in particular might benefit from the learning of a regular language such as Esperanto, and they praised the quality of the teaching and learning resources provided by the project team as well as the support available to them. In sum, then, it would appear that the 'Springboard' programme achieved its broad aims of enhancing the participating children's metalinguistic awareness as well as fostering some cross-cultural awareness.

3.3 Metalinguistic Awareness in the Primary-School Classroom

While the language awareness programmes described in the previous section have primarily educational aims, there are also a (relatively small) number of research studies that have empirically investigated the role of metalinguistic awareness in instructed child L2 learning. The focus in this section is on research involving children at primary or elementary level, that is, from the ages of 5 to 6 up to the age of 12 years. In particular, recent empirical work has examined both different ways of enhancing children's metalinguistic awareness and the effectiveness of explicit, form-focused teaching of specific L2 structures on children's subsequent learning and use of these structures. Approaches aimed at raising metalinguistic awareness include training children in error analysis (Bouffard & Sarkar, 2008), investigating how children make use of L1/L2 contrasts (Ammar, Lightbown, & Spada, 2010; Horst, White, & Bell, 2010), and teaching children a 'starter language' prior to further L2 learning (Tellier, 2015; Tellier & Roehr-Brackin, 2013a, 2013b, 2017) in keeping with the approach used in the 'Springboard to languages' project (Tellier, 2012) and the idea of a language apprenticeship (Hawkins, 2005), as outlined above. Two representative studies will be described to illustrate the first two approaches, followed by an outline of the rationale and research into the 'starter language' approach.

Bouffard and Sarkar (2008) conducted a study in which 8-year-old children were trained to notice and repair L2 errors, to identify the language features involved, to negotiate form, and to perform grammatical analyses. The setting for the study was a French immersion programme in Canada, where English-speaking children are educated in a French environment from ages 5 to 6 onwards. In this environment, children typically achieve good levels of reading and listening comprehension, but their L2 productive skills remain below desired standards. The researchers set out to trial a form-focused approach aimed at improving children's oral and written language development via prior enhancement of their metalinguistic awareness. The reported study is based on the assumption that a teacher can train even young learners to engage in metalinguistic questioning and exploration, as long as guidelines are provided to prompt and assist the learners.

Accordingly, the study focused on whether it is possible to train 8-year-old French immersion learners to (1) notice and repair their errors, (2) use metalinguistic terminology to identify forms, and (3) analyse errors using (meta)language as a tool, with a view to improving their metalinguistic awareness. The participants were 8 to 9-year-old English-speaking immersion students in two Grade 3 classes. One of the authors was their teacher, who provided the training that proceeded in three stages over three months. In Stage 1, communicative classroom activities were video-recorded on 23 occasions. Corrective feedback – mostly elicitation, metalinguistic clues and repetition – was provided for lexical, phonological, grammatical and L1 transfer errors in order to prompt self-repair. In Stage 2, the video footage was edited to obtain 287 isolated clips of error-feedback-repair

54 Metalinguistic Awareness in Language Education

sequences extending over 167 minutes in total. In Stage 3, the participating children were audio-recorded over 28 sessions in which they were prompted to analyse the videotaped error sequences with teacher guidance. Each session involved 4–7 children, with a total of 38 participants. The aim was "to push participants to achieve grammatical analysis through collaborative discussion" (Bouffard & Sarkar, 2008, p. 8).

Each error–feedback–repair episode and its associated discussion were coded in a data-driven manner according to level of metalinguistic awareness/grammatical analysis. The levels that were identified actually corresponded closely to the focus of the research question: (1) noticing and repair of errors; (2) use of metalinguistic terminology to identify forms; (3) ability to analyse errors. Phonological errors were not analysed, since they were very rare. Instead, the researchers concentrated on lexical errors, grammatical errors and L1 transfer errors, with the latter including unsolicited use of the L1, lexical mapping errors and word order errors. Overall, the results show an improvement over time in children's metalinguistic abilities regarding the discussion of errors. General patterns indicate that lexical errors often occurred when children used light verbs such as *faire* instead of choosing more precise alternatives. In the teacher-led discussion sessions, the children proved able to use strategies to enhance their metalinguistic awareness. They acknowledged differences between L1 English and L2 French and were able to attend to the negotiation of form. Grammatical errors were analysed in terms of noun phrase and verb phrase errors. Children demonstrated knowledge of the gender of nouns and determiners, and they were able to pinpoint the absence of grammatical gender in English. Verb phrase errors proved to be more challenging. Children's concepts relating to verbs and tenses seemed somewhat confused, although collaborative analysis helped them with identifying forms. Towards the end of the data collection period, instances of more independent successful metalinguistic analysis began to appear. In the area of L1 transfer, lexical mapping errors occurred when an L1 word corresponded to more than one L2 word, e.g. *know* and *savoir/connaître*. With prompting, the children were able to compare L1 and L2 and thus showed facility in identifying the likely cause of such errors. Word order errors proved challenging and required teacher guidance in order to be identified and labelled metalinguistically.

In summary, the data suggested three developmental phases that broadly corresponded to the research issue outlined above. In the earliest phase, the learners were able to correct errors, but required extensive prompting to achieve error identification. In the second phase, the learners began to make metalinguistic guesses and tried to use metalinguistic terminology. These strategies led to the realisation that error analysis was possible. Negotiation of form came more easily, and the children began to move into the final stage, in which they used metalinguistic terminology appropriately. They were able to identify, correct and analyse errors, and occasionally were able to propose explanations. Thus, over the three months of the study, the teacher-led small-group discussions enabled the children to analyse their developing L2 systems metalinguistically.

L1 transfer errors in particular were found to lead quite readily to an awareness of language patterns. The children demonstrated an understanding of language mapping and displayed suitable strategies to address mapping errors. Comparisons between L2 and L1 proved to be a helpful route towards understanding both word order errors and other errors in argument structure. Consequently, Bouffard and Sarkar (2008) conclude that children as young as 8 years can be trained in metalinguistic awareness and show an understanding of how the L2 system works, especially in comparison with the L1. They acknowledge, however, that improved metalinguistic awareness cannot necessarily be equated with development in the sense of improved L2 use. While it is expected that metalinguistic awareness will prove facilitative, the researchers did not show this empirically, given the design of the study.

As a matter of fact, the second example study to be considered (Ammar et al., 2010) aimed to provide just such empirical proof. The researchers investigated 10 to 11-year-old learners' metalinguistic awareness of differences in L1 French and L2 English question formation as well as how such awareness related to learners' L2 performance regarding this grammar point. Question formation in French and English has been examined as a structure exemplifying misleading similarities between L1 and L2. Drawing on their own previous work, the researchers point out that L1 French learners typically have considerable difficulty with recognising and using correct L2 English questions. In a study using a grammaticality judgement task, for instance, students were asked to provide explanations for incorrect items. Although 570 items were judged to be incorrect, explanations were offered for only 56 of them, and no more than 15 of the proposed explanations were related to the targeted structure. The measure was in a written format, however, which may have prevented students from verbalising their metalinguistic awareness in full.

In the present study, Ammar et al. (2010) sought to investigate any L1 influence on learners' ability to judge and form questions in the L2, learners' awareness of differences between French and English interrogatives, and the relationship between awareness and success in judging and constructing questions. The participants were L1 French learners of L2 English in a Canadian immersion context who took part in intensive English classes running over five months of the school year. Prior to these intensive classes, the pupils had had only 60–120 hours of English instruction using a communicative approach. There were 58 participants in total from one intact Grade 6 (age 11) and two intact Grade 5 (age 10) classes. In order to measure learners' knowledge of question formation, the researchers employed a written grammaticality judgement task (GJT), a scrambled-questions task carried out in pairs, and oral interviews with half of the sample to explore their metalinguistic awareness of the targeted structure. The GJT presented question items in pairs, with participants required to choose whether one, both or neither of the two given options were correct. The scrambled-questions task made use of eight envelopes containing words on cards. In pairs, participants were

56 Metalinguistic Awareness in Language Education

required to form as many questions as possible, discuss their answers as they went along, and write down any questions they had formed. Metalinguistic awareness interviews were completed individually with 29 participants.

The results show that on the GJT, the participants were significantly more accurate when the subject of a question was a pronoun than when it was a noun. If *yes/no* and *wh-* questions were analysed separately, significant differences were in evidence as well, with pupils performing best on *yes/no* questions with pronoun subjects and worst on *wh-* questions with noun subjects. The learners tended to reject inversion with noun subjects even after having begun to accept it with pronoun subjects. On the scrambled-questions task, the children produced many questions with declarative word order and fronting, i.e. they placed a question word or *do/does* at the beginning of a declarative sentence. These patterns suggest L1 influence on L2 performance.

The interview analysis focused on the use of *do/does*. Nearly 60% of interviewees thought that *do/does* translated into the invariant French question form *est-ce que*. Interviewees were also asked directly whether there were any differences between French and English question forms. Almost a third of the learners (31%) saw no difference and/or was unable to offer any explanation of perceived differences, 48% provided partial explanations of the differences, and only 21% were able to provide correct explanations. This relatively low level of metalinguistic awareness is attributed to the communicative orientation of the English classes the students were attending. The researchers conclude that learners have incomplete knowledge not only of L2 metalinguistic rules, but also of how interrogatives work in the L1.

Importantly, Ammar et al. (2010) report a significant positive correlation between learners' metalinguistic awareness as measured by the oral interview and their performance on the GJT and scrambled-questions task. Although correlations cannot prove cause and effect, it is possible to argue that the two language tasks encouraged the use of explicit knowledge, and any explicit knowledge that the learners had at their disposal helped with successful task performance. The researchers recommend that learners should be guided towards identifying potentially problematic relationships between L1 and L2 structures – something that can be achieved by means of contrastive form-focused instruction, for instance.

Unlike the previous two example studies which were conducted in immersion classrooms in Canada, a series of empirical studies examining the effect of a 'starter language' on children's metalinguistic awareness and their subsequent L2 learning has been carried out in the limited-input setting of primary-school L2 classrooms in England. The rationale for a 'starter language' approach is closely connected with the issue of implicit vs. explicit learning in individuals of different ages. Researchers generally assume that child L2 learners, who have not yet reached cognitive maturity, learn primarily implicitly. Moreover, evidence from age-of-onset studies that have compared individuals who began L2 learning in naturalistic settings either early (i.e. as children) or late (i.e. as adolescents or adults) suggests that children learn very successfully in input-rich environments that offer both intensive and extensive L2 exposure (DeKeyser, 2000; J. S. Johnson & Newport, 1989). Although children initially learn more slowly than adults, they eventually reach higher levels of proficiency than older learners with a later starting age (Birdsong, 2006; Hyltenstam & Abrahamsson, 2003).

In classroom settings that offer limited L2 input only, however, a different performance pattern can be observed. Research looking at the attainment of learners exposed to classroom-based L2 instruction has shown that later starters consistently outperform younger starters on measures of L2 achievement. Put differently, older children and adolescents do better than younger children on a variety of performance measures after the same amount of L2 exposure, if input is limited to a few hours per week over the school year (Cenoz, 2003; García Mayo, 2003; Harley & Hart, 1997; Larson-Hall, 2008; Muñoz, 2008, 2009, 2006). In an input-poor environment, explicit learning is particularly useful because explicit processes are fast and efficient, unlike implicit learning, which requires considerable exposure to input over a longer period of time in order to be maximally successful (DeKeyser, 2003). Explicit learning is conscious and intentional, though, and it thus requires attention, awareness and effort. Put differently, explicit learning is cognitively demanding, which is why cognitively more mature learners (e.g. adolescents) are better able to cope than cognitively less mature learners (e.g. young children).

While this line of argument is generally uncontroversial, it is worth noting that children do not exclusively learn implicitly, just as adults do not exclusively learn explicitly. Recent research suggests that younger children cannot only draw on, but can also benefit from explicit knowledge and learning (e.g. Harley, 1998; Lichtman, 2013, 2016; Milton & Alexiou, 2006). Researchers investigating the potential effects of a 'starter language' approach (Tellier, 2015, 2012; Tellier & Roehr-Brackin, 2013a, 2013b, 2017) hypothesise that if young children's developing metalinguistic awareness and their developing capacity to learn explicitly could be enhanced, then their classroom-based L2 learning could potentially be made more successful. In other words, children who are better able to learn explicitly at an early age would be better able to benefit even from limited L2 input.

Specifically, learning an 'easy' language that lends itself especially well to metalinguistic inspection, reflection and analysis may help sharpen a learner's metalinguistic abilities (Fettes, 1997), and it may thus help accelerate the development of explicit learning capacity. The constructed language Esperanto was designed to be easy to learn and use. It has highly regular morphology and syntax, and it is characterised by direct phoneme-grapheme correspondence. The language has just 16 key rules of grammar and a transparent morphological system. In lexical terms, Esperanto draws on the main European languages, with a particularly heavy influence from the Romance languages. In the context of classroom-based child

L2 learning in the 21st century, the introduction of Esperanto may also be considered as a more egalitarian tool than the introduction of a language such as Latin, which has traditionally been regarded as a suitable means for raising language learners' metalinguistic awareness (e.g. Sparks, Ganschow, Fluharty, & Little, 1995–6). Unlike Latin, Esperanto is a continually evolving language with third- and fourth-generation speakers, and it therefore arguably lends itself more readily than Latin to a focus on all four skills, including speaking and listening (Tellier & Roehr-Brackin, 2013a).

In a study seeking to establish whether Esperanto would indeed be easier to learn than a non-constructed L2, Tellier and Roehr-Brackin (2013b) compared two groups of 8 to 9-year-old English-speaking children who were instructed in either Esperanto (N = 14) or French (N = 14) over a school year. The researchers found that all children achieved statistically significant gains on measures of language learning aptitude, metalinguistic awareness and L2 proficiency in the course of the year. However, effect sizes in the Esperanto group were larger throughout, and this group also exhibited greater homogeneity of performance. Moreover, the Esperanto group showed a closer association between aptitude, metalinguistic awareness and L2 proficiency at the end of the treatment. Importantly, Esperanto proved significantly easier to learn than French, with larger gains in L2 proficiency achieved by the Esperanto group compared with the French group. Language-analytic ability was a significant predictor of L2 achievement in the sample as a whole.

In a further study (Tellier & Roehr-Brackin, 2013a), the same researchers compared two groups of 11 to 12-year-old English-speaking children on a measure of metalinguistic awareness. The first group (N = 35) had learned Esperanto and a European L2 in Years 3–4 and Years 5–6 of primary school, respectively, while the second group (N = 168) had learned various combinations of European and non-European L2s in Years 3–6 of primary school. Differences in overall level of metalinguistic awareness did not reach statistical significance, but the group that had been exposed to Esperanto significantly outperformed the comparison group on one of the eleven metalinguistic tasks included in the measure of metalinguistic awareness. This group also displayed a more homogeneous performance pattern, indicating that learning Esperanto may have a lasting levelling effect that reduces differences between children with varying (metalinguistic) abilities. The researchers suggested that exposure to Esperanto as a 'starter language' may be of particular benefit to children exhibiting lower and/or as yet less developed cognitive abilities because such children may be better able to cope with a regular and transparent language, they may experience greater success when attempting to acquire such a language, and they may feel encouraged and more confident in their capacity as L2 learners.

More recently, Tellier and Roehr-Brackin (2017) addressed the 'starter language' hypothesis directly in the context of a quasi-experimental study with 8 to 9-year-old English-speaking children (N = 178). The researchers compared

Metalinguistic Awareness in Language Education **59**

children exposed to the constructed language Esperanto plus a dedicated focus-on-form element (Group E+) with children exposed to Esperanto (Group E), German (Group G) and Italian (Group I) without dedicated focus on form for half a school year. Subsequently, all children followed the same instructional programme in French (with focus on form) for the second half of the school year. The researchers examined the effect of the different 'starter language' programmes on children's development of metalinguistic awareness as measured by a specifically designed instrument (Tellier, 2013, see Chapter 6 for details) as well as their development of L2 French proficiency. They also examined whether children with lower language learning aptitude in particular would benefit from being exposed to Esperanto as a 'starter language'.

The results show that Group E+ exhibited significantly greater gains than Group I and marginally greater gains than Group G on the measure of metalinguistic awareness at the end of the first half of the treatment. All groups progressed significantly in French proficiency during the second half of the treatment and showed no attrition on a delayed post-test. Between-group differences in French proficiency gains were statistically non-significant, but Group E+ and Group E exhibited greater homogeneity of performance in French at post-test. This finding appears to lend further support to the argument that learning Esperanto as a 'starter language' may have a levelling effect in mixed-ability groups of children who are taught together in the classroom. However, the absence of any advantage in L2 French gains for the Esperanto groups indicates that in the context of this study at least, Esperanto did not convey any particular benefits for subsequent L2 learning. This finding was further borne out by the fact that language learning aptitude played a significant role in the development of French knowledge in all groups, with no advantages in evidence for children of lower aptitude who had been exposed to Esperanto as opposed to Italian or German.

Given the significantly greater gains of Group E+ in terms of metalinguistic awareness, the researchers argue that exposure to teacher-led form-focused activities in an age-appropriate 'starter language' programme targeting all four skills can have a beneficial effect on children's development of metalinguistic awareness – a result which is consistent with the view that young children can and do develop metalinguistic abilities. What is not clear from the present study, of course, is whether form-focused activities provided in connection with a non-constructed L2 would have led to the same result. Nevertheless, the finding suggests that explicit instruction comprising deductive, form-focused activities can be effective even with young learners (Tellier & Roehr-Brackin, 2017).

The latter point has been supported by a number of studies which exposed primary-level L2 learners to explicit, form-focused instruction on selected L2 structures in the context of quasi-experimental research. Most studies have been carried out with learners in later years of primary school, i.e. at ages 10, 11 and 12. Work in Canadian immersion classrooms has shown that children in that age

60 Metalinguistic Awareness in Language Education

range can benefit from form-focused instruction on question formation (L. White, Spada, Lightbown, & Ranta, 1991), a structure that is notoriously difficult for L1 French learners of L2 English (see also Ammar et al., 2010 discussed above), as well as form-focused instruction on the accurate use of the English possessive determiners *his* and *her*, another persistent source of error for L1 French learners of English (J. White, 2008; J. White & Ranta, 2002). Research in input-limited classrooms in Europe has produced comparable results. In a replication of J. White and Ranta's (2002) study, for instance, Serrano (2011) reports some positive effects on Spanish/Catalan bilingual learners' metalinguistic knowledge and accurate use of the English possessive determiners *his* and *her*, while Hanan (2015) found lasting positive effects of explicit, input-based instruction on the written and oral use of L2 German accusative case in 9 to 11-year-old English-speaking learners. One of the most interesting studies in this research tradition is perhaps the work carried out by Harley (1998), which involved children aged just 7 to 8 years and thus set the age boundary for explicit, form-focused instruction to an unusually low level.

Harley (1998) carried out her study with English-speaking children in Grade 2 in an intensive French immersion programme in Canada. The targeted L2 feature was grammatical gender, and in particular the gender-relevant information provided by determiners and morphophonological clues in certain French noun endings. As in the studies mentioned in the previous paragraph, the targeted feature was chosen because of the challenge it typically poses to learners. Apart from the low salience and communicative redundancy of the form, English-speaking learners in particular do not have a similar concept in their L1 and are therefore not primed to attend to grammatical gender in the L2. What is more, immersion learners are exposed to much misleading input from their peers who also struggle with accurate use of the form.

Six intact classes with between 19 and 26 children per group participated in the study. The children were exposed to the experimental instructional treatment for 20 minutes per day over five weeks. The learners were pre-tested and post-tested immediately after the end of the treatment and again after a delay of six months. The form-focused activities used in the treatment were designed to make attention to grammatical gender task-essential by enhancing the salience of the form in the input and providing opportunities for focused output. In terms of format, the activities were primarily adaptations of language games already known to the children, e.g. 'I spy', 'Bingo' and 'Simon says'. The presentation of metalinguistic rules was avoided because it was deemed inappropriate for children of such a young age.

The measures used included four tests: an aural discrimination task (Test 1), an aurally administered multiple-choice task requiring children to choose the correct article for nouns they heard (Test 2), an individual production task in which children had to assign grammatical gender to novel nouns (Test 3), and an individual production task asking children to name items (determiner and noun) for which the vocabulary was already known (Test 4). The latter two tasks were administered to a random sub-sample of 8 children per class. The comparison cohort comprised children from six intact classes of the preceding school year who had participated in the same tests. They had not been pre-tested, however, so the researcher compared the delayed post-test scores of the experimental group with the end-of-year scores of the control group.

The results show that the experimental group made significant progress over time on Tests 1, 2 and 4. Progress continued at a slower rate (Tests 1 and 2) or stabilised (Test 4) between the immediate and delayed post-tests. There was no significant progress in evidence on Test 3, which required generalisation to novel nouns. This finding may indicate that the children relied on item-based rather than system learning, possibly because there was insufficient input available to allow them to identify and generalise predictive patterns. In other words, the young learners were not yet familiar with a sufficiently large number of exemplar nouns to derive abstractions beyond the item level. This null result apart, however, the experimental group significantly outperformed the control group on Tests 1, 2 and 4. Accordingly, Harley (1998) argues that providing explicit instruction on grammatical gender in the context of form-focused activities which make attention to the targeted structure task-essential is beneficial and helpful even for 7 to 8-year-olds.

4

METALINGUISTIC AWARENESS AS EXPLICIT KNOWLEDGE AND LEARNING

Theoretical Premises

4.1 The Interface of Explicit and Implicit Knowledge

In the last section of the previous chapter, a small number of studies investigating the potential benefits of form-focused, explicit instruction for child L2 learners were introduced. Research looking at the effects of explicit instruction in adolescent and adult L2 learners is much more common, which is unsurprising, given that the ability to make maximum use of explicit knowledge and learning has been linked with cognitive maturity, that is, fully developed capacities in terms of working memory, language-analytic, reasoning and strategic abilities. In other words, learners from approximately age 13 onwards are much better able than younger learners to utilise metalinguistic awareness in the sense of explicit knowledge about language, although this improvement is not sudden or abrupt, of course, with metalinguistic abilities developing gradually during childhood (see Chapter 2). Still, adolescents and adults are better equipped than young children to draw on explicit knowledge as both a product of and a primer for explicit learning in the context of explicit instruction because of the demanding and resource-intensive nature of the cognitive processes involved. These processes are the focus of this chapter; as we shall see, there has been extensive theorising in the field of instructed SLA, but a number of controversies remain, not least owing to the challenges involved in the empirical verification of some of the hypothesised constructs.

As we saw in Chapter 1, a key defining characteristic of explicit knowledge, memory and learning is conscious awareness on the part of the speaker/learner; conversely, a key defining characteristic of implicit knowledge, memory and learning is the absence of conscious awareness. A detailed breakdown of properties distinguishing implicit and explicit knowledge has been put forward (R. Ellis,

2004; R. Ellis et al., 2009), according to which implicit knowledge is tacit and intuitive, whereas explicit knowledge is conscious. By the same token, implicit knowledge is procedural, whereas explicit knowledge is declarative. L2 learners' procedural rules may or may not be target-like, while declarative rules are said to be often imprecise and inaccurate. Implicit knowledge is available through automatic processing, whereas explicit knowledge is generally accessible only through controlled processing. Default L2 production relies on implicit knowledge, but difficulty in performing a language task may result in learners attempting to exploit explicit knowledge. Implicit knowledge is only evident in learners' verbal behaviour, whereas explicit knowledge can be verbalised, i.e. talked about, often by making use of technical metalanguage, though knowledge of metalinguistic terminology is not considered an essential component of explicit knowledge. L2 learners utilise a combination of implicit and explicit knowledge. As learners exploit both systems in performance, they may develop both implicit and explicit knowledge of the same linguistic feature, although this is not necessarily the case (R. Ellis, 2004; R. Ellis et al., 2009).

It is immediately obvious that the properties of explicit knowledge all relate in one way or another to conscious awareness, and explicit and implicit instruction can be contrasted along similar lines. Explicit instruction draws on the learner's metalinguistic awareness, either by providing metalinguistic descriptions and explanations of the linguistic feature that is the target of instruction, or by asking learners to attend to the targeted linguistic feature with the aim of arriving at metalinguistic generalisations of their own (Norris & Ortega, 2001). The former approach is typically labelled deductive, the latter approach inductive (R. Ellis et al., 2009; Hulstijn, 2005). A deductive teaching sequence typically moves top-down from pedagogical rule presentation to practice with concrete linguistic instances, whereas an inductive teaching sequence moves bottom-up from engagement with concrete linguistic instances to the pedagogical grammar rule (R. Ellis & Shintani, 2014). Unlike explicit instruction of either the deductive or the inductive kind, implicit instruction is aimed at enabling learners to infer patterns without awareness; it exposes learners to linguistic instances, but the focus is exclusively on meaning, not form (R. Ellis et al., 2009).

Clearly, there is a difference between instruction, knowledge and learning: We cannot be sure that explicit instruction will lead to explicit learning and knowledge, or that implicit instruction will lead to implicit learning and knowledge. Instead, it is a fair assumption that both explicit and implicit learning will take place, though to varying degrees, depending on the type of instruction that is offered in the learning context as well as individual learner variables. It has been shown empirically that both implicit and explicit knowledge are implicated in learners' L2 proficiency (R. Ellis, 2006b), and it is highly likely that cognitively mature L2 learners will attempt to learn explicitly and/or acquire explicit knowledge at least some of the time, especially (though not exclusively) if they are exposed to explicit instruction. This is attributable to the fact that instructed

64 Theoretical Premises of Explicit Knowledge/Learning

adolescent and adult learners typically expect a certain focus on form in the classroom and generally consider such an approach useful and necessary for successful learning (Loewen et al., 2009; Scheffler, 2009; Schulz, 2001; Thepseenu & Roehr, 2013). Researchers tend to agree that the process of explicit learning results primarily in explicit knowledge, while implicit learning results primarily in implicit knowledge (Hulstijn, 2005; Rebuschat, 2013). In view of the fact that explicit instruction draws on learners' metalinguistic awareness, encourages explicit learning and is thus expected to lead to primarily explicit knowledge, a crucial concern in SLA research is the question of whether explicit instruction, learning or knowledge can contribute to the development of implicit knowledge (Dörnyei, 2009) – the tacit, intuitive knowledge source that allows a speaker/ learner to engage in fluent, automatic and effortless language use.

When considering this issue, researchers have traditionally distinguished between three so-called interface positions that represent different views on the relationship between explicit and implicit knowledge and learning (see, e.g., R. Ellis et al., 2009; Hulstijn & de Graaff, 1994). According to the non-interface position, which is typically associated with early work by Krashen (1981, 1982; Krashen & Terrell, 1983) arguing for the distinction between non-conscious 'acquisition' and conscious 'learning', and sometimes also more recent work by Paradis and colleagues (e.g. Paradis, 2004) focusing on language representation and processing in neuroanatomical terms, explicit and implicit knowledge are stored and accessed independently and cannot influence each other. According to the opposing strong-interface position, which is typically associated with researchers applying skill acquisition theory as conceptualised in the so-called ACT (Adaptive Control of Thought) model (J. R. Anderson, 1993, 1995, 1996, 2000; Segalowitz, 2003) to L2 learning (e.g. DeKeyser, 2007; K. Johnson, 1996), explicit or declarative knowledge can be proceduralized through extensive practice. A third point of view is the weak-interface position, which appears to have become the consensus view adopted in most current SLA research. The weak-interface position has common ground with the non-interface position in that it regards explicit and implicit knowledge as separable and distinct. It also shares common ground with the strong-interface position because it argues that explicit knowledge can be conducive to the development of implicit knowledge. The weak-interface position thus offers a compromise view that is likely to be acceptable to most (if not all) parties, thus arguably rendering the traditional interface debate moot.

The weak-interface position has been articulated in most detail by Nick Ellis and colleagues (N. C. Ellis, 2002, 2005, 2011, 2015; N. C. Ellis & Larsen-Freeman, 2006) and has subsequently been espoused by a number of other researchers (e.g. Dörnyei, 2009; R. Ellis et al., 2009; Roehr, 2008a). In essence, the weak-interface position argues that explicit learning and knowledge can contribute indirectly to implicit learning and knowledge. However, it is not a question of declarative or metalinguistic rules being converted into implicit knowledge; instead, sequences of language that have been comprehended or constructed with the help of such

Theoretical Premises of Explicit Knowledge/Learning **65**

explicit rules may be automatized and thus become part of a learner's implicit knowledge. Specifically, explicit knowledge, which includes metalinguistic information provided by means of corrective feedback, can help the learner focus their attention on L2 forms in the input that might otherwise be disregarded, it can enable the learner to compare input features with features they produce in their spoken or written output, it can help solve comprehension difficulties, facilitate output practice via the controlled use of declarative knowledge, and it can thus provide further (auto-)input (Dörnyei, 2009; N. C. Ellis, 2011; R. Ellis et al., 2009). In sum, then, a number of facilitative functions are posited. But how does the weak interface happen? Or, put differently, what are the cognitive processes involved in allowing a learner to make use of explicit knowledge and learning for the development of implicit knowledge?

The interface between explicit and implicit knowledge and learning has been described as dynamic, situated and contextualised, since it happens transiently during conscious processing, but with an enduring influence on implicit cognition. Thus, consciousness itself provides the weak interface, or, to be more precise, the psychological processes of the interface are synchronous with consciousness (N. C. Ellis, 2011). Consciousness involves limited information that creates access to a large number of unconscious sources of knowledge: "Consciousness is the publicity organ of the brain. It is a facility for accessing, disseminating, and exchanging information, and for exercising global coordination and control. This is the interface, the 'stuff' of learning" (N. C. Ellis & Larsen-Freeman, 2006, p. 571). In his in-depth discussion of the interface between explicit and implicit learning, Nick Ellis (2005) argues that implicit learning occurs during fluent comprehension and production, whereas explicit learning occurs during conscious efforts to negotiate meaning and achieve successful communication. Modularisation of the representational system into explicit and implicit components is seen as emergent, with implicit, non-conscious learning processes taking place automatically during language use. Such processes are necessary for developing fluency, but explicit processes are needed as well, since many aspects of the L2 are acquired only very slowly or not at all through implicit processes alone. Although explicit and implicit knowledge are distinct and dissociated in the sense that they involve different types of representation and are sub-served by different parts of the brain, they still interact, with the psychological processes of interface happening during conscious processing, as stated above. During fluent language processing, our implicit systems automatically handle the input, while our conscious selves can concentrate on the meaning rather than the form of an utterance. However, in unpredictable situations, e.g. when comprehension difficulties arise, explicit processes take over, and consciousness is used to organise existing knowledge in new ways. Consciousness is achieved through unification as evidenced in the neurological process of binding: "Neural systems in the hippocampus bind disparate cortical representations into unitary episodic representations" (N. C. Ellis, 2005, p. 308).

66 Theoretical Premises of Explicit Knowledge/Learning

Implicit, non-conscious learning is associative learning during which the learner keeps track of the frequency distributions of input features. It is pointed out that the psycholinguistic evidence for the importance of such implicit tallying, priming and strengthening of connections in language acquisition is increasingly being supported by neurobiological research, which has identified the areas of the brain involved in non-conscious processing. Nick Ellis (2005) writes that the neural correlates of consciousness are a coalition of forebrain neurons implicated in working memory and planning. Competition between coalitions of neurons leads to a winner-takes-all situation, i.e. consciousness gives clout. When processes compete for control, the one with the greatest clout dominates the scene until it is displaced by a process with even greater clout. A discrete epoch of consciousness lasts between 20 and 200 milliseconds before it is replaced by another coalition in an ongoing stream of 'snapshots'. Conscious processing is spread widely over the brain, unifying otherwise disparate areas in a synchronised focus of activity. Accordingly, conscious activity gives scope for long-range associations, bringing about a whole new level of potential learning outcomes.

By contrast, implicit learning occurs largely within a single modality and involves representations and routines within a single module. While a vast number of unconscious neural processes happen simultaneously at any given moment, conscious capacity represents a narrow bottleneck. However, consciousness appears to be a gateway that creates global access to any part of the nervous system. Our state of mind reflects complex dynamic interactions of implicit and explicit knowledge. While thinking in the sense of the manipulation of data and concepts is largely unconscious, images, tones, silent speech and feelings are conscious parts of thought (N. C. Ellis, 2005). Biological systems are described as accretive (N. C. Ellis, 2005), that is, development and growth is the consequence of gradual addition. Thus, while the speech system is overlaid on a set of organs that supported breathing, eating and simple vocalisation in earlier mammals, language is overlaid on systems for the visual representation of the world. Although the symbolic representations of language are different from the analogue representations of vision, both are believed to interact, which allows us to produce mental images by linguistic means. Possibly, the global broadcasting property of consciousness may be overlaid on earlier, primarily sensorimotor functions.

According to Nick Ellis (2005), implicit learning can be compared with multivariate statistical analysis, in the sense that the correlated variables will become apparent as long as the number of observations is large enough. The greater the number of potential variables, the greater the sample size required for the computation of robust estimates, and the slower the learning process. The learner has at their disposal attention-focusing biases acquired through word-learning heuristics, e.g. the whole-object constraint (new words often apply to whole objects), the mutual-exclusivity constraint (new words are likely to refer to things for which a name is not already known), and the tendency for words to relate to things distinguished by shape or function rather than colour or texture, for instance. These word-learning principles emerge from general cognition including attention and rational inference, i.e. knowledge of the world and the ways language usually refers to it, as well as the learner's existing repertoire of linguistic constructions. As language is a social construction, the ways in which language refers to the world are culturally determined.

At the point of incomprehension in language learning, conscious resources are brought to bear. The primary mechanism of explicit learning is in the initial registration of pattern recognisers for linguistic constructions, since conscious awareness is relevant in the initial consolidation of a unitary representation. Through attention, features can be bound to form newly integrated objects. Working memory is involved in both the initial encoding and the ultimate recall of explicit knowledge.

The encoding of episodic memories is mediated by two brain components, namely a frontal-lobe component whose operations are strategic, organisational and accessible to consciousness and voluntary control, and a medial temporal or hippocampal component whose operations are essentially automatic. There is ample evidence for the role of working memory in the formation of new memories. Explicit memories are consolidated with the help of neural systems in the hippocampus and related limbic structures. Unitised memory representations constitute pattern recognition units for new stimulus configurations; they also help consolidate new bindings, which are adopted by neocortical regions of the brain, where they are subsequently tuned implicitly.

As the neocortex gradually integrates new information with existing knowledge, it has a slow learning rate. The hippocampus, on the other hand, learns rapidly through assigning distinctive sparse representations to input patterns which encode the episodic details of specific events. The initial representation of a form-meaning association usually involves consolidation of a specific explicit memory, i.e. a formula, which underlies subsequent more schematic linguistic constructions. As exemplars accumulate, analysis becomes possible. Analysis may occur at the explicit level of hypothesis formation and analogy in working memory, and/or at the implicit level of categorisation, distributional analysis, and frequency-based pattern abstraction. Once a form–meaning mapping has been consolidated, there is scope for implicit learning on every subsequent occasion of use. Through usage, the elements in the construction are primed and made more available as a result. All the elements that are activated during processing are bound more tightly together as a whole, and conscious awareness on the part of the learner is no longer necessary (N. C. Ellis, 2005).

Context plays an important role in determining the content of consciousness. For instance, most English words have multiple meanings, yet we can only become conscious of one meaning at a time. Metalinguistic information can have a priming function for conscious interpretations, since it can provide the context that serves as a powerful constraint on the processing of subsequent forms. In this

68 Theoretical Premises of Explicit Knowledge/Learning

sense, metalinguistic knowledge interacts with implicit learning via a dynamic interface. Explicit knowledge can also be brought to mind to construct utterances. Thus, the learner may use explicit memories to scaffold the building of linguistic constructions in working memory. Formulas may be used for analogical reasoning and conceptual blending. The processes and the results of explicit construction can then feed into implicit learning. Moreover, declarative knowledge can facilitate monitoring. Learners can monitor their own output during production because their utterances may remind them of various forms of other relevant knowledge. In this sense, metalinguistic knowledge is used to counter erroneous implicit habits. Put differently, if metalinguistic knowledge comes to consciousness at the appropriate moment, it can influence the processing of a language form and its corresponding interpretation and thus indirectly impact on implicit language knowledge. Through corrective feedback such as recasts, communication partners can help scaffold both comprehension and production. A helpful L1 speaker may provide focused feedback to flawed output which highlights the relevant element of the form while the desired meaning to be expressed is still active in the L2 learner's working memory.

Working memory plays a crucial role in consciousness. Somewhat quirkily, Nick Ellis (2005, p. 337) describes working memory as being "like 221b Baker Street: It is the home of explicit deduction, hypothesis formation, analogical reasoning, prioritization, control and decision-making. It is where we develop, apply, and hone our metalinguistic insights into an L2". The different components of working memory seem to be differentially involved in implicit and explicit learning processes. Phonological short-term memory should contribute to the memory of form at both an implicit and an explicit level and to the ability to hold phonological feedback. Explicit memory and its ready access in the episodic buffer should facilitate conscious construction of output and monitoring. The supervisory system of the central executive should relate to explicit learning and the analysis of language temporarily represented in the phonological loop or episodic buffer, as well as in conscious construction of output. Nevertheless, the various components of working memory clearly work together and partially overlap in different tasks. Nick Ellis (2005) concludes his extensive overview with a summary of the main claim of the weak-interface position: While the systems of implicit and explicit processing are functionally and anatomically separate, they are dynamically involved with each other in every cognitive task and every learning episode, with consciousness serving as the interface.

The concept of consciousness is complex and arguably constitutes a research field in its own right, with cognitive scientists, psychologists and philosophers still grappling with and debating its definition and measurement. Baddeley (1997) distinguishes three approaches to the study of consciousness, that is, (1) consciousness as a mystical entity that is the essence of the human mind, (2) the nature of conscious experience: Why do we experience the world as we do? How can we account for the 'qualia' that constitute our conscious sensory

Theoretical Premises of Explicit Knowledge/Learning **69**

awareness?, and (3) consciousness as a biological phenomenon whose function and manner of operation can be investigated in the same way as any other complex biological phenomenon. Favouring the latter approach (3), Baddeley (1997) regards consciousness as an emerging property of certain patterns of physical and neural development, thus obviating the need for any supplementary metaphysical, mystical or theological assumptions. He writes that our subjective feeling that our experience of the world is central to our being is believed to have led Descartes to postulate *cogito ergo sum*. Yet, the solidity and stability of personal experience is only apparent, and it may possibly be illusory. Drawing on linguistic analysis, it can be shown that the concepts of mind and consciousness only appeared in the mainstream European languages following Descartes' influential work. The concept of consciousness is also lacking in Ancient Greek and Chinese – languages associated with major philosophical traditions.

Baddeley argues that consciousness is most usefully regarded as an evolutionary solution to a biological problem. In this approach, the phenomena that are attributed to consciousness reflect the way in which the human brain has evolved, demonstrating one way of solving a number of cognitive problems. Consciousness is thus viewed as a difficult and intriguing problem, but not as a problem that is qualitatively different from other questions in cognitive psychology. Baddeley proposes a speculative account of consciousness: Humans are born in a vulnerable state, but with a substantial capacity to adapt through learning, with consciousness representing an important part of this survival skill. The need to perceive and categorise the world in terms of integrated objects is obvious; if relevant sensory channels are bound together through conscious awareness, objects can be perceived as whole units. In conscious awareness, information from a range of correlated variables is simultaneously available. As multimodal information is available as phenomenological experience, we can use attentional processes to selectively focus and reflect on one object or one aspect of the environment. Individual pieces of information about separate episodes or experiences can be stored and recalled, thus usefully complementing implicit learning processes in which individual instances may become absorbed in overall schemas. Episodic memories are relevant in many circumstances, not least in social interaction where it is of interest and import to know who did what to whom and when. Indeed, it has been proposed that conscious, explicit memory has primarily evolved because of its role in social interaction.

Accumulated information that is consistent across repeated experiences is described as the basis of semantic memory. While such episodes can initially be retrieved as individual memories, their accumulation seems to contribute to knowledge of the world that is maintained long after the capacity to recall independent episodes has been lost. In sum, "episodic memory is based on the encoding of conscious experience [and] it offers the possibility of retrieving aspects of such experiences, given the appropriate cue" (Baddeley, 1997, pp. 332–333). Through consciousness and episodic and semantic memory, humans not only have some

70 Theoretical Premises of Explicit Knowledge/Learning

command of their environment and their past, but can also plan for the future by taking advantage of learned knowledge and accumulated experience. A series of goals can be set up, pursued, and modified on the basis of subsequent information. Working memory seems to have evolved as a process for achieving this. The use of mental models allows us to deal with the environment in a flexible way that goes beyond simple reaction. We can reflect, plan, select, and thus act constructively. It is conceded that conscious awareness may not be the only way of solving the problem of perceiving the world coherently and using the past to plan for the future. However, it appears to be the evolutionary path along which humans have evolved (Baddeley, 1997).

As we have seen in the preceding paragraphs, if consciousness is viewed as an essentially biological phenomenon, it can be conceptualised as a unifying force (Dienes & Perner, 2003) that binds together representations across modalities – a cognitive state that is brought about through synchronised neuronal activity. The idea of binding is discussed in the fields of both psychology and cognitive science, and it is relevant to researchers working in neural network modelling, philosophy of mind and cognitive neuroscience (Engel, 2003). Encoding and retrieval of information in neuronal networks requires a mechanism which allows for the expression of specific relationships between elementary processors. This binding problem arises for several reasons. As processing underlying specific cognitive functions is distributed across network elements, it is necessary to identify those nodes that participate in the same process. Perception and action in complex environments requires the parallel processing of information relating to different events which have to be kept apart to allow for sensory segmentation and goal-directed behaviour. However, specific yet flexible binding appears to be needed to enable systematic and productive cognitive processes to occur. Indeed, many cognitive functions require the context-dependent selection of relevant information from a rich set of available data, for which appropriate binding may be a prerequisite. By the same token, a binding mechanism may be critical for the establishment of conscious mental states. This view is based on the intuition that consciousness requires integration and coherence of mental contents, and the suggestion that conscious recall of memory contents requires the binding of distributed information stored in spatially separate areas of the brain. According to this view, only appropriately bound neuronal activity can enter working memory and become available for access to phenomenal consciousness (Engel, 2003).

In his discussion of this issue, Engel (2003) focuses on sensory awareness, a basic form of phenomenal consciousness which most higher-order mammals are thought to share with humans. Phenomenal consciousness is considered basic in the sense that it does not extend to higher-order features such as language or an elaborated self-model. Sensory awareness as the basic form of phenomenal consciousness involves selective attention to relevant information, working memory for short-term storage of episodic contents, and the capacity for structured representation, defined as "the ability to achieve coherence of the contents of mental states and to establish specific relationships between representational items" (p. 133). Empirical evidence suggests that temporal binding, or precisely synchronised neuronal discharges, may be crucial for generating such functionally effective representational states, as well as for the selection of relevant information. Thus, the binding problem is solved by exploiting the temporal aspects of neuronal activity. It is assumed that synchrony among neurons is subject to both bottom-up and top-down influences. In other words, it is determined by the stimulus as well as factors like expectation, attention, and knowledge about the situational context. Highly selective temporal structures would allow for the establishment of a distinct representational pattern or so-called assembly for each object, so that the visual system could achieve figure-ground segregation. The temporal binding model as developed for the visual modality may be generalised to other cortical systems. Moreover, synchrony should occur between different systems. In sum, it is proposed that temporal binding in the sense of synchronisation of assemblies is a necessary but not a sufficient condition for conscious awareness (Engel, 2003).

Apart from cognitive scientists seeking to understand the neural correlates of consciousness (Block, 2005; Engel, 2003), philosophers of mind have also tackled the problem of consciousness. Their focus is not so much on consciousness as a biological phenomenon, but on the nature of conscious experience, although the concept of unification remains prominent. According to Bayne and Chalmers (2003), when a person has multiple conscious experiences at the same time, these experiences can be described as unified, in the sense that they are aspects of a single encompassing state of consciousness. Therefore, for instance, a person may simultaneously have the visual experience of a red book, the auditory experience of birds singing, and the emotional experience of melancholy. Although these experiences are distinct and could occur in isolation, they seem to be tied together when experienced all at once. The authors examine the idea of the unity of consciousness from a philosophical perspective, arguing that there are in fact four distinct notions of unity, namely objectual unity, spatial unity, subject unity and subsumptive unity. Two states of consciousness are objectually unified when they are directed at the same object. Thus, when watching a blue car go down the road, we have a unified experience of colour (blue), shape (car), motion (along the road) and possibly sound (engine noise). Accordingly, objectual unity can cross different sensory domains. This phenomenon is also referred to as binding. Objectual unity is clearly important, but it cannot account for all our conscious states.

Two conscious states are spatially unified when they represent objects as being part of the same space. When seeing a red book on a table and observing a blue car going down the road, our experiences of the book and the car are not directed at the same object, but both objects are represented as part of the same visual scene. However, as experiences such as emotions have no spatial content, spatial unity does not suffice either. Two conscious states are subject-unified when they are had by the same subject at the same time. This is described as trivial, however, since it is true by definition. Experiences are unified simply

72 Theoretical Premises of Explicit Knowledge/Learning

because they are had by the same person, so subject unity is not an informative notion. Two conscious states are subsumptively unified when they are subsumed by a single state of consciousness. This "singularity behind the multiplicity" would subsume perceptual, bodily, emotional, cognitive and any other experiences in a single state of consciousness (Bayne & Chalmers, 2003, p. 27). Subsumptive unity is distinct from neurophysiological unity, since more than a single area or mechanism of the brain may be involved, and it is seen as the most relevant notion for the unity thesis.

Accordingly, one may consider what is involved in the idea of one conscious state being subsumed by another. For this purpose, further distinctions are made. Access unity and phenomenal unity are characterised as distinct concepts. A mental state is described as access-conscious "if by virtue of having that state, the content of the state is available for verbal report, for rational inference, and for the deliberate control of behavior. When I look at a red book, I can report the presence of the book ('there's a red book'), I can reason about it (e.g., concluding that I must have put it there when reading yesterday), and I can use its presence in deliberately directing my behavior (e.g., picking up the book and putting it back on the shelf)" (Bayne & Chalmers, 2003, p. 28). Put differently, the subject is access-conscious of the relevant object.

A mental state is described as phenomenally conscious "when there is something it is like to be in that state" (Bayne & Chalmers, 2003, p. 28), i.e. being in that state involves some sort of subjective experience. The mental state thus has a phenomenology, or phenomenal properties ('qualia') which characterise what it is like to be in them. Phenomenal consciousness tends to be regarded as the most important type of consciousness. However, it is also the type of consciousness that poses the most difficulty for scientific explanation. While access consciousness is defined in terms of the causal role a state plays, phenomenal consciousness is defined in terms of the way the state feels. It follows from this line of argument that two conscious states can be described as access-unified when they are jointly accessible, that is, when a person has access to the contents of both states at once. Two conscious states are phenomenally unified when they are jointly experienced, that is, when there is something it is like to be in both states at once.

By the same token, subsumptive phenomenal unity and subsumptive access unity can be distinguished. Two conscious states are subsumptively access-unified if the conjunction of their contents is available for verbal report, reasoning, and the deliberate control of behaviour, i.e. if a person is access-conscious of the conjunction of their contents, or if the conjunctive mental state subsumes the original mental states, which may be visual, auditory, bodily, emotional etc. (e.g. looking at a red book and feeling a pain in one's shoulder). Typically, our conscious states are not jointly accessed, but jointly accessible.

The thesis that any two access-conscious states of a subject at a time are necessarily access-unified is described as false because access bottlenecks have been shown to occur in cognitive systems. Given our limited cognitive resources, joint access may well occur ordinarily, but it does not hold necessarily. However, a breakdown in access unity does not entail a breakdown of phenomenal unity. Although access consciousness and phenomenal consciousness tend to correlate for simple contents, they will not always correlate for complex contents. Access to a total phenomenal state is therefore sometimes piecemeal, but one cannot infer a breakdown of phenomenal unity from a breakdown in access unity. Two conscious states are subsumptively phenomenally unified if there is something it is like for a person to be in both states simultaneously. In other words, two states are phenomenally unified when they have a conjoint phenomenology which subsumes the phenomenology of the individual states. The phenomenal unity thesis states that, necessarily, any set of phenomenal states of a subject at a time is phenomenally unified. Hence, unlike access unity, phenomenal unity cannot break down. It is argued that much of the reason for accepting the idea of unity comes from the fact that its denial seems inconceivable, so the unity thesis may be a conceptual truth. It may be that our most basic concept of consciousness is a total phenomenal state, with simple phenomenal states being a derivative. Bayne and Chalmers (2003, p. 57) conclude that "there is at least some plausibility in the idea that the concept of consciousness, and states of consciousness, are fundamentally holistic rather than atomistic. And this squares well with our intuition that consciousness is necessarily unified."

While this conclusion to the philosophical discussion appears to complement the cognitive scientists' explanation of consciousness as a biological phenomenon, it is important to note that the defining property of phenomenological consciousness, the elusive concept of 'qualia', or "subjective experiences that no-one else can experience as we ourselves experience them" (Cattell, 2006, p. 89), such as the taste of coffee, the sound of a cello, the smell of new-mown grass, or the experience of viewing a particular painting, remains unsolved, both from a philosophical and from a neuroscientific perspective. There is little doubt that the complexity and relative intractability of the concept of consciousness is the reason why L2 researchers often prefer to refer to awareness when discussing explicit knowledge and learning.

4.2 Attention, Awareness and Metalinguistic Understanding

Up to this point, terms such as attention, noticing and awareness have been used without further conceptual elaboration, and it is now time to consider them in detail. The widespread use of these terms in SLA (for an overview of attention in the context of different SLA theories, see Leow, 2015) can be traced back to the so-called 'noticing hypothesis' (Schmidt, 1990, 1993, 1994, 2001). Although first formulated more than 25 years ago, the impact of the noticing hypothesis on L2 research concerned with explicit knowledge and learning continues to be profound. In the seminal article that brought the noticing hypothesis into the public domain, Schmidt (1990) critiques the terminological vagueness associated with the concept of consciousness. In order to achieve greater clarity, he proposes a three-way distinction of consciousness as awareness, consciousness as knowledge and consciousness as intention. Consciousness as awareness is identified as a key notion in SLA. It is thought to operate on three levels which are conceptualised hierarchically, namely (1) perception, (2) noticing or focal awareness and (3) understanding. Perception is not necessarily conscious and involves "the ability to create internal representations of external events" (Schmidt, 1990, p. 132). Noticing refers to the momentary subjective experience of stimuli; this experience is potentially available for verbal report, provided that lack of memory or inadequate metalanguage do not get in the way. Understanding involves reflection on an experience, comprehension and insight.

Schmidt (1990, 1993) explores the three levels of awareness he has posited in the context of SLA research in order to establish whether subliminal learning is possible (Can we learn without attention or noticing?), whether incidental learning is possible (Can we learn without 'trying' or paying attention?), and whether implicit learning is possible (Can we learn without awareness at the level of understanding?). Schmidt claims that subliminal learning of new information in the sense of learning without attention is not possible, although subliminal perception of familiar stimuli is considered feasible. It is argued that focused attention is required for input to become intake, which is then available for further mental processing. Attention also controls access to conscious experience. If the attentional threshold for storage in memory and the threshold for conscious awareness are the same, then all learning would be accompanied by awareness, i.e. noticing. This assumption is the basis of the noticing hypothesis, which postulates that the subjective experience of noticing is the necessary and sufficient condition for the conversion of input to intake.

By way of evidence, Schmidt makes reference to a diary study documenting his own acquisition of Portuguese (Schmidt & Frota, 1986). In his evaluation of his diary entries and tape recordings of his oral L2 performance, he concludes that presence and frequency of input cannot explain all the features of his language output, and that there appeared to be a close connection between noticing a particular language form and producing it. Methodological weaknesses are acknowledged, however. Diary entries require a high level of self-awareness, i.e. the awareness that one has noticed something and needs to record this. Thus, it is likely that not all sources of learning are specified. Nonetheless, a mismatch between learning outcomes and diary entries cannot be interpreted as evidence of learning without noticing.

With regard to incidental vs. intentional learning, it is argued that a learner can deliberately control the focus of their attention, but that it is likewise possible to direct a learner's attention without relying on their volition. Attention and noticing are seen as being constrained by a number of factors, such as learner expectations, individual learner characteristics, the type of instruction provided, task demands, and the frequency and salience of linguistic features in the input. As learning tasks

Theoretical Premises of Explicit Knowledge/Learning **75**

can be designed in such a way that a learner's attention is directed towards specific L2 features, it is argued that incidental learning is possible. However, if the task does not focus the learner's attention on what needs to be learned, intentional learning will be superior to incidental learning. With regard to implicit vs. explicit learning, Schmidt (1990) argues that understanding and insight into linguistic systematicities will be facilitative for L2 learning, but are not essential. Thus, implicit learning is possible.

As we have seen, noticing has been defined as detection with focal attention accompanied by awareness, and it can thus be described as equivalent to conscious perception (Schmidt, 2001). It is distinguished from detection without awareness, that is, the mere registration of stimuli. The use of the term detection shows that at this point, the field of SLA had taken on board research in cognitive science concerned with the notion of attention, which argues that attention is limited, selective, and partially subject to voluntary control. Furthermore, it controls access to consciousness and is essential for action control and learning. The lasting influence of a cognitive-psychological approach to the concept of attention in L2 research is to a large extent attributable to a single but highly influential paper by Tomlin and Villa (1994).

Tomlin and Villa (1994) state that in cognitive science research, attention is differentiated from consciousness and awareness in both theoretical and empirical terms (see also Carr & Curran, 1994). The human attentional system is considered to be a limited resource, although it is a matter of debate as to whether this limitation is due to capacity limits or control of attentional focus (for a discussion of this issue, see Robinson, 1995, 2003). Humans can perform two tasks simultaneously, provided that one of the tasks does not require attention, or both tasks, though attention-demanding, are compatible. Attention in the sense of action control refers to the allocation of attention to some information and the inhibition of attention with regard to other information. Tomlin and Villa (1994) argue that the human attentional system can be described more precisely in terms of three separate but interrelated networks or functions, that is, alertness, orientation and detection.

Alertness refers to an overall readiness to deal with incoming stimuli or information. In the context of SLA, the role of alertness is equally general in that learners simply need to be ready to process information. Orientation refers to the direction of attentional resources towards specific cues (at the exclusion of others) that are common to a class of information. Stimuli that are not the subject of attentional orientation are thus inhibited; they may still be detected, but only with additional effort. In SLA, orientation is an important process because learners need to orient to both form and function for successful acquisition. Detection refers to "the cognitive registration of sensory stimuli" (Tomlin & Villa, 1994, p. 192). Through the process of detection, a particular piece of information is selected or engaged. Detection requires considerable attentional resources; once information is detected, it can be processed further. In SLA, detection involves the registration of exemplars in memory, thus making them accessible for further learning. "Detection is the process that deals with specific and particular moments of acquisition, with the current utterance in some interaction, and it is ultimately on this level that acquisition must operate" (Tomlin & Villa, 1994, p. 193).

Tomlin and Villa (1994, p. 193) define awareness as "a particular state of mind in which an individual has undergone a specific subjective experience of some cognitive content or external stimulus". In order to demonstrate awareness, three criteria should be met: Individuals must exhibit (1) a behavioural or cognitive change due to the experience, (2) report that they were aware of the experience, and (3) be able to describe the subjective experience. Importantly, none of the components of attention – alertness, orientation or detection – requires awareness. Consciousness may be equated with awareness, but the former term is associated with a number of concepts, including perception, understanding and intention. It is therefore preferable to use the term awareness, which is more limited in its definition, as stated above. Awareness requires attention, but attention does not require awareness. Awareness may follow attention, but it can also be a cognitive means to increase alertness and/or set an orientation prior to detection.

In the context of SLA, alertness can be considered together with motivation, language interest and general preparedness to learn. In other words, it refers to a learner's general readiness to deal with a task at hand. In a classroom context, a teacher's charisma may enhance alertness, for example. Orientation is in evidence when a learner's sensitivity is heightened with regard to a specific cue or stimulus characterising a class of information. Input flooding might cue the learner to orient towards a particular formal linguistic feature common to a class, for example. Orientation and alertness enhance the likelihood of detection to occur, but neither orientation nor alertness is a necessary prerequisite for detection. Awareness in the context of explicit instruction, for example, may enhance alertness or orientation and may thus play a role in detection as well. Detection is the key process that is necessary for learning, but, as already stated, it does not depend on awareness. In summary, then, awareness can be used to enhance both alertness and orientation, but neither awareness nor alertness nor orientation is required for detection to occur. Once the learner has detected a particular linguistic instance of a pattern in the input, it becomes available for further processing and thus for acquisition. Eventually, the learner will generalise over a number of instances. This is achieved by the detection of mappings between form and meaning and by registering these associations – a process that depends on exposure to multiple relevant exemplars (Tomlin & Villa, 1994).

The recommendation to apply findings from cognitive science with regard to the attentional sub-processes of alertness, orientation and detection to SLA has been welcomed by many L2 researchers (Leow & Bowles, 2005), met with caution by others (Schachter, 1998), and been challenged outright in some quarters (Simard & Wong, 2001). In the latter case, it has been argued that the role of attentional processes should be investigated from a more interactive perspective which takes into account SLA-relevant variables such as task type, the nature of the linguistic feature to be acquired and individual learner differences such as working memory capacity, learning style and motivation. It is extremely difficult or perhaps even impossible to operationalise the three attentional functions in an L2 learning context. Operationalisations in the field of cognitive science have focused on visual orienting to spatial locations and may thus only be of limited relevance to SLA. What is more, the separable nature of the sub-systems of attention as identified in such research refers to anatomical dissociations as captured with the aid of neuroimaging of brain activity. Even though they are located in distinct areas of the brain, the three attentional networks tend to be activated simultaneously, especially when higher-order cognitive tasks such as the processing of language data are carried out. It is further proposed that attention and awareness be viewed as "graded properties" rather than discrete "all-or-none entities" (Simard & Wong, 2001, p. 118), since SLA studies suggest that different degrees of attention lead to differential learning outcomes (see also the explicitness hierarchy proposed by Dienes & Perner, 2003).

More recent research in cognitive science concerned with attention has considered the potentially graded nature of the construct (Montemayor & Haladjian, 2015), and the different levels of awareness acknowledged in the context of the noticing hypothesis certainly satisfy this criterion. In the preceding paragraphs, we considered attention and awareness at the level of noticing; let us now turn to the highest level of awareness in Schmidt's (1990) hierarchy, that is, awareness at the level of understanding. Researchers generally agree that, unlike noticing, awareness at the level of understanding is not a necessary condition for L2 learning to take place, though it is regarded as beneficial. If learners are able to explicitly analyse language, reflect on its uses and come to appreciate the relationship between form and function – i.e. if learners develop and utilise metalinguistic awareness – L2 learning will be facilitated, not least because understanding may confer a sense of accomplishment (Larsen-Freeman, 2003) and a feeling of control over a complex stimulus domain, and it may thus increase the learner's levels of confidence and self-efficacy. Metalinguistic awareness in the sense of awareness at the level of understanding is closely connected with the notion of pedagogical grammar.

In pedagogical terms, grammar has been defined as "a system of rules which governs how words (and smaller morphemes) can be combined to form sentences" (Keck & Kim, 2014, p. 33). Clearly, however, grammar description may go beyond the sentence level and thus involve more than morphology and syntax. Indeed, pedagogical grammar may refer to any aspect of language that can be described in a systematic manner, which extends the notion to all linguistic domains, including phonology, semantics, pragmatics and discourse (Chalker, 1994; Westney, 1994). In this sense, a language rule can be regarded as an "observed regularity with predictive value" (Westney, 1994, p. 74). It is noteworthy that proficient speakers of a language have a potentially vast number of choices as to how to express a meaning, yet they settle on just one option. The question is how they make that choice. If one takes this into account, grammar is not so much a set of rules, but a resource for speakers – a circumstance which means that grammatical description must necessarily extend beyond morphosyntax. Thus, the starting point for analysis may not be an individual sentence, but the communicative situation or register. In order to identify situational factors, one must consider the mode, participants and purpose of communication, for instance. Proficient speakers or writers are able to use language forms for specific purposes in a range of social contexts, so their speech or writing is not just grammatical, but also appropriate and effective. This means that L2 learners need to acquire the possible structures in a language as well as learn which forms are appropriate and typical in a particular communicative context (Keck & Kim, 2014).

Larsen-Freeman (2003) addresses this issue by proposing the three inter-dependent dimensions of form, meaning and use which learners should be taught and acquire knowledge of. Thus, metalinguistic information should go beyond mere descriptive rules and additionally include an explanation of why a particular form might be chosen over other forms with the same meaning. It is argued that grammar is a skill – 'grammaring' – rather than just a knowledge domain because it allows learners to use linguistic structures accurately, meaningfully and appro-priately. If students have both rules and reasons, they can not only begin to understand the underlying logic of language and its motivated use, including exceptions to rules, but also have the tools to understand utterances in specific contexts and express their own ideas in the way they want to.

Applied linguists concerned with the notion of pedagogical grammar have identified the properties of language rules that are likely to be useful to L2 learners. Typically, pedagogical language rules are distinguished from descriptive or theoretically-driven language rules, with pedagogical grammars essentially constituting simpler, shorter and more accessible versions of descriptive grammars (Chalker, 1994; McDonough, 2002; Westney, 1994). Swan (1994) proposes six criteria that characterise a good pedagogical grammar rule: truth, demarcation, clarity, simplicity, conceptual parsimony and relevance. At the same time, it is acknowledged that some of these criteria are necessarily in conflict with one another. The truth criterion states that rules should be true in that language rules provided to learners should correspond as closely as possible to the linguistic facts. Admittedly, though, the facts are not always known, and the truth criterion may need to be compromised for the sake of clarity, simplicity and conceptual parsimony (see also Chalker, 1994). The demarcation criterion states that a rule should show clearly the limits on the use of a given form. Language rules should not only state what things are, but also what they are not; otherwise they have little defining or predictive value, and the learner will not know when to (not) use a form. The clarity criterion states, unsurprisingly, that rules should be clear, in the sense that vague terminology and ill-defined concepts should be avoided. By the same token, the simplicity criterion states that rules should be simple. While clarity relates to how an explanation is worded, simplicity relates to the way it is constructed. Simplicity can be improved by reducing the number of categories and subdivisions in a rule, or by ignoring details in order to make a description more manageable.

Simple and clear rules are regarded as psychologically valuable because they allow students to feel that they can understand and control complex material. The conceptual parsimony criterion states that rules should make use of the conceptual framework available to the learner. If it is necessary to add to this, one should aim for as little intervention as possible. Terminology should be chosen for its familiarity rather than its precision. If new concepts are needed to get a point across, these should be kept at a minimum. Finally, the relevance criterion states that rules should answer the question that the learner is asking. It is argued that as pedagogical grammar is about the interaction between language and language learners, a good rule is not just a neutral analysis of a set of linguistic data, but should answer a real or potential question that is relevant to a learner's developing L2. Thus, pedagogical rules describing the same linguistic feature may differ according to the context in which they are introduced, depending on a learner's L1, their stage of development, and individual difficulties. Overall, pedagogical grammar rules are considered useful to the learner, despite their limitations, in keeping with the argument that "a little truth goes a long way when one is off one's ground" (Swan, 1994, p. 54).

This practice-oriented analysis of pedagogical grammar in the context of L2 instruction has been complemented by a theoretically-driven analysis in the context of SLA research. Roehr (2008a; see also Roehr, 2010) discusses the potential advantages and disadvantages of pedagogical grammar in L2 learning by contrasting the characteristics of explicit metalinguistic knowledge with the characteristics of implicit linguistic knowledge as conceptualised in a usage-based approach to language and language learning. Specifically, it is argued that while implicit linguistic knowledge is characterised by exemplar-based categories, explicit metalinguistic knowledge relies on so-called Aristotelian categories. Exemplar-based categories are flexible, highly contextualised and subject to prototype effects, whereas Aristotelian categories are stable, discrete and clearly delineated. In addition to positing qualitatively distinct category structures, it is further argued that the processing mechanisms operating on implicit linguistic and explicit metalinguistic knowledge representations are qualitatively different. While implicit linguistic knowledge is stored in and retrieved from an associative network during parallel-distributed, similarity-based processing, explicit metalinguistic knowledge is processed sequentially with the help of rule-based algorithms. It is suggested that these differences between linguistic and metalinguistic knowledge representations and processes affect the way in which the two types of knowledge can be utilised in L2 learning and use.

Roehr (2008a) points out that in the usage-based approach, categorization is a key mechanism. Furthermore, it is accepted that both conceptual and linguistic

80 Theoretical Premises of Explicit Knowledge/Learning

categories are subject to context and prototype effects. Linguistic knowledge is conceptualised in terms of constructions, i.e. conventionalised form-meaning mappings varying along the parameters of specificity and complexity. Just like linguistic constructions, metalinguistic descriptions also vary along the parameters of specificity and complexity, so L2 learners' metalinguistic knowledge can be more or less specific as well as more or less complex. A metalinguistic description may refer to specific items (e.g. '*Since* requires the present perfect tense': *Mark has lived in Colchester since 2010*), or it may be wholly schematic and include no specific exemplars at all (e.g. 'The default word order in English statements is subject – verb – object'). Both of these metalinguistic descriptions are complex in the sense that they state relations between categories. Metalinguistic descriptions may also be minimal (e.g. 'verb').

While metalinguistic knowledge is comparable with linguistic constructions in terms of complexity and specificity, explicit metalinguistic knowledge differs qualitatively from implicit linguistic knowledge in terms of categorization. The usage-based approach assumes that implicit cognitive categories, whether conceptual or linguistic, are flexible and context-dependent, sensitive to prototype effects and have fuzzy boundaries. By contrast, explicit metalinguistic knowledge appears to be characterized by stable, discrete and context-independent categories with clear-cut boundaries. Put differently, metalinguistic knowledge relies on Aristotelian categorization. This point can be illustrated by contrasting the linguistic construction [NOUN] and the metalinguistic description 'noun'. The linguistic construction [NOUN] is a form-meaning pairing which has been abstracted over a large number of exemplars which the learner/speaker has experienced over time. As a consequence, the linguistic construction [NOUN] is associated with the semantics of its most frequent exemplars, so in the average learner/speaker of English, constructions such as *people, car, coffee* or *bread* are more strongly linked with the schema [NOUN] than constructions such as *somnambulism* or *kedgeree*. Therefore, the linguistic schema [NOUN] has a flexible and context-dependent category structure which accounts for prototype effects. Conversely, the metalinguistic description 'noun' has an Aristotelian category structure which is based on clear yes/no distinctions and does not take into account frequency, contextual information or prototypicality. Hence, in metalinguistic terms, the constructions *car, bread, somnambulism* and *kedgeree* are all equally good examples of the Aristotelian category 'noun'.

Use of Aristotelian categorization does not mean that learners/speakers are unaware of the potential shortcomings of such an approach. This awareness is acknowledged in pedagogical grammar rules that are qualified by frequency adverbs such as *usually, in general*, etc., contain statements about specific usage contexts or lists of exceptions to a rule. It is also worth noting that metalinguistic descriptions are not immune to prototype effects, given that descriptions of prototypical functions of L2 forms will occur more often than descriptions of less prototypical functions of the same form, for instance. However, these prototype effects only concern the presentation and/or our perception of metalinguistic descriptions and do not have any bearing on the internal category structure of explicit knowledge representations or the processing mechanisms operating on these representations. Indeed, metalinguistic knowledge requires conditions of stability and discreteness because otherwise it would be of little practical value. A learner needs to be able to decide categorically whether a specific linguistic construction is to be classified as a noun or not, otherwise a metalinguistic description such as 'the verb needs to agree in number with the preceding noun or pronoun' cannot be utilised.

Roehr (2008a) further argues that the contrasting category structures of implicit linguistic and explicit metalinguistic representations are reflected in the processing mechanisms operating on these representations during language learning and use, with implicit and explicit mental operations seemingly analogous with what is respectively termed similarity-based and rule-based processing in cognitive psychology. Rule-based processing is characterised by compositionality, productivity, systematicity, commitment, and a drive for consistency. A set of operations is compositional when more complex representations can be built out of simpler components without a change in the meaning of the components. Productivity means that there is no limit to the number of such new representations. An operation is systematic when it applies in the same way to a whole class of objects. Rule-based processing entails commitment to specific kinds of information, while contextual variations are neglected because rule-based operations involve only a small subset of an object's properties which are selected for processing. A strict match between an object's properties and the properties specified in the rule has to be achieved, so rule-based judgements are more consistent and more stable than similarity-based judgements.

These properties of rule-based processing are in keeping with the characteristics of Aristotelian category structure, i.e. stability, discreteness, lack of flexibility, as well as selective and categorical decision-making. The characteristics of rule-based processing can be contrasted with the characteristics of similarity-based processing, which involves a large number of an object's properties that only need to be partially matched with the properties of existing representations to allow for successful categorization. Moreover, similarity-based processing is flexible, dynamic, open and susceptible to contextual variation. These attributes reflect the characteristics of implicit linguistic categories assumed in the usage-based approach.

Metalinguistic knowledge based on Aristotelian category structure is at its best when it pertains to highly frequent and entirely systematic patterns whose usage is largely independent of context and may be described in terms of one or a few relations between categories, e.g. as in the case of the metalinguistic description 'In English, an -s needs to be added to present tense verbs in the third person.' Conversely, metalinguistic knowledge is less useful when less frequent or more item-based constructions exhibiting complicated form-meaning relations need to be captured, since the required number of categories and propositions specifying

82 Theoretical Premises of Explicit Knowledge/Learning

relations between categories grows rapidly with every specific usage context that diverges from the regular pattern.

In conclusion, the complexity, flexibility and context-dependency of language in use mean that general and truthful metalinguistic descriptions are inevitably rather rare – a statement which echoes the point made by researchers analysing pedagogical grammar from a practice-oriented perspective, as discussed above. Inevitably, metalinguistic descriptions will exhibit a trade-off between accuracy or truth on the one hand and simplicity and clarity on the other hand. Importantly, whether the scales are tipped one way or the other will determine the learning difficulty of explicit metalinguistic knowledge.

4.3 Learning Difficulty

The question of learning difficulty was first discussed at length in the 1994 edition of the AILA Review, when SLA researchers considered the issue in rather global terms and from a primarily hypothetical perspective. Hulstijn and de Graaff (1994) identified a number of properties that would not only determine the learning difficulty of grammar rules and linguistic features, but would also interact differentially with explicit instruction. They argued that the complexity of a grammar rule is dependent on the number and/or the type of criteria that need to be applied in order to arrive at the correct L2 form, hypothesising that explicit instruction would be more beneficial in the case of complex rules than in the case of simple rules. The property of scope relates to the number of cases covered by a grammar rule, while reliability describes the extent to which the rule holds true (see also DeKeyser, 1994 on categorical vs. prototypical rules). It is further hypothesised that explicit instruction will be more effective in the case of rules with a large scope and high reliability. The concept of rule learning vs. item learning refers to the rule-based nature of a linguistic feature as opposed to the requirement for learning and retrieval by item, with explicit instruction deemed more beneficial if rules can be applied. Finally, it is argued that semantic or communicative redundancy is a property impacting on learning difficulty, with linguistic features that are of little importance for successful communication particularly difficult to acquire. It is hypothesised that explicit instruction will be of particular benefit for developing comprehension when there is no semantic redundancy, and that it will be of particular benefit for developing production when there is semantic redundancy (Hulstijn & de Graaff, 1994). Thus, in summary, the overall hypothesis is that in some cases explicit instruction will be particularly effective when the learner is faced with greater complexity (complex grammar rules, semantic redundancy in production), but mostly it will be particularly effective when learning difficulty is relatively low (reliable grammar rules with a large scope, rule-based learning, no semantic redundancy in comprehension).

This practical but ultimately intuitive approach to learning difficulty was subsequently refined by DeKeyser (2003, 2005), who hypothesises that explicit

Theoretical Premises of Explicit Knowledge/Learning 83

instruction is not likely to be useful in the case of extremely easy grammar rules, since it is unnecessary, or in the case of very difficult rules, which are not considered to be amenable to explicit instruction. In the case of moderately easy rules, explicit learning processes may be accelerated through explicit instruction, while ultimate attainment may be furthered in the case of moderately difficult rules. Explicit instruction of difficult rules is thought to lead to enhanced implicit acquisition at later stages through increased chances of noticing.

With regard to the properties determining learning difficulty, DeKeyser (2003, p. 334) argues that "the harder it is to learn something through simple association, because it is too abstract, too distant, too rare, too unreliable, or too hard to notice, the more important explicit learning processes become." There appear to be three overarching factors that play a role in determining grammatical difficulty, i.e. complexity of form, complexity of meaning and complexity of the form-meaning relationship (DeKeyser, 2005). Moreover, the difficulty of grasping the form-meaning relationship while processing an L2 sentence seems to be relevant too. This difficulty depends on the transparency of the relationship, that is, the degree of importance of a linguistic form for the meaning it expresses. In particular, a morpheme may be the one and only cue to the meaning it expresses, or it may be largely or completely redundant in semantic terms. L2 meaning can also be a source of difficulty because of novelty, abstractness, or both. Elements of grammar such as articles, classifiers, grammatical gender and verbal aspect are hard to acquire for learners with L1s that do not instantiate these notions because they are highly abstract and difficult to infer from the input either explicitly or implicitly. L2 form can be a source of difficulty because of complexity in the sense of the number of choices involved in selecting the right morphemes and allomorphs to express certain meanings and putting them in the right place. While basic word order is thought to be relatively unproblematic, L2 learners' failure to use morphology appropriately is a well-known and widely studied phenomenon.

L2 form-meaning mappings can be a source of difficulty if the link between form and meaning lacks transparency because of redundancy, optionality or opacity. A form is redundant if it is not semantically necessary because its function is also expressed by another element in the sentence. Examples of optional forms are null subjects in Spanish and Italian and case marking in Korean. Opacity refers to a low form-meaning correlation, i.e. when a morpheme has different allomorphs and is also homophonous with other morphemes, so different forms stand for the same meaning, and/or the same form stands for different meanings. This is the case for English -s, which can mark the third person singular of a verb, the plural of a noun or the genitive of a noun. The relationship between the order of subject and verb in Spanish is an example of opacity in syntax. To L2 learners, cases of opacity may appear as instances of optionality. Frequency is described as another factor which plays a role in determining ease or difficulty of learning form-meaning mappings. The importance of frequency seems to depend on the transparency of the mapping, with minimal exposure sufficient for acquiring

84 Theoretical Premises of Explicit Knowledge/Learning

transparent mappings and even maximal exposure insufficient for acquiring very obscure mappings (DeKeyser, 2005).

More recent research has gone beyond listing characteristics of grammatical rules and/or linguistic features that may determine learning difficulty and has instead attempted to arrive at a principled definition of the concept of learning difficulty through theoretical analysis, empirical investigation, or both. Collins, Trofimovich, White, Cardoso and Horst (2009) review a number of different approaches that can be taken in order to determine L2 learning difficulty. They distinguish between what they label the acquisition perspective, the linguistic perspective, the pedagogical perspective and the psycholinguistic perspective (for a similar categorisation, see also Spada & Tomita, 2010). The acquisition perspective takes the view that early acquired structures are easy to learn, whereas late acquired structures are difficult to learn. The authors acknowledge that in this view actual learner behaviour is taken into account, but the approach is descriptive rather than explanatory. According to the linguistic perspective, the L2 construction to be learned is compared and contrasted with the equivalent L1 construction. There is some evidence for L1 influence, but it is likewise known that difference does not always equal difficulty. Marked structures are more difficult to learn than unmarked structures, and complex structures that require more transformations are more difficult than less complex structures that require fewer transformations. It is a clear advantage that such precise predictions can be formulated and tested empirically, but the empirical evidence to date does not necessarily support the predictions made, indicating lack of psychological validity, e.g. of the construct of transformation.

The pedagogical perspective argues that more complex pedagogical rules describing and/or explaining L2 structures result in greater difficulty than less complex pedagogical rules. On the plus side, this view takes into account actual instructional input, which is indicative of ecological validity. However, easy rules are not necessarily easy to acquire, and metalinguistic rules are likely to be more relevant for explicit learning than for implicit learning, so the exclusive focus on grammatical rules is a disadvantage. Finally, the psycholinguistic perspective is concerned with the interaction between learners and the L2 input, with learners' knowledge of language emerging from their experience with language in use, as posited in the usage-based approach. Structures which can be accessed easily in the input are easier to learn than structures which are difficult to access in the input. Factors influencing accessibility include transparency of form-meaning mapping, communicative redundancy, selective attention and salience. Bearing in mind not only the theoretical analysis presented here, but also initial supporting evidence from their own empirical work, Collins et al. (2009) favour this latter approach to conceptualising learning difficulty.

Taking a similarly theoretical stance, some SLA researchers have sought to define learning difficulty by trying to disentangle the meaning of this term from the notion of complexity (Bulté & Housen, 2012; Dietz, 2002). Specifically, it has been suggested that the term complexity be used in a structural or absolute sense and the term difficulty in a relative or psychological sense. Complexity in a structural or absolute sense refers to the number of discrete components that a language structure or system consists of, as well as the number of connections between these components, i.e. categories and relations between categories in Roehr's (2008a) terms. It is an objective and quantitative notion. Conversely, difficulty refers to complexity in relation to the language learner/user operating in a specific learning context, that is, it refers to how cognitively resource-intensive and taxing the processing of a particular language structure or system might be. It is thus a subjective notion (Bulté & Housen, 2012; Dietz, 2002). Therefore, learning difficulty is ultimately determined by the interaction of characteristics of the L2 target to be learned, the characteristics of the learner him/herself, and the context in which learning takes place (DeKeyser, 2016; N. C. Ellis, 2016; Housen & Simoens, 2016).

A recent approach that takes into account the characteristics of the linguistic target in context proposes a differentiation between learning difficulty as implicit and as explicit knowledge (R. Ellis, 2006b; Housen, Pierrard, & Van Daele, 2005; Roehr & Gánem-Gutiérrez, 2009a). Rod Ellis (2006b) argues that the learning difficulty of L2 features as implicit knowledge depends on at least five factors, that is, frequency in the input, salience, functional value (with non-redundant forms mapping onto a single function the easiest to learn), regularity (with regular features easier to learn than irregular features) and processability (Pienemann, 1999). Conversely, the learning difficulty of L2 features as explicit knowledge is discussed in terms of declarative grammar rules. Critical criteria are conceptual clarity and technicality of metalanguage. Moreover, structures for which clear and true pedagogical grammar rules can be formulated are learned more easily than structures involving item-based learning. Finally, prototypical rules are easier to learn than peripheral rules. With regard to metalanguage, it is hypothesized that the more technical the metalanguage involved in a rule, the more difficult the rule will be to learn (R. Ellis, 2006b).

The criteria accounting for implicit and explicit learning difficulty proposed by Rod Ellis were subsequently adapted to make them applicable in practice, that is, to allow learning difficulty judgements of particular linguistic constructions and metalinguistic descriptions to be made (Roehr & Gánem-Gutiérrez, 2009a). Practical applicability requires the avoidance of composite criteria such as conceptual clarity; furthermore, notions that are dependent on a specific theoretical framework such as processability were excluded. The resulting taxonomy of criteria for the prediction of implicit and explicit learning difficulty by means of expert judgements comprises nine criteria. Six criteria refer to the learning difficulty of linguistic constructions, or learning difficulty as implicit knowledge: frequency, perceptual salience, communicative redundancy, opacity of form-meaning mapping (one form, x meanings), opacity of meaning-form mapping (one meaning, x forms) and schematicity.

Frequency describes how frequently a construction occurs in the input, and perceptual salience refers to how easily a construction can be perceived in spoken input. High frequency and high perceptual salience are expected to decrease learning difficulty. Communicative redundancy pertains to how much a construction contributes to the communicative intent of a message. Opacity of mapping refers to the extent to which a form maps onto a single or multiple functions or meanings, and the extent to which a function or meaning maps onto a single or multiple forms. High communicative redundancy and high opacity of mapping are expected to increase learning difficulty. Schematicity refers to the extent to which a linguistic construction is schematic or specific, and also to whether a metalinguistic description covers a schematic or a specific construction. High schematicity is expected to decrease both implicit and explicit learning difficulty, so this criterion applies to learning difficulty as both implicit and explicit knowledge.

Three further criteria determine the learning difficulty of metalinguistic descriptions, or learning difficulty as explicit knowledge: conceptual complexity, technicality of metalanguage and truth value. Conceptual complexity refers to the number of elements that are taken into account in a metalinguistic description, i.e. the number of categories and relations between categories that are included. Technicality of metalanguage refers to the relative familiarity and abstractness of the metalanguage used in a metalinguistic description. High conceptual complexity and high technicality of metalanguage are expected to increase learning difficulty. Last but not least, truth value refers to the extent to which a metalinguistic description applies without exception. High truth value is expected to decrease learning difficulty (Roehr & Gánem-Gutiérrez, 2009a).

4.4 Metalinguistic Awareness and Language Learning Aptitude

The notion of learning difficulty as discussed in the previous section pertains to the (meta)linguistic input learners are exposed to. As we have seen, the characteristics of this input can be expected to interact not only with an individual's implicit learning and knowledge, but also, and importantly, with their explicit learning and the acquisition and use of explicit metalinguistic knowledge. By the same token, researchers have argued that characteristics of the learner can be expected to relate to the development and use of metalinguistic awareness. The learner variable that is mentioned most frequently in this respect is language learning aptitude, defined as a specific capability for learning L2s quickly and with ease. Aptitude shows variation between learners and is therefore an individual difference variable (for a detailed review, see, e.g. Dörnyei, 2005). Language learning aptitude is typically conceptualised in terms of John B. Carroll's classic model, which comprises four aptitude components: (1) phonetic coding ability, or the ability to identify sounds in the L2, (2) grammatical sensitivity, or the ability to recognise how words function grammatically in sentences, (3) inductive language learning ability, or the ability to induce grammatical rules from language

Theoretical Premises of Explicit Knowledge/Learning **87**

examples, i.e. the ability to identify patterns of correspondence and form-meaning relationships, and (4) associative memory, or the ability to recognise and remember words and phrases (Carroll, 1962, 1981, 1990).

More recently, researchers have tended to combine the components of grammatical sensitivity and inductive language learning ability into a single component termed language-analytic ability (Skehan, 1998, 2002), defined as the ability to infer linguistic systematicities from the input and make generalisations. Other recent developments in aptitude research include the consideration of working memory capacity as a potential component of aptitude (Miyake & Friedman, 1998; Sawyer & Ranta, 2001; Wen, 2012), as well as the proposal of so-called aptitude complexes which break down the concept into a number of specialised cognitive capacities that are related to L2 processing under different task conditions (Robinson, 2001, 2007). Most recently, and following on from the idea of aptitude complexes, a distinction between aptitude for explicit learning vs. aptitude for implicit learning has been proposed (Granena, 2013, 2016; Linck et al., 2013; Suzuki & DeKeyser, 2017). Understandably, research in L2 learning that has drawn links between aptitude and metalinguistic awareness is primarily concerned with the notion of language-analytic ability, that is, a component of aptitude for explicit learning.

Some researchers have simply stated in general terms that language learning aptitude and metalinguistic awareness are partially overlapping constructs (Herdina & Jessner, 2002; Jessner, 2006). In the context of multilingualism, for instance, Jessner (2006, p. 68) writes that

> language aptitude and metalinguistic abilities or skills present related concepts which might be interpreted as identical concepts under certain circumstances. The more language systems that are involved in the acquisition process, the more difficult it is to decide whether language aptitude or metalinguistic awareness influence the language acquisition process, in particular when one does not adhere to a theory of innate language aptitude.

Others have focused more specifically on the concept of language-analytic ability, which, like metalinguistic ability, refers to the ability to handle language in a decontextualized manner, that is, the ability to treat language as an object of reflection, to reason analytically about language, and to look through meaning at linguistic form (Ranta, 2005; Sawyer & Ranta, 2001). In this sense, language-analytic ability and metalinguistic skill can be regarded as two sides of the same coin (Ranta, 2002). Unlike Jessner (2006), however, Ranta (2002) considers language learning aptitude as an innate and relatively stable trait that affects the development of metalinguistic awareness, thus positing a one-way cause-effect relationship rather than any bilateral influence or cyclical interplay between the two variables. In addition to language-analytic ability, it has been argued that the aptitude component of phonetic coding ability is likely to be related to

88 Theoretical Premises of Explicit Knowledge/Learning

phonological awareness, i.e. the dimension of metalinguistic awareness that is crucial for the development of literacy, both in L1 and L2 (Kormos, 2013; Sparks & Ganschow, 2001).

Theoretical argumentation positing a close relationship or partial overlap between (components of) language learning aptitude and metalinguistic awareness is certainly in keeping with the observation that the specific role of different aptitude components may change as individuals mature (Abrahamsson & Hyltenstam, 2008; DeKeyser, 2000, 2012). For instance, there is evidence suggesting that language-analytic abilities become more relevant as predictors of L2 achievement in older children, with memory abilities more relevant in younger children (Dörnyei & Skehan, 2003; Harley & Hart, 1997; Muñoz, 2014; Robinson, 2005; Tellier & Roehr-Brackin, 2013b) – a circumstance which can be linked quite straightforwardly with the notion of explicit learning and the development of metalinguistic skills as individuals mature. Still, findings are not entirely convergent, with recent work suggesting that phonetic coding ability and language-analytic ability as components of aptitude for explicit learning can be crucially important for children as young as ages 8 to 9 (Roehr-Brackin & Tellier, 2016), and sequence learning ability as a component of aptitude for implicit learning may be equally important for child and adult learners (Granena, 2013).

Having established the theoretical premises underlying research into explicit knowledge and learning, the next chapter discusses the evidence that has arisen from empirical studies concerned with explicit knowledge and learning in SLA.

5

METALINGUISTIC AWARENESS AS EXPLICIT KNOWLEDGE AND LEARNING

Empirical Evidence

5.1 Effects of Explicit Learning and Teaching on L2 Knowledge and Use

One of the key findings that has arisen from empirical research into the effectiveness of instructed L2 learning over the past decades is that, reassuringly, language teaching works, in the sense that any L2 instruction is better than no L2 instruction (Collentine, 2000; Doughty & Long, 2003; R. Ellis, 2006a; Norris & Ortega, 2001). At first glance, this may be considered unsurprising or perhaps even trivial. However, if we take into consideration that learning contexts, learners and L2 targets vary widely across time and across the locations in which SLA takes place, it is arguably an issue that required empirical verification before more specific questions can be investigated. The next issue of interest to us is whether explicit teaching and learning drawing on metalinguistic awareness are more effective than their counterparts, implicit teaching and learning.

In practice, researchers often operationalise explicit vs. implicit instruction in terms of form-focused vs. meaning-focused instruction, although it should be noted that the terms explicit and form-focused on the one hand and implicit and meaning-focused on the other hand are not direct equivalents, as will become apparent further below. Form-focused instruction refers to "any planned or incidental instructional activity that is intended to induce language learners to pay attention to linguistic form" (R. Ellis, 2001, pp. 1–2). In this sense, form-focused instruction can include traditional teaching approaches based on a structural syllabus as well as more communicatively-oriented approaches where a focus on form arises out of largely meaning-based activities. In historical terms, empirical research into form-focused instruction can be traced back to early classroom investigations carried out in the 1960s and 1970s, when researchers with an interest in pedagogy tended to compare teaching methods at a global level (Doughty, 2003; R. Ellis, 2001). At around the same time, SLA researchers focused on the comparison of classroom L2 learning with naturalistic L2 learning outside the classroom. This avenue of research led to the identification of seemingly universal sequences, or the so-called 'natural order', according to which certain morphological and syntactic features were typically acquired. On the one hand, it became clear that instructed learners acquired language more rapidly and generally achieved higher levels of proficiency – and certainly higher levels of grammatical accuracy – than non-instructed learners. On the other hand, all learners appeared to follow similar sequences of acquisition. Thus, researchers proposed that form-focused instruction would likely work by facilitating rather than changing the processes involved in naturalistic L2 learning (R. Ellis, 2001).

Empirical studies conducted in the 1980s and 1990s addressed the question of whether form-focused instruction really did work in this way. Overall, findings showed that grammatical forms are amenable to instruction, especially if learners are developmentally ready to acquire the targeted structures. From the early 1990s onwards, SLA research began to draw more heavily on theories from the field of cognitive psychology, especially information processing and skill acquisition. The concepts of attention, noticing and awareness at the level of understanding found their way into studies examining the question of whether some types of form-focused instruction might work better than others, and which types of corrective feedback might be particularly beneficial for L2 learning. Both classroom-based and laboratory-based studies focused on comparing various explicit and implicit learning conditions, for instance. A finding that emerged consistently from this line of research is that form-focused instruction effectively promotes L2 learning (R. Ellis, 1997, 2001).

It has been argued that form-focused and meaning-focused instruction differ in terms of whether language is viewed as an object of scrutiny or as a tool, and in terms of the role the learner is invited to play: student of the language or user of the language. It is worth noting here that form not only refers to morphosyntax or grammar, but also includes phonological, lexical and pragmatic aspects of language. In the literature on form-focused instruction, a three-way distinction has become the norm, that is, focus on forms (FonFS), focus on form (FonF) and focus on meaning (FonM). FonM instruction makes no attempt to overtly direct learners' attention to linguistic form. By contrast, FonFS is evident in traditional approaches to grammar teaching which assume that language learning is a process of accumulating knowledge of distinct morphosyntactic entities. During FonFS instruction, both teacher and student are aware of the fact that a pre-selected form is to be learned and that the learner must focus their attention on the form in order to do so. By contrast, FonF is largely embedded in communicative language teaching, but overtly draws learners' attention to linguistic elements as and when necessary, either incidentally or in a pre-planned manner.

Planned FonF instruction may involve enhanced input highlighting the targeted form, or an input flood with plentiful exemplars of the targeted form. Task design can make the targeted feature useful, natural or essential to successful performance, with task-essentialness usually aimed for, but most difficult to achieve. A targeted feature is considered task-essential if the task creates obligatory contexts for its use (Loschky & Bley-Vroman, 1993). Incidental FonF instruction can be either pre-emptive or reactive. In the pre-emptive case, the teacher and learner take time out from a communicative activity to attend to a form that is perceived to be problematic, although no error or breakdown in communication has occurred. In the reactive case, the teacher provides corrective feedback in response to a learner error (R. Ellis, 2001; Norris & Ortega, 2001).

The effectiveness of form-focused instruction (FonF or FonFS vs. FonM) as well as the effectiveness of L2 learning under explicit vs. implicit conditions has been the focus of a large number of empirical studies conducted over the past four decades. In fact, this particular research domain has proved sufficiently developed to be the subject of meta-analyses, that is, secondary research in the research synthesis tradition aimed at identifying cumulative results arising from a body of primary studies.

In their seminal and much-quoted meta-analysis, Norris and Ortega (2001) report cumulative findings from empirical studies into the effect of different types of L2 instruction published between 1980 and 1998. The studies in question investigated whether an implicit or an explicit approach to L2 instruction is more effective, whether raising metalinguistic awareness or focus on form is beneficial, whether and which type of corrective feedback facilitates language learning, and if comprehension and production practice are equally effective. Empirical studies typically operationalise instructional approaches in accordance with the focus of the teaching materials and thus distinguish between focus on meaning (FonM), exclusive focus on forms (FonFS), and focus on form (FonF), that is, selected forms made salient as needed, but integrated in a meaningful context, as discussed above. Form-focused instruction is used as a more general term to refer to any interventions that are aimed at focusing learners' attention on particular forms within a meaningful context, regardless of whether this is done proactively or reactively, obtrusively or unobtrusively. Instructional treatments can be further classified as rule-based (e.g. inductive and deductive grammar teaching or expla-nation, consciousness-raising activities, dictogloss), feedback-based (e.g. recasts, models, metalinguistic feedback), input-based (input flood, enhanced input), or practice-based (structured input in processing instruction, output practice).

The overall aim of the meta-analysis reported by Norris and Ortega (2001) is to summarise findings about variables of general interest within the research domain of instructed SLA, so that a useful empirical context is provided for the meaningful interpretation of future primary research. The meta-analysis addresses the following specific research questions: (1) How effective is L2 instruction overall? (2) What is the effectiveness of different types of L2 instruction? (3) Does

92 Empirical Evidence for Explicit Knowledge/Learning

type of outcome measure have an influence on observed instructional effectiveness? (4) Does length of instruction have an influence on observed instructional effectiveness? (5) Are instructional effects durable? These questions are answered by means of a meta-analysis of studies with an experimental or quasi-experimental design investigating the effectiveness of instructional treatments on the acquisition of specific L2 forms and functions. A total of 77 studies are identified and coded according to their independent and dependent variables as well as a number of methodological features.

The independent variable codes categorise the studies as to whether the instructional treatment was explicit, implicit, FonF, FonFS, FonM, or a combination of these features. An instructional treatment was considered explicit "if rule explanation comprised any part of the instruction (…) or if learners were directly asked to attend to particular forms and to try to arrive at metalinguistic generalizations of their own" (Norris & Ortega, 2001, p. 167). In the absence of either of these criteria, the treatment was considered implicit. FonF instruction showed evidence of an integration of form and meaning, while FonFS instruction required the focus of learner attention on a particular structure. FonM, by contrast, did not involve any attempts at focusing learners' attention on the targeted structure.

The dependent variable codes classify the outcome measures, which include metalinguistic judgements (acceptability or grammaticality judgements), selected response measures (multiple-choice tests), constrained constructed response measures (e.g. combining two sentences with relative pronouns, converting an active sentence into the passive voice), and free constructed response measures (e.g. oral interviews, written compositions). The classification of methodological features includes information on the participants, the instructional settings, the research design, and the methods of statistical analysis used.

The majority of the 77 studies identified were published between 1990 and 1998. About half of the studies had English as the targeted L2, and most studies involved adult learners, typically in a university setting. Altogether, the primary researchers operationalised more than 20 different instructional treatments. The majority of studies had a quasi-experimental design rather than a classic experimental design with random selection of participants. Sample sizes varied widely from N = 6 to N = 319, with a mode of 34, and group sizes ranged from 5 to 35. Treatment length also varied, ranging from less than an hour to 50 hours of instruction. Most studies used more than one outcome measure, and in general measures focused on whether participants were able to recognise the targeted L2 feature, to produce it, and/or to explain its rule-governed nature. Most studies were quantitative in nature, which is unsurprising, given the selection criterion of a (quasi-)experimental design. Over 90% of the studies reported statistically significant results, which may hint at a publication bias in favour of findings disconfirming the null hypothesis.

For the purpose of the meta-analysis, Norris and Ortega (2001) computed the magnitude of relationships or effects observed in the primary research. This was done by calculating effect sizes based on the Cohen's d statistic, which can be arrived at with the help of certain descriptive statistics. For the meta-analytic comparisons, effect sizes were combined to form averages. The trustworthiness of findings was assessed by means of confidence intervals. In general, if an effect size falls within a 95% confidence interval, it is deemed trustworthy. The narrower the confidence interval, the more robust the observed effect, with any confidence intervals that do not include the value of zero indicating that the observed effect differs probabilistically from the null hypothesis of no effect. Of the 77 studies identified for potential inclusion in the quantitative meta-analysis, only 49 unique sample studies reported sufficient descriptive data to allow for the calculation of effect sizes.

Across these 49 studies, 70% of the instructional treatments were categorised as explicit, and 30% were categorised as implicit. A total of 56% of instructional treatments were coded as FonFS, 80% of which included explicit techniques. Of the 44% that were classified as FonF, 58% included explicit techniques. Effect sizes were calculated for four categories of independent variable, i.e. implicit instruction, explicit instruction, FonF instruction and FonFS instruction. The average effect size across all treatments was d =.96, showing a large effect (>.80). FonF treatments showed slightly greater effect sizes than FonFS treatments, but both led to large effects. Explicit treatments were substantially more effective (d = 1.13) than implicit treatments (d =.54), which showed a medium effect (>.50, but <.80). The observed difference between explicit and implicit treatments can be considered trustworthy, as confidence intervals do not overlap.

Across combined categories, effectiveness patterned as follows: FonF explicit (large effect) > FonFS explicit (large effect) > FonF implicit (medium effect) > FonFS implicit (small effect, and confidence interval including zero). However, the confidence intervals were found to be overlapping, so the differences between the four types of instructional treatment are not deemed trustworthy. It must therefore be concluded that FonF and FonFS as operationalised in the primary studies are equally effective. Conversely, explicit instruction is more effective than implicit instruction.

Taking a different approach to the question of instructional effectiveness with a sub-set of 19 unique sample studies, effect sizes were also calculated for pre-test values compared with post-test values. The same pattern was observed, but it is worth noting that control or comparison conditions exhibited development too, with a medium effect size. More specifically, about 18% of change from pre-test to post-test can be attributed to something other than the instructional treatment, e.g. practice effects, exposure only effects, or general maturation of the control or comparison groups.

With regard to outcome measures, constrained constructed responses were most popular, while free constructed responses were used least often. On average, individual studies used two to three types of different outcome measures, thus compensating to some extent for the bias towards certain test formats. Effect sizes

94 Empirical Evidence for Explicit Knowledge/Learning

for metalinguistic judgements and free constructed response measures were noticeably lower than those for selected response and constrained constructed response measures. Confidence intervals overlap, however, so these differences may not be trustworthy. It is acknowledged that different outcome measures may yield different observations about the effectiveness of a treatment, and in particular that more controlled outcome measures may favour explicit knowledge (see also Doughty, 2003). However, given the widespread use of more than one measure per study, it is unlikely that outcome measures can account for cumulative differences among different instructional treatments (Norris & Ortega, 2001).

With regard to the duration of instructional treatments, two major categories were compared, that is, treatments lasting for less than two hours (accounting for 68% of all treatments) and treatments lasting for three hours or more (accounting for 32% of all treatments). Shorter-term treatments produced larger effects than longer-term treatments, although confidence intervals were found to be overlapping, indicating a difference that may not be trustworthy. Regarding the durability of instructional treatments, a sub-set of 22 unique sample studies provided data on immediate and delayed post-tests. Overall, the observed treatment effects were maintained, with only minimal attrition between immediate and delayed post-tests. This is offset by the observed maturation of control groups, of course. Hence, it can be said that instructional effects remained robust in that they lasted beyond immediate post-tests.

In conclusion, the research questions can be answered briefly as follows. Regarding the question about the effectiveness of L2 instruction overall, Norris and Ortega (2001) conclude that L2 instruction is indeed effective. As for the effectiveness of different types of L2 instruction, the researchers conclude that explicit instruction is more effective than implicit instruction, while FonF and FonFS instruction are equally effective. With regard to the question of whether type of outcome measure has an influence on observed instructional effectiveness, it appears to be the case that selected response and constrained constructed response formats yield greater effects than metalinguistic judgements and free response formats. However, further research is needed to uncover possible moderator variables that may be (partly) responsible for this pattern. Regarding the question of whether length of instruction has an influence on observed instructional effectiveness, shorter treatments seem to yield greater effects than longer treatments, but again further research is needed to uncover possible moderator variables that may be (partly) responsible for this. As to the durability of instructional effects, the meta-analytic findings indicate that L2 instruction has lasting effects, although it needs to be borne in mind that the sub-set of studies included in this particular analysis was relatively small (Norris & Ortega, 2001).

The meta-analysis performed on primary research published between 1980 and 1998 (Norris & Ortega, 2001) is complemented by a more recent meta-analysis of primary research in the same domain published between 1999 and 2011 (Goo, Granena, Yilmaz, & Novella, 2015). The latter focuses on the effects of explicit vs. implicit instructional treatments, addressing the following research questions: (1) How effective is L2 instruction overall? (2) Is there any difference between explicit and implicit treatments in their overall effectiveness on L2 learning? (3) To what extent do potential moderator variables mediate the effectiveness of implicit and/or explicit treatments?

The researchers draw on a total sample of 34 primary studies, including 11 studies published between 1993 and 1998 that were among the primary research meta-analysed by Norris and Ortega (2001), as well as 23 new studies published between 1999 and 2011. All 34 studies have an experimental or a quasi-experimental design and directly compare implicit with explicit treatments, including treatments involving corrective feedback, on the development of specific L2 features in adolescent or adult participants. Goo et al. (2015) coded the studies for explicitness of instructional treatment using the same definitions as Norris and Ortega (2001). If more than two treatment conditions were operationalised in the same study, the researchers only included data from the most explicit and the least implicit condition. The moderator variables included experimental vs. quasi-experimental design, type of treatment (feedback vs. non-feedback vs. combined), mode of instruction (oral vs. written vs. combined), type of target feature (grammatical vs. lexical vs. pragmatic) and type of outcome measure (metalinguistic judgement vs. selected response vs. constrained constructed response vs. free constructed response). The timing of post-testing was categorised as immediate (0–7 days), short-term delayed (8–29 days) or long-term delayed (> 30 days). The majority of the studies were published after 2000, and just over half of the studies had a quasi-experimental design, the others a classic experimental design. The mean age of participants was 21.9 years, with most of them university students.

In answer to the first research question which concerned the overall effectiveness of L2 instruction, Goo et al. (2015) report that the instructional treatments as operationalised in the primary research studies had a large positive effect on learner performance. A large effect was obtained for both immediate and short-term post-tests, while a medium effect was obtained for long-term post-tests. This pattern of results confirms the findings reported by Norris and Ortega (2001) and thus provides further evidence that L2 instruction is indeed beneficial.

The second research question was concerned with the effectiveness of explicit vs. implicit treatments. The meta-analysis reveals that explicit instruction resulted in a large effect overall, whereas implicit instruction was slightly less effective, resulting in a medium effect overall. Both types of instruction yielded large effects on immediate post-tests, though the effect size for explicit instruction was noticeably greater. On short-term delayed post-tests, explicit instruction led to a large effect and implicit instruction to a medium effect. On long-term delayed post-tests, explicit instruction led to a medium effect and implicit instruction to a small effect. Goo et al. (2015) state that their results generally show larger effects than the ones identified by Norris and Ortega (2001). This may be due to more powerful interventions in more recent studies, or it may be

96 Empirical Evidence for Explicit Knowledge/Learning

due to differences in selection, coding and analytic techniques used in the two meta-analyses.

The third research question asked to what extent potential moderator variables might mediate the effectiveness of implicit and/or explicit treatments. With regard to mode of instruction, a combination of oral and written treatment in an explicit condition led to a large effect size and resulted in larger effects than a purely oral mode of treatment. A combined mode was also most effective in implicit conditions, so overall learners benefited most if both oral and written input were available. A likely explanation for this result is the fact that input in two modalities will suit the needs and preferences of a greater number of learners. Moreover, a combined approach seems to be particularly critical if the treatment is implicit, with written-only treatments such as input enhancement or input floods perhaps less useful than expected. Along similar lines, a combination of feedback-based and non-feedback-based treatment yielded the largest effect sizes in both explicit and implicit conditions. Non-feedback studies contributed more to learning than feedback-only studies in explicit and implicit conditions, though in the latter case the difference was not statistically significant. Hence, it appears that learners may benefit less if the instructional treatment is based on feedback only, although it should be borne in mind that a sub-set of only 9 studies was included in this analysis, so the finding cannot be regarded as conclusive.

With regard to outcome measures, in explicit conditions the largest effect size was obtained for selected response formats, followed by constrained responses, free production, and lastly metalinguistic judgements. In implicit conditions, a similar pattern was found, with selected responses followed by free and then constrained responses and lastly metalinguistic judgements. The fact that the effect of instructional treatments varied by outcome measure is consistent with the findings reported by Norris and Ortega (2001), but the large effect sizes obtained for free response formats in more recent research are new. However, Goo et al. (2015) point out that the types of free responses solicited in the primary studies seems to have played a role. Specifically, more than half of the free responses were provided in a written modality, and instructions given to participants often encouraged a focus on form. Taken together with the fact that the vast majority of outcome measures used in the primary studies in both meta-analyses had a constrained response format, there is evidence of a certain bias in favour of explicit knowledge. This circumstance may have widened the gap in the observed effectiveness of explicit vs. implicit treatments.

Finally, for a direct comparison between explicit and implicit conditions, explicit instruction was treated as the experimental condition and implicit instruction as the control condition. In this comparison also, explicit instruction was found to be more effective than implicit instruction, with a medium effect size. The same applies to performance on immediate and short-term delayed post-tests, though the effect size is only small on long-term delayed post-tests. On all other moderator variables, explicit instruction was once more shown to be

Empirical Evidence for Explicit Knowledge/Learning **97**

more effective than implicit instruction, although effect sizes varied from small to large (Goo et al., 2015).

In sum, the two meta-analyses of (quasi-)experimental research covering more than 30 years provide powerful evidence that explicit instruction is more effective than implicit instruction when specific L2 features are targeted, and that instructional effects are generally durable. However, empirical evidence for the durability of instructional effects is still somewhat limited, due to the fact that only a minority of studies to date has incorporated delayed post-tests. Moreover, studies with a truly longitudinal design are still in very short supply. Indeed, two classroom-based studies that were not included in the meta-analyses considered above provide useful insights into instructed learners' morphosyntactic development over the long term (Klapper & Rees, 2003; Macaro & Masterman, 2006), as will become clear in the following paragraphs.

Klapper and Rees (2003) report on a four-year longitudinal study with advanced university-level learners of L2 German (N = 57) which examined the impact of focus-on-form (FonF) and focus-on-forms (FonFS) instruction as well as the effects of L2 immersion during a period of residence abroad. The participating leaners were either following a specialist degree in German language or studying German as non-specialists in conjunction with another subject. The specialist students attended language and culture classes, with some of their language classes providing explicit grammar instruction that is described as FonFS. The non-specialist students received a similar amount of L2 input, but their language classes were more meaning-oriented and only involved FonF-type engagement with L2 structures. However, the non-specialist students had access to explicit grammar through pedagogical grammar books and optional computer-based self-study. The participants completed a grammar test and a C-test assessing their L2 proficiency at the beginning of Year 1, at the end of Year 2, and at the start of Year 4 of their degree programme. The grammar test consisted of 125 gap-fill items covering 13 topics of pedagogical grammar, e.g. adjective endings, word order, prepositions, passive, etc. Year 3 of the degree programme involved residence abroad in a German-speaking country for either 12 or 6 months. Language marks achieved in the final university exams at the end of Year 4 were also recorded.

At the start of the degree programme, the participant sample was essentially homogeneous in terms of their L2 proficiency and scores on an IQ test, although the non-specialist students achieved marginally higher scores on all measures than the specialist students. At the end of Year 2, the specialists who had received FonFS instruction outperformed the non-specialists on both the grammar and the C-test. After residence abroad the rates of progress achieved on both tests were higher for the non-specialist group, however. Although this group had been lagging behind at the end of Year 2, it had nearly caught up with the specialists by the beginning of Year 4 on C-test performance and outperformed the specialists on the grammar test. Throughout the degree programme, the FonFS students seemingly had an advantage in terms of overall progress, but both

98 Empirical Evidence for Explicit Knowledge/Learning

specialists (FonFS) and non-specialists (FonF) were similar in terms of outcome at the end of the degree programme.

By analysing the subcategories of their grammar test, the researchers identify certain topics of pedagogical grammar which may be particularly amenable to explicit FonFS instruction, namely strong verbs, word order, modal expressions, adjective endings, prepositions, use of tenses, and relatives. With regard to the relative difficulty of different L2 structures, the researchers write that "those topics which at the start of the programme posed greatest difficulties remained difficult at the end, while those which proved more accessible early on, remained so" (Klapper & Rees, 2003, p. 303). In general, and perhaps unsurprisingly, the students performed better on L2 structures that had been the subject of instruction than on topics that had not been a focus of their classes. However, naturalistic exposure during residence abroad compensated for the lack of tuition in many cases, facilitating acquisition in all areas, including improvements in grammatical accuracy. The researchers conclude that explicit FonFS instruction, if offered in conjunction with meaning-based communicative activities, has a useful role to play, especially in settings where naturalistic L2 exposure is limited. Overall, naturalistic exposure building on FonF instruction proved just as effective as immersion following preparatory FonFS instruction. However, in view of the advantages enjoyed by the specialists before the period of residence abroad, Klapper and Rees (2003) argue in favour of a FonFS approach for L2 programmes which do not include extensive naturalistic exposure.

The second study we will consider (Macaro & Masterman, 2006) was likewise conducted in a university setting. It involved learners of L2 French who had performed poorly on a university admissions grammar test. The study investigated whether these learners would benefit from intensive explicit FonFS instruction on a range of L2 structures. The specific research issues addressed refer to whether an intensive course in explicit French grammar is a sufficiently powerful intervention to bring about improvements in grammatical knowledge and a reduction in written production errors, whether there are any long-term benefits, whether any reduction in production errors can be achieved without detrimental effects on other aspects of writing proficiency, and whether the intervention group (N = 12) will perform differently from the control group (N = 10) in the long term. All participating students achieved similarly low scores on the admissions grammar test in French and were about to embark on the first year of a specialist degree in French language. The intervention group participated in an intensive 30-hour FonFS course covering a range of L2 structures over two weeks, while the control group did not.

The researchers administer a pre-test, an immediate post-test one week after the end of the intervention, and a delayed post-test 12 weeks after the end of the intervention. Four L2 grammar topics are assessed, that is, verbs/tenses/aspect, relative clauses, agreement and prepositions. The measure comprises a grammaticality judgement requiring the identification and correction of errors, an error correction and rule explanation task, a sentence-level L1-to-L2 translation task, and a written composition of about 250 words which required participants to narrate a story based on a set of pictures.

The results show that on the immediate post-test, the mean ability of the intervention group to identify, correct and explain errors improved significantly, whereas the control group did not show any significant improvement. However, neither group improved significantly on the translation task, and both groups improved significantly on the composition task. On the delayed post-test, the two groups differ significantly on one task only, namely the error correction and rule explanation task, on which the intervention group outperformed the control group. In addition to analysing group means, the researchers also look at the performance patterns of individual students. With regard to the constrained response tasks, the intervention group seems to consist of two types of student, i.e. students who show most improvement immediately after the intensive course, and students who show little immediate improvement, but then leap ahead later on. Thus, in the case of the latter type of student, the intensive course seems to have had a delayed effect, or it may have worked together with subsequent L2 study and exposure.

Taking a conservative stance, Macaro and Masterman (2006) conclude that the intensive FonFS course did not in itself bring about significantly greater improvements in the intervention group compared with the control group. Moreover, students who improved in the short term did not sustain this improvement in the long term. However, some students did improve in the long term. The researchers attribute this finding to a combined effect of awareness-raising through the intensive FonFS course and further L2 exposure and study. Overall, it appears that individual learner differences were at the root of the differential effects of the FonFS intervention.

Taken together, and despite the diverging overall interpretations offered by the respective researchers, the findings reported by both Klapper and Rees (2003) and Macaro and Masterman (2006) show that FonFS instruction can have beneficial effects on the L2 development of relatively advanced learners studying an L2 at university level, as long as the FonFS instruction is complemented by L2 exposure in meaning-oriented and communicative settings, as exemplified by the non-FonFS classes in both studies and additionally the period of residence abroad in the first study. It is also clear, however, that individual learner characteristics have a role to play in how different students respond to FonFS instruction and make use of metalinguistic knowledge in their L2 learning. Moreover, different L2 structures may be more or less amenable to form-focused instruction. Before returning to these points further below, and having considered findings from (quasi-)experimental research, let us look at findings from correlational studies aimed at identifying the relationship between learners' explicit knowledge about the L2 and their L2 proficiency.

5.2 Relating Explicit Knowledge, L2 Achievement and Use

Empirical research into the relationship between cognitively mature learners' metalinguistic knowledge in the sense of explicit knowledge about the L2 and their L2 proficiency typically operationalises metalinguistic knowledge as learners' ability to correct and explain L2 errors. Measures include grammaticality judgements that require participants to identify accurate vs. inaccurate instances of targeted L2 structures followed by correction of any inaccurate instances, correction tasks that provide only incorrect instances, sometimes with the targeted mistakes already highlighted, as well as description and explanation tasks that require participants either to explain instances of correct or incorrect L2 use by means of pedagogical grammar rules, ideally with the help of appropriate technical terminology, i.e. metalanguage, or to illustrate given pedagogical grammar rules by formulating example L2 sentences (see Chapter 6 for further details).

Research to date has shown that adolescent and adult L2 learners who have experienced explicit, form-focused instruction are not only able to acquire metalinguistic knowledge, but sometimes exhibit quite extensive knowledge of both pedagogical grammar rules and metalanguage (Hu, 2011). How well learners perform on specific metalinguistic tasks may vary, however, and appears to depend at least in part on exactly how correction and explanation ability are measured (Alderson, Clapham, & Steel, 1997; Clapham, 2001; Gutiérrez, 2016). Thus, a study involving 300 L1 German learners of L2 English at school and university level who had been exposed to form-focused instruction for between 3 and 12 years yielded divergent results with regard to participants' correction and explanation abilities (Green & Hecht, 1992). The participants were presented with twelve L2 sentences containing errors commonly made by German learners. The errors were highlighted, and the participants were required to supply corrections and state the pedagogical grammar rules that had been violated. The results show that participants had not necessarily learned the rules they had been taught, although grammar school and university students were found to achieve significantly higher scores than the other groups of school learners. Thus, the acquisition of metalinguistic knowledge was linked to academic achievement (see also Sorace, 1985), whereas length of instruction seemingly had no role to play in the sample. The researchers further report that almost all the participants who produced an appropriate rule were able to provide an adequate correction as well. However, a large number of successful corrections were carried out without the learners being able to supply appropriate rules (Green & Hecht, 1992).

A more recent study reveals a different pattern of results pointing towards convergence between language use, grammaticality judgement and explanation ability (Scheffler & Cinciała, 2011). The researchers examined whether 16- to 18-year-old L1 Polish secondary-school learners of L2 English (N = 20) could provide pedagogical grammar rules for L2 structures which they were able to use accurately in spontaneous oral performance. Each participant was interviewed for up to half an hour on a range of everyday topics. In addition, each participant was asked to orally describe two pictures. Transcripts of the participants' oral performance were coded for accuracy of use on a range of L2 structures, with 75% accuracy considered the cut-off point for proficient performance. The researchers focused on structures for which learners had encountered pedagogical grammar rules in the context of their L2 classes, that is, tenses, modal verbs and pronominal forms. Structures that resulted in accuracy scores of 75% or above were then used to develop tailor-made tests of metalinguistic knowledge.

Each learner was presented with a selection of accurate sentences they had produced as well as with matched inaccurate sentences designed by the researchers, with the matched sentences containing errors in the targeted structures. Learners were asked to identify the correct and the incorrect sentence in each matched pair and to provide a metalinguistic explanation which accounted for the contrast between the correct and the incorrect sentence. Results show that learners were generally successful in identifying correct vs. incorrect sentences; they were likewise good at providing appropriate rules. In 81% of cases, correct identification was associated with a correct rule. In only 15% of cases a correct sentence was associated with an incorrect rule. Correct rules were hardly ever associated with an incorrect identification, accounting for fewer than 1% of cases (Scheffler & Cinciała, 2011).

While studies such as these reveal cognitively mature learners' ability to acquire and demonstrate metalinguistic knowledge, they do not provide any direct insight into how such knowledge relates to L2 achievement. The question of whether learners' levels of metalinguistic knowledge are associated with their levels of L2 proficiency has been addressed in a number of correlational studies (Absi, 2014; Alderson et al., 1997; Elder & Manwaring, 2004; Elder, Warren, Hajek, Manwaring, & Davies, 1999; Gutiérrez, 2016; Renou, 2000; Roehr, 2008b). In sum, these studies show that learners' metalinguistic knowledge and their L2 proficiency are significantly and positively correlated, although reported correlation coefficients vary in strength, ranging from moderate (e.g. Alderson et al., 1997; Elder et al., 1999) to strong (e.g. Roehr, 2008b).

Mixed patterns of results are also in evidence, as exemplified by the study reported by Elder and Manwaring (2004), which examined the metalinguistic knowledge of English-speaking learners of L2 Chinese (N = 91) at an Australian university. The sample included both ab-initio learners and learners who had previously studied Chinese for four years at secondary school. The participants completed a custom-made Chinese metalinguistic assessment test that required them to match metalinguistic terms for parts of speech with the appropriate parts of speech in Chinese example sentences as well as to correct and explain errors in Chinese sentences. End-of-semester achievement tests that included written and oral components were used to assess L2 achievement.

The results show that learners generally scored low means on the metalinguistic assessment test and exhibited highly variable performance on all components. The

102 Empirical Evidence for Explicit Knowledge/Learning

easiest items were those that targeted grammatical features which exist in both English and Chinese. Participants had particular difficulty with providing metalinguistic explanations and using metalinguistic terminology appropriately. Moreover, correction and explanation ability did not always go hand in hand. Finally, and perhaps surprisingly, the ab-initio learners performed significantly better on all parts of the metalinguistic assessment test than the post-secondary learners. By way of explanation, Elder and Manwaring (2004) state that, according to the participants' language teachers, post-secondary students by and large have some degree of communicative competence, but often little explicit understanding of Chinese grammar. Conversely, ab-initio learners are exposed to explicit, form-focused instruction as soon as they start their university course. The observable differences may therefore be due to differences in instructional emphasis as well as the potentially greater maturity and motivation of ab-initio learners to engage with explicit grammar. In the case of the ab-initio learners, metalinguistic test scores and L2 achievement scores were positively and significantly correlated, with slightly larger coefficients in evidence for reading and writing. In the case of the post-secondary learners, less consistent correlational patterns were found, with both significant and non-significant relationships in evidence (Elder & Manwaring, 2004).

These findings suggest that in the relationship between metalinguistic knowledge and L2 proficiency, moderator variables are likely to be at play. Apart from the question of measurement which pertains to both the operationalisation of metalinguistic knowledge and how L2 proficiency is assessed (Gutiérrez, 2016), a number of other factors may impact on the strength and statistical significance of any observed associations. Relevant factors include the typological distance between L1 and L2 (Elder & Manwaring, 2004), participants' language learning experience (Roehr & Gánem-Gutiérrez, 2009b) and individual learner differences in terms of (meta-)cognitive variables such as language learning aptitude and beliefs about L2 learning. We will revisit these points in the final section of this chapter.

If L2 learners can acquire and demonstrate metalinguistic knowledge, and if metalinguistic knowledge is related to L2 achievement, the next question that arises is whether metalinguistic knowledge is instrumental in L2 performance. Specifically, how do L2 learners make use of metalinguistic knowledge while engaging in L2 tasks? This issue has been addressed in a number of studies taking a cognitive perspective (e.g. Butler, 2002; Golonka, 2006; Hu, 2002) or a sociocultural theoretical perspective (e.g. Gánem-Gutiérrez & Nogués Meléndez, 2013; Gánem-Gutiérrez & Roehr, 2011; Swain, 1998). Work by Hu (2002), which was conducted within a cognitive framework, offers a useful case in point.

Hu (2002) investigated to what extent instructed learners' metalinguistic knowledge is involved in L2 production as well as the psychological constraints on access to metalinguistic knowledge in L2 performance. The theoretical foundations of the study are derived from cognitive psychology and draw on skill acquisition theory and prototype theory. According to skill acquisition theory, declarative knowledge – in this case metalinguistic knowledge – can be automatized through practice. According to prototype theory, category structures are asymmetric, so that some category members are better examples than others. Put differently, some members are more prototypical of a category, while other members are less prototypical. Prototypes are established on the basis of two principles, namely maximisation of cue validity or distinctness from contrasting categories, and maximisation of category resemblance or representativeness within a category. In other words, "members of a category that share the most features with other members of the same category but the least features with members of contrasting categories emerge as prototypes" (Hu, 2002, p. 354).

Prototypical members of a category are generally acquired earlier and with greater ease than peripheral members, and they tend to be processed more quickly and more accurately. Linguistic constructions are subject to prototype effects, and these are expected to influence learners' acquisition and use of L2 structures. By the same token, the acquisition and use of metalinguistic knowledge is expected to be mediated by category structure (see also Roehr, 2008a). In sum, Hu (2002) assumes that three interacting factors will mediate real-time access to metalinguistic knowledge, that is, learners' attentional focus, processing automaticity, and linguistic prototypicality. This leads to the following hypotheses: (1) Given correct metalinguistic knowledge about a target structure, learners' accuracy of use of the structure will increase in proportion to the degree of attention to form allowed by a production task. (2) Given correct metalinguistic knowledge about different uses of a target structure, learners will be more accurate with prototypical uses than with peripheral uses. (3) Given correct metalinguistic knowledge about different uses of a target structure, learners' accuracy with peripheral uses will be more affected by attention to form than their accuracy with prototypical uses.

The empirical component of the study involves L1 Chinese learners of L2 English aged between 18 and 21 (N = 64). All learners had been exposed to several years of form-focused instruction that included ample metalinguistic information. In terms of proficiency, the learners are described as being at an upper-intermediate level. The targeted L2 structures are use of the definite article, the simple present, simple past, and present perfect tense, as well as two sets of pedagogical grammar rules describing more prototypical and more peripheral uses of these structures. Relative prototypicality was established on the basis of expert opinions, occurrence in textbooks, learners' own judgements, and the occurrence of structures in learner productions as collected during a pilot study. Learners' metalinguistic knowledge is assessed by means of an explanation task aimed at eliciting the targeted pedagogical grammar rules. Once the adequacy of leaners' metalinguistic knowledge has been established, participants carry out four spontaneous writing tasks comprising two narratives and two argumentative essays. Two tasks are completed before and two after a set of consciousness-raising error

104 Empirical Evidence for Explicit Knowledge/Learning

correction tasks. The error correction tasks focus on the target structures and are intended to manipulate participants' attention, directing it towards form. The error correction tasks are followed up with a post-study questionnaire in order to ascertain whether the desired focus on form was indeed achieved. The error correction and spontaneous writing tasks are administered once in a timed condition and once in a non-timed condition.

The results support the researcher's three hypotheses. Prototypical uses of the target structures were supplied more accurately than peripheral uses, and significantly greater accuracy was achieved for both uses in the absence of time pressure. When participants performed under time pressure, accuracy for prototypical uses was significantly less affected than accuracy for peripheral uses. Moreover, differences in attention to form had a significantly greater effect on peripheral than on prototypical uses of the target L2 structures.

By way of explanation, the researcher suggests that processing of metalinguistic knowledge about prototypical uses can be regarded as more automatized than processing of metalinguistic knowledge about peripheral uses, making the former less susceptible to attentional and time pressure than the latter. It is argued that the findings arising from the study are consistent with the proposals that, first, metalinguistic knowledge is indeed involved in L2 performance, and second, that it operates within certain psychological constraints. It appears that attentional focus on form in the absence of time pressure facilitated participants' access to any metalinguistic knowledge that was not fully automatized. In addition to the allocation of attention, prototypicality was an important mediating factor. Prototypical uses consistently resulted in higher levels of accuracy, arguably because the association between the respective pedagogical grammar rules and the uses they described was stronger and thus less susceptible to processing constraints brought about by time pressure. Last but not least, it is concluded that the usefulness of metalinguistic knowledge in L2 task performance is not an either/or phenomenon, but a matter of degree (Hu, 2002).

The research evidence we have considered so far about the acquisition of metalinguistic knowledge, the relationship between metalinguistic knowledge and L2 achievement and the use of metalinguistic knowledge in L2 task performance has been gleaned exclusively from measures assessing the product of cognitive processes. In order to arrive at a better understanding of how learners put to use their metalinguistic knowledge and how this affects L2 development, the use of process-oriented measures should provide us with further insights. In particular, studies employing verbal protocols in addition to test-based measurement have sought to uncover the relative benefits of focused attention, awareness at the level of noticing and awareness at the level of metalinguistic understanding (Camps, 2003; Leow, 1997, 2000; Roehr, 2006).

A study reported by Camps (2003) illustrates such process-oriented research well, not least because it makes use of two types of verbal protocol, concurrent think-aloud and retrospective recall. The study involved L1 English learners of L2

Spanish (N = 74) from first-semester and second-semester university-level Spanish classes and targeted third-person direct object pronouns. The first-semester students completed the experimental task shortly after being introduced to the target L2 structure in the context of their regular classes, while the second-semester students had encountered the target structure some weeks earlier when they were in their first semester. The main research questions are (1) whether participants who notice the target form will obtain higher scores in the experimental task than those who do not notice it, and (2) whether results will vary depending on students' semester.

The experimental task consists of a short narrative text with 16 blanks. The participants must complete the blanks by choosing from three multiple-choice options. Learners need to attend to both form and meaning, since the correct pronoun option not only has to agree in terms of gender and number with the respective referent in the task sentence, but it also has to make sense in the communicative context of the sentence and the text as a whole. The learners are provided with a vocabulary list as well as a set of instructions; they further participate in a brief training session on think-aloud protocols. The learners then perform the experimental task, verbalising their thoughts as they go along. Immediately after task completion, they are asked to record an additional retrospective protocol in which they describe how they went about the multiple-choice activity.

Noticing is operationalised as mentioning the target L2 structure in a verbal protocol. Thus, the concurrent and retrospective protocols are coded according to specific mentions of object pronoun forms as well as general references to gender and/or number. Overall, the target structure is referred to more often in the concurrent than in the retrospective protocols. Unsurprisingly perhaps, the concurrent protocols contain more specific references, while the retrospective protocols contain more general comments. For the purpose of statistical analysis, the participants are divided into two groups according to whether they mentioned the targeted L2 feature during their verbal reports or not. Camps (2003) reports that only 6 out of 29 first-semester students and 10 out of 45 second-semester students referred to pronouns and/or their agreement features, that is, a proportion of about 25% of participants. ANOVA-based analyses reveal that in the context of the concurrent protocols, only the interaction between participant grouping (mention vs. no mention) and language level (first vs. second semester) is significant. Analyses based on data from the retrospective protocols do not yield any statistically significant results.

A comparison of the two participant groups (mention vs. no mention) reveals significant differences in accuracy on the experimental task for the second-semester students, but not for the first-semester students. References to the target feature co-occur with accurate performance in 92% of cases; no references of the target feature still co-occur with accurate performance in 69% of cases. When considering the sample as a whole, learners who mention the targeted feature do not

106 Empirical Evidence for Explicit Knowledge/Learning

obtain higher scores than learners who do not mention it. If considered on their own, however, the second-semester students who mention the targeted feature do better than those who do not mention it. In view of this pattern of results, Camps (2003) concludes that the second-semester students who noticed and mentioned the targeted form achieved the best results on the experimental task. He suggests that the lower proficiency level of the first-semester learners may have prevented them from making use of the information they attended to, so the same effect did not obtain for them.

Thus, while earlier studies with university-level learners of Spanish indicate that higher levels of awareness are associated with improved performance (Leow, 1997, 2000), more recent work offers a somewhat more nuanced outlook. Specifically, it appears to be the case that noticing and awareness, though beneficial in many cases, do not necessarily and uniformly warrant success, but that moderator variables such as level of L2 proficiency impact on the usefulness or otherwise of metalinguistic awareness in L2 task performance (Camps, 2003; Roehr, 2006). Moreover, recent work has led to a more fine-grained conceptualisation and operationalisation of levels of awareness inferred from verbal report data, as discussed in Chapter 6 below.

The empirical research we have considered so far has shown convincingly that all else being equal, explicit teaching and learning facilitate L2 development in cognitively mature learners, that such learners can acquire metalinguistic knowledge, that learners' level of metalinguistic knowledge correlates positively with their level of L2 achievement, and that metalinguistic knowledge can be utilised in L2 task performance. However, all else is rarely equal. Indeed, research into explicit teaching and learning has identified a number of moderating variables that appear to interact with metalinguistic knowledge and its role in L2 teaching, learning and use. The moderating variables we have encountered so far pertain to characteristics of the (meta-)linguistic input as well as to characteristics of the learner. Input factors include the typological distance between L1 and L2, the prototypicality of L2 constructions as well as properties impacting on learning difficulty. Learner factors include L2 learning experience and language history, L2 proficiency level as well as psychological variables in the cognitive and affective domain, including language learning aptitude and learners' beliefs and perceptions, for instance. Let us now turn to the as yet rather small body of research that has sought to uncover the role of such moderator variables.

5.3 The Role of Learner and Input Variables

In view of the conceptual closeness of metalinguistic ability on the one hand and language-analytic ability as a component of language learning aptitude on the other hand, as discussed in the previous chapter, it is somewhat surprising that there is relatively little empirical research that has examined the relationship between metalinguistic knowledge and language learning aptitude (Alderson et al., 1997; Brooks & Kempe, 2013; Roehr & Gánem-Gutiérrez, 2009b). A study by Roehr and Gánem-Gutiérrez (2009b) addressed the issue directly. Working with L1 English university-level learners of L2 German and L2 Spanish (N = 39), the researchers administered a battery of measures, including a test of metalinguistic knowledge, the Modern Language Aptitude Test (MLAT, Carroll & Sapon, 2002) and reading span tests in L1 English and L2 German or Spanish in order to measure participants' working memory capacity. The MLAT operationalises the classic model of aptitude comprising phonetic coding ability, language-analytic ability and associative memory by means of five sub-tests labelled number learning (phonetic coding, associative memory), phonetic script (phonetic coding), spelling clues (phonetic coding, L1 lexical knowledge), words in sentences (language-analytic ability) and paired associates (associative memory). The test of metalinguistic knowledge required the participants to correct, describe and explain highlighted errors in L2 sentences as well as identify the grammatical role of parts of speech in L2 sentences.

The results show a moderate positive correlation between participants' metalinguistic knowledge and their overall level of language learning aptitude. Analyses by sub-test reveal that the relationship is driven by the words-in-sentences sub-test of the MLAT, that is, the measure of language-analytic ability. MLAT scores are moderately correlated with working memory as measured by the L1 reading span test. Metalinguistic knowledge is not associated with working memory as measured in either L1 or L2. A principal components analysis reveals four distinct components, with the metalinguistic knowledge test loading on one component, the working memory measures loading on another component, and the MLAT sub-tests loading on two further components. This suggests that metalinguistic knowledge, language learning aptitude and working memory are distinguishable constructs. Specifically, language-analytic ability in L1 as measured by the words-in-sentences sub-test of the MLAT and language-analytic ability in L2 as measured by the second section of the metalinguistic knowledge test do not cluster together.

A regression analysis with metalinguistic knowledge as the dependent variable results in four significant predictors. The participants' language learning experience, operationalised as years of study of L2 German or Spanish and cumulative years of study of other L2s, explains an impressive 45% of the variance in metalinguistic knowledge scores, thus proving by far the most powerful predictor. Performance on the words-in-sentences and paired-associates sub-tests of the MLAT explain a further 15% of the variance in the participants' metalinguistic knowledge. Given that the metalinguistic knowledge test was administered in a written modality and did not draw on phonetic abilities, the latter result is arguably unsurprising (Roehr & Gánem-Gutiérrez, 2009b). More interestingly perhaps, it appears to be the case that language learning experience can compensate to some extent for individual differences in aptitude, making long-term exposure to and engagement with a number of L2s the strongest predictor of metalinguistic development in the participating university-level learners.

In a longitudinal case study with an L1 English learner of L2 German, Roehr-Brackin (2014, 2015) examines the role of a number of learner and input variables and their interaction with both the participant's L2 development and his use of explicit knowledge and processes. The study covers a period of more than three years during which the participant takes L2 classes on an individual basis; the classes are characterised by form-focused instruction with practice in all four skills. The data set that is analysed comprises audio-recordings of the participant's oral performance in interaction with his tutor as well as measures of language learning aptitude, learning style, language learning strategy use and metacognition, with the latter accessed via diary entries in which the learner comments on his perceptions of the learning task. The results are interpreted from a usage-based and complexity-theoretic perspective, i.e. in terms of theoretical approaches that emphasise the dynamic interaction of multiple variables during L2 development.

In summary, the findings reveal that explicit knowledge and processes have a powerful impact on the participant's L2 learning and use, allowing him at times to seemingly override the default implicit path of development that predicts a bottom-up trajectory from linguistic items to more abstract schemas. Instead, the participant is able to use explicit knowledge and processes to take a top-down approach, applying the (simplified) schemas provided by pedagogical grammar to new instances in the input. This suggests that explicit knowledge can function as a so-called control parameter that brings about phase shifts, i.e. qualitative changes in behaviour that lead the learner's L2 system into a new and desirable attractor state. At the same time, however, use of explicit knowledge and processes is not necessarily and automatically beneficial because it can occasionally lead to overgeneralisation errors and/or to cognitive overload (Roehr-Brackin, 2014).

With regard to the moderating variables that were measured in the study, metalinguistic knowledge appears to be used as a tool for mediating the apparent tension between the learner's aptitude profile which shows relatively weak grammatical sensitivity and stylistic preferences which result in discomfort with spontaneous oral use of the L2 on the one hand, and stylistic preferences for accuracy, diligence and reflection on the other hand. Judicious use of explicit knowledge and processes alongside suitable language learning strategies seemingly permit the learner to follow a successful developmental path that shows gradually decreasing reliance on his tutor and steadily increasing progress in terms of L2 accuracy in an oral modality (Roehr-Brackin, 2015).

Apart from the study just reviewed which took into consideration the participating learner's metacognition through an analysis of his diary entries, a number of other studies have investigated learners' metacognition by examining beliefs about explicit knowledge, learning and teaching (Loewen et al., 2009; Scheffler, 2009, 2013; Schulz, 2001; Thepseenu & Roehr, 2013). Scheffler (2009), for instance, addresses the relationship between learners' beliefs about the usefulness of (explicit) instruction in conjunction with perceived learning difficulty. The researcher administered a questionnaire to two groups of L1 Polish learners of

L2 English at a college of modern languages. The participants in Group A (N = 50) were asked to rate the perceived difficulty of selected English grammar points on a five-point scale ranging from 'very easy' to 'very difficult'. The participants in Group B (N = 50) were asked to rate the perceived usefulness of instruction on the same grammar points on a five-point scale ranging from 'not useful at all' to 'very useful'. Overall, the results show that the learners tend to perceive English grammar as fairly easy, while the usefulness of instruction is generally rated quite highly. The findings further suggest an overlap between the perceptions of the two groups of participants. In general, if an area of grammar is considered difficult, instruction is considered useful. Only two grammar points do not fit in with this pattern: prepositions and -*ing* forms and infinitives are regarded as both difficult and not amenable to instruction. Nonetheless, the general conclusion is that instruction in areas perceived as difficult is seen as particularly useful (Scheffler, 2009).

Using a more complex research design, Thepseenu and Roehr (2013) investigated the relationship between learners' beliefs about the usefulness of explicit instruction and learning difficulty by drawing not only on participants' perceptions, but also on their actual performance. Moreover, the researchers employed more extensive measures, including tests, questionnaires and interviews. The participants were L1 Thai university-level learners of L2 English (N = 64) who on average had learned English for almost 13 years, yet only achieved mean L2 placement test scores at an elementary level of proficiency. The participants completed a test of meta-linguistic knowledge (Ziętek & Roehr, 2011) targeting 12 grammar points that had previously been categorised as high vs. low learning difficulty by means of the taxonomy of learning difficulty put forward by Roehr and Gánem-Gutiérrez (2009a) and reviewed in Chapter 4. The test required participants to correct, describe and explain highlighted errors at sentence level. A questionnaire aimed at eliciting beliefs about metalinguistic knowledge asked participants to judge the difficulty and indicate the usefulness of instruction of the targeted grammar points using the same five-point scales employed by Scheffler (2009). Furthermore, participants were asked to indicate their (dis-)agreement with a number of statements about the teaching and learning of grammar. Finally, two open-ended items asked participants to describe why they (dis-)liked the study of grammar. Semi-structured follow-up interviews with a sub-sample of participants (N = 9) allowed for a more in-depth discussion of the perceived usefulness of the teaching and learning of L2 grammar, advantages and disadvantages, likes and dislikes, etc.

The results show that the participants did better on grammar points categorised as exhibiting low explicit learning difficulty than on grammar points categorised as exhibiting high explicit learning difficulty, as expected. The participants' own difficulty judgements were consistent with the test designers' judgements in that the learners judged the designated low-difficulty items to be significantly easier than the high-difficulty items. With regard to the relationship between perceived difficulty and perceived usefulness of instruction, a very strong negative correlation was obtained, indicating that the easier a grammar point was judged to be,

110 Empirical Evidence for Explicit Knowledge/Learning

the more useful instruction was perceived to be. Interestingly, this finding is in direct contrast with the result reported by Scheffler (2009). Of course there are a number of differences between the two studies, including the participants' L1s, their level of L2 English proficiency, and perhaps most importantly the fact that the learners in Thepseenu and Roehr's (2013) study were tested on the grammar points they were asked to judge immediately prior to making their judgements, unlike the learners in Scheffler's (2009) study.

Regarding the explicit teaching and learning of grammar more generally, the participants held many positive beliefs pertaining to the importance of grammar for L2 mastery and for accurate use of the L2 in reading and writing but also speaking and listening, including self-correction, as well as for building up confidence, both in terms of gaining and maintaining cognitive control over the complex linguistic domain that is the L2 system, and in terms of self-efficacy. Negative beliefs referred to the sometimes limited usefulness of explicit knowledge during speaking and listening activities and to the potential for confusion arising from a sometimes overwhelming number of pedagogical grammar rules to be memorised. In sum, the findings show that learners' beliefs were not only quite differentiated, but also reveal a correspondence between participants' perceptions and their actual performance with regard to the learning difficulty of specific L2 grammar points (Thepseenu & Roehr, 2013).

Beyond learners' own perceptions, the issue of learning difficulty has also been addressed in terms of expert judgements made by L2 teachers and L2 learning researchers (Rodríguez Silva & Roehr-Brackin, 2016b; Scheffler, 2011). In a recent study, Rodríguez Silva and Roehr-Brackin (2016b) asked L1 Mexican Spanish university-level learners (N = 30), their teachers (N = 11) and applied linguistics experts (N = 3) to judge the learning difficulty of 13 English grammar points. In addition, the learners' explicit and implicit knowledge of the targeted grammar points was assessed by means of a test of metalinguistic knowledge and an oral elicited imitation task, respectively. In order to make their difficulty judgements, the learners and their teachers used the same five-point scale ranging from 'very easy' to 'very difficult' previously employed in other studies (Scheffler, 2009; Thepseenu & Roehr, 2013), while the applied linguists used the more elaborate taxonomy of learning difficulty put forward by Roehr and Gánem-Gutiérrez (2009a). The results show that whereas the experts' learning difficulty judgements did not lead to significant predictions of learners' performance, the learners' own difficulty rankings correlated significantly with their performance on the measure of explicit knowledge. Although correlations based on teachers' difficulty rankings did not reach statistical significance, the judgements of this group were the only ones which showed trends towards successful prediction of learners' performance on both the implicit and the explicit L2 measure. Thus, the teachers exhibited a trend towards the best overall prediction ability when compared with the learners themselves and the L2 learning researchers (Rodríguez Silva & Roehr-Brackin, 2016b).

Ziętek and Roehr's (2011) investigation into the relationship of L2 learners' metalinguistic knowledge and their stylistic preferences is the only published empirical study concerned with cognitive style as a potential moderating variable interacting with explicit knowledge and learning. The researchers worked with 18-year-old L1 Polish secondary-level learners of L2 English (N = 20) who were experienced language learners. The participants completed the same test of metalinguistic knowledge used by Thepseenu and Roehr (2013; see above). In addition, their stylistic orientation on the wholist/analytic dimension of cognitive style was assessed by means of the Extended Cognitive Style Analysis – Wholist/Analytic measure (Peterson & Deary, 2006; Peterson, Deary, & Austin, 2003).

The results reveal a fairly strong negative correlation between participants' performance on the test of metalinguistic knowledge and their wholist/analytic style ratio, indicating that greater metalinguistic knowledge was associated with a more wholist orientation. This was contrary to the researchers' initial expectation of finding a relationship between improved metalinguistic knowledge and a more analytic orientation. However, Ziętek and Roehr suggest that a possible explanation for the finding may lie in the nature of the metalinguistic test the learners were asked to complete. Specifically, the correction task presented highlighted errors in the context of L2 sentences and thus offered linguistic exemplars. The description/explanation task required the articulation of propositions underlying corrections of the errors and thus drew on inferencing. Inductive tasks, that is, tasks where (linguistic) observations are given and (metalinguistic) principles must be inferred are thought to suit wholistic individuals. Such individuals also have a preference for organising information at a global level and getting a sense of the big picture. This orientation seemingly helped with successful performance on the particular metalinguistic test used in the study. Stylistic orientation was not associated with performance on an independent measure of L2 proficiency, as expected (Ziętek & Roehr, 2011).

The research we have considered so far mostly addressed a single moderator variable (for exceptions see Brooks & Kempe, 2013; Roehr & Gánem-Gutiérrez, 2009b). Studies incorporating multiple moderator variables and their interplay with explicit knowledge, learning or teaching (Robinson, 1997; Rodríguez Silva & Roehr-Brackin, 2016a; Roehr-Brackin, 2014, 2015; Yalçın & Spada, 2016) are still very much in short supply, presumably because of the necessarily greater methodological and practical challenges associated with operationalising several learner and input variables within the same research design. A recent study aimed at investigating the role of language learning aptitude (a learner variable) in the explicit learning of two L2 structures differing in learning difficulty (an input variable) illustrates how these challenges may be addressed.

Yalçin and Spada (2016) hypothesised that aptitude would play a greater role in the explicit learning of a difficult structure than in the explicit learning of an easy structure. Their empirical study is conducted with 13 to 14-year-old L1 Turkish learners of L2 English (N = 66) in three intact Grade 8 classes, i.e. the participant

112 Empirical Evidence for Explicit Knowledge/Learning

sample comprises learners who are at the threshold of cognitive maturity. The targeted L2 structures are the passive voice, described as difficult, and the past progressive tense, described as easy. The passive was considered difficult because its production requires a number of grammatical operations, because it is less frequent in the input, and because it is late acquired by L1 learners. By comparison, the past progressive is more frequent and exemplifies a transparent form-meaning relationship. Finally, the passive was perceived as more difficult than the past progressive by the learners themselves. The targeted L2 structures are taught for four hours each. The instruction is form-focused in nature, providing explicit information about the formal properties of the target structures as well as opportunities for communicative practice. Aptitude is assessed by means of the computer-administered LLAMA battery (Meara, 2005; Rogers et al., 2016). Explicit L2 knowledge is measured by means of two written untimed grammaticality judgement tasks (GJT) with 40 items each and one GJT focusing on each target structure. Learners must make a judgement ('correct', 'incorrect', 'don't know') and provide the correct form for any items judged to be ungrammatical. Productive use of the target structures is measured by means of two picture-cued oral tests, administered on an individual basis. The researchers argue that this task type draws more on implicit knowledge, given its focus on meaning, but they make no categorical claim that only implicit knowledge will be used.

The results for the passive, i.e. the difficult structure, show a significant moderate correlation between GJT pre- and post-test scores. Moreover, GJT post-test scores are moderately correlated with the LLAMA F sub-test (grammatical inferencing, or language-analytic ability) and the LLAMA E sub-test (sound-symbol recognition). In a regression analysis, LLAMA F explains 12% of the variance in GJT post-test scores after controlling for pre-test scores. The oral pre-test and post-test scores are likewise moderately correlated, but there are no correlations with any of the LLAMA sub-tests, so no regression analysis is run. The results for the past progressive, i.e. the easy structure, show a relatively strong correlation between GJT pre- and post-test scores. The LLAMA E sub-test (sound-symbol recognition) is weakly correlated with post-test scores. In a regression analysis, LLAMA E does not emerge as a significant predictor once pre-test scores are controlled for. The oral pre- and post-test scores are strongly correlated. Post-test scores also correlate with the LLAMA B sub-test (vocabulary learning, or associative memory). In a regression analysis, LLAMA B explains 6% of the variance in oral post-test scores once pre-test scores are controlled for.

The researchers argue that when learners performed the GJT targeting the difficult structure, they relied to a greater extent on aptitude, in particular grammatical inferencing ability. This is in keeping with the hypothesis that explicit learning of difficult structures is dependent on aptitude. The result is also in keeping with the information processing model of L2 development proposed by Skehan (2002), according to which language-analytic ability is particularly important at the patterning stage. The learners may have been at that stage with regard to the passive, which was a novel structure for them. By contrast, associative memory predicted a small amount of the variance of accurate use of the easy structure in the oral production task. The fact that the past progressive was easy may help explain why aptitude played no role on the GJT targeting this structure. Previous learning of this structure, which was not new to the learners, may have levelled out any differences in aptitude. The result is described as being consistent with Skehan's (2002) model as well. The model claims that memory plays a greater role at later stages of development, in particular the lexicalising stage. According to the researchers, the participants may have reached that stage, given that they had already been familiar with the structure prior to the experimental treatment. Overall, it is concluded that aptitude was a facilitator for the difficult structure while it had a minimal effect on outcomes for the easy structure. Moreover, different aptitude components contributed differentially to the learning of difficult and easy structures in the adolescent learners taking part in the study (Yalçın & Spada, 2016).

In conclusion, though still limited in scope and number at this point in time, studies investigating the role of moderator variables in explicit learning and teaching have shown that (components of) language learning aptitude can predict the acquisition of metalinguistic knowledge as well as L2 performance on measures drawing on either explicit or implicit knowledge. Learners' performance seems to be moderated by the relative learning difficulty of the targeted L2 structures as well as by their language learning experience. Cognitively mature learners' own judgements of learning difficulty are associated with their performance on measures of explicit knowledge, with structures judged to be more difficult resulting in lower levels of success than structures judged to be easier. Furthermore, the use of explicit knowledge and processes in L2 learning can be a powerful tool whose deployment can have both advantages and disadvantages. Advantages include the potential for fast-track learning, thus allowing a learner to essentially side-step the gradual implicit path from item to schema, while disadvantages include inappropriate overgeneralisation and possible cognitive overload. However, the use of metalinguistic knowledge is mediated by individual learner differences in language learning aptitude and metacognition including learners' beliefs, as already noted, as well as by stylistic preferences. Last but not least, it is worth bearing in mind that the role of moderating variables in L2 learning and use and their interaction with metalinguistic knowledge is necessarily influenced by how specific variables are operationalised in empirical research. Therefore, we will now turn to the important issue of measuring metalinguistic awareness.

6

MEASURING METALINGUISTIC AWARENESS

6.1 Tests and Self-Report as Measures of Explicit Knowledge

Seminal work in the area of measuring both explicit and implicit knowledge in L2 learning has been carried out by Rod Ellis and colleagues (R. Ellis, 2004; R. Ellis et al., 2009). It is argued that explicit and implicit knowledge can be distinguished according to a number of criteria (see Chapter 4), that is, awareness or the absence thereof (conscious vs. intuitive), type of knowledge (declarative vs. procedural), accessibility of knowledge (controlled vs. automatic processing), use of knowledge, with implicit knowledge being used during fluent performance and explicit knowledge to resolve difficulties, systematicity and certainty of knowledge, availability or otherwise for self-report, and learnability, with explicit knowledge being potentially learnable at any age given sufficient cognitive maturity and implicit knowledge being subject to maturational constraints (R. Ellis, 2005). Accordingly, if explicit knowledge is to be operationalised in line with these criteria, a test measuring explicit knowledge would have a primary focus on form, the use of metalanguage would be encouraged, it would require or at least encourage learners to respond in line with known pedagogical grammar rules, and it would not impose any time pressure.

Application of these criteria was attempted in a validation study with university-level participants in New Zealand (R. Ellis, 2005), including L2 learners of English from different L1 backgrounds and at varying levels of L2 proficiency (N = 91) and a control group of L1 English speakers (N = 20). These participants completed a battery of tests targeting 17 English structures which are known to be problematic for L2 learners at different stages of development: modal verbs, plural -*s*, verb complements (*to* + infinitive vs. gerund), regular past tense, *yes/no* questions, *since* vs. *for*, indefinite article, possessive -*s*, third person -*s*, adverb placement, comparatives, dative alternation, embedded questions, ergative verbs, question tags, relative clauses, and unreal conditions. The test battery comprised five measures: an elicited imitation test presented orally (see also Erlam, 2006; Spada, Shiu, & Tomita, 2015; Suzuki & DeKeyser, 2015), an oral narrative test with written presentation and an oral response, a computer-administered timed grammaticality judgement task (GJT) with written presentation, a computer-administered untimed GJT with written presentation, certainty ratings and source attributions asking participants to report whether they relied on 'rules' or 'feel', and a written metalinguistic knowledge test. It was hypothesised that the elicited imitation test, the oral narrative test and the timed GJT would tap implicit knowledge, whereas the untimed GJT and the metalinguistic knowledge test would tap explicit knowledge.

Based on this hypothesis, a factor analysis with a two-factor solution is conducted. The elicited imitation test, the oral narrative test and the timed GJT load at 0.7 or above on Factor 1, explaining about 58% of the variance. The untimed GJT and the metalinguistic knowledge test load at 0.7 or above on Factor 2, explaining about 16% of the variance. However, the untimed GJT also loads at above 0.5 on Factor 1. Interestingly, it seems to be the case that grammatical and ungrammatical sentences function differently in the untimed GJT. Accordingly, separate correlations are run for grammatical and ungrammatical sentences in the untimed GJT. It is found that scores achieved on grammatical sentences correlate more strongly with the oral and timed tests, while scores achieved on ungrammatical sentences correlate more strongly with the metalinguistic knowledge test. Therefore another factor analysis is carried out with scores for grammatical sentences on the untimed GJT removed. The result shows that the cumulative variance explained is similar, but the factor loadings are now more clearly divided, with each test score loading strongly on a single factor only.

Further results reveal that the designated tests of explicit knowledge led to fuller use of metalinguistic knowledge than the designated tests of implicit knowledge. Moreover, drawing on confidence ratings and source attributions, the designated tests of explicit knowledge encouraged the use of rules, whereas the designated tests of implicit knowledge encouraged the use of feel, with the exception of the ungrammatical items on the untimed GJT. However, the tests of implicit knowledge did not lead to more certainty or more systematic responses than the tests of explicit knowledge, so the criteria of certainty and systematicity of knowledge may not be sufficient in themselves to allow us to distinguish whether explicit or implicit knowledge was used. Finally, it is argued that time-pressured tests require learners to rely on their implicit knowledge, while untimed tests permit learners to draw on both types of knowledge. As a consequence, the non-speeded measures resulted in overall higher scores. The findings are seen as supporting the overall validity of the five tests which appear to provide relatively separate measures of implicit and explicit knowledge. Further support for the proposed test battery has since been provided by a partial replication study with L1 Chinese learners of L2 English incorporating an elicited imitation test, timed and untimed GJTs and a metalinguistic knowledge test targeting the same 17 structures (Zhang, 2015), as well as a small-scale conceptual replication study using L2 Spanish versions of all five tests included in the original study (Bowles, 2011). Overall, it can be concluded that the elicited imitation test (implicit knowledge) and the test of metalinguistic knowledge (explicit knowledge) potentially offer the clearest distinction between the two knowledge types (R. Ellis, 2005).

In point of fact, tests of metalinguistic knowledge are relatively widely-used measures of explicit knowledge in classroom-based L2 learning research. Metalinguistic knowledge tests are typically administered in an untimed written modality and may include metalinguistic labelling tasks, error correction, description and explanation tasks, and/or rule illustration tasks. A metalinguistic labelling task (Alderson et al., 1997; Clapham, 2001; Elder & Manwaring, 2004; Elder et al., 1999; Roehr, 2005) presents participants with stretches of L2 text, typically at sentence level, but potentially in shorter units such as clauses or longer units such as connected discourse, and requires them to label relevant linguistic exemplars with appropriate metalinguistic terms such as 'present tense verb', 'singular noun', 'preposition', 'subordinating conjunction', etc. The technical terms are generally provided, so participants must recognize their meaning and then identify L2 instances to which the terms apply.

A rule illustration task (Absi, 2014; Rodríguez Silva & Roehr-Brackin, 2016b; Scheffler, 2011; see also Scheffler & Cinciała, 2011) is perhaps more demanding because it involves both recognition and production. Such a task provides participants with pedagogical grammar rules and asks them to write L2 sentences illustrating the rules in question. Hence, participants must understand the given rule, think of a suitable L2 sentence that is captured by the rule, and produce that sentence accurately, making sure that all categories and relations included in the rule are fully illustrated. For instance, the pedagogical grammar rule that one should use the simple past tense in English to refer to a finished event in the past would be fully illustrated by the sentence *John went to the cinema yesterday*, but not by the sentence *John went to the cinema* because there is no indication as to whether the event is finished. Without further context, *John has gone to the cinema* would be equally acceptable, while **John has gone to the cinema yesterday* clearly is not.

An error correction, description and explanation task (Akakura, 2012; Alderson et al., 1997; Elder & Manwaring, 2004; Elder et al., 1999; Erlam, 2013; Green & Hecht, 1992; Rodríguez Silva & Roehr-Brackin, 2016b; Roehr, 2008b; Roehr & Gánem-Gutiérrez, 2009a, 2009b; Thepseenu & Roehr, 2013; Ziętek & Roehr, 2011) presents participants with L2 sentences that contain an erroneous instance of the targeted structure. This may be an error of form or an error of use, or both in combination. For instance, if the target is the English plural -*s*, the learner may be presented with *Helen went to the market and bought a bunch of **banana***. The learner may be required to identify the error, or the error may be highlighted to ensure that the learner is focused on the target right away, as in the given example. The task is to correct the error (*a bunch of bananas*) and to describe and explain the correction. Describing the correction will require or at least encourage the use of metalinguistic terminology (What form is used?), while explaining the correction will require a justification (Why is that form used?). In other words, the learner is essentially asked to provide a pedagogical grammar rule.

Early research sometimes combined correction, description and explanation with the use of a GJT (e.g. Bialystok, 1979; Sorace, 1985), but this is much less common in current work. The reason for avoiding prior judgement tasks, for highlighting targeted errors and even for excluding a correction score altogether and focusing on description and explanation alone is the fact that description and explanation tasks require the use of metalanguage and the recall, reconstruction or ad-hoc construction of pedagogical grammar rules, which are explicit by definition. By contrast, error correction may be achieved by drawing on explicit knowledge, implicit knowledge, or both. Gutiérrez (2016) makes this point slightly differently by referring to the distinction between analysed knowledge and knowledge of metalanguage. Analysed knowledge is equated with knowledge that is available to consciousness, but not necessarily for verbal report, while knowledge of meta-language comprises knowledge of technical terminology and entails the ability to verbalise analysed knowledge. It is argued that analysed knowledge can exist independently of knowledge of metalanguage, i.e. learners may be aware of a grammatical systematicity, but may be unable to articulate it.

This argument is supported empirically by means of a study that compares L2 learners' performance on a test of analysed knowledge and a test of knowledge of metalanguage (Gutiérrez, 2016). The relationship between performance on these tests and on various measures of L2 proficiency is examined. The participants are Canadian university-level learners of L2 Spanish (N = 49) at roughly B1 level of the Common European Framework of Reference (CEFR). The learners are regularly exposed to form-focused instruction that includes explicit grammar teaching. Analysed knowledge is measured by means of an untimed GJT that requires learners to judge the acceptability of sentences and correct ungrammatical sentences; only error correction is scored in order to assess analysed knowledge. Knowledge of metalanguage is measured by means of a metalinguistic knowledge test that requires learners to correct highlighted errors and provide relevant pedagogical grammar rules explaining the corrections. The tests target 16 Spanish grammar points the learners had been taught. L2 proficiency is measured by means of university-internal course-based assessments, which comprise two written compositions, an oral exam and two term exams, mid-term and end-of-term. The latter test listening and reading comprehension, vocabulary, grammar and writing.

The results indicate that the participants did significantly better on the meta-linguistic knowledge test (mean 60%) than on the GJT (mean 46%), with a large effect size. The two measures are moderately correlated, which indicates that they tap related but separate constructs. The researcher explains the difference in performance by referring to the demands of the GJT, which are considered to be higher in terms of both analysis of knowledge and control of processing. The error correction part of the metalinguistic knowledge test yielded a high score (mean 82%), much higher than the error correction task on the GJT, where learners had to identify ungrammatical sentences, pinpoint the error and then provide the correction. Thus, the way analysed knowledge was measured affected performance.

The participants did well on the measures of L2 proficiency, with all mean scores above 75%. The composition score was strongly correlated with the GJT and moderately correlated with the metalinguistic knowledge test. The oral exam score was moderately correlated with the GJT. The term exams were strongly correlated with both the GJT and the metalinguistic knowledge test. Given the correlations between explicit knowledge and L2 proficiency, it is argued that both analysed knowledge and knowledge of metalanguage are important components of L2 proficiency (see also R. Ellis, 2006b). However, the individual correlations show that analysed knowledge was a better predictor of L2 achievement than knowledge of metalanguage. Metalanguage was primarily relevant in measures focused on grammatical accuracy. By contrast, awareness of how grammar features work can be regarded as more useful in language use of any kind. Thus, the results are consistent with the idea of a continuum of usefulness for explicit knowledge (Gutiérrez, 2016), with speaking and listening at one end (Absi, 2014) and writing and grammar at the other (Roehr, 2008b).

The discussion so far suggests that whereas tests of metalinguistic knowledge constitute a valid and reliable measure of explicit L2 knowledge, GJTs present a more complex picture, not only because it is unclear exactly which type of knowledge may be used to make an acceptability judgement in timed or untimed conditions, but also because L2 learners' response patterns seem to differ according to whether they attempt to judge grammatical or ungrammatical sentences. While traditional SLA research informed by a nativist theoretical paradigm has put much faith in GJTs (Mandell, 1999; Schütze, 1996; Schütze & Sprouse, 2013; Winitz, 1996), many contemporary applied linguists are more wary of this kind of instrument, and rightly so, it seems. Two recent studies (Godfroid et al., 2015; Gutiérrez, 2013) have followed up the intriguing results reported previously in the context of Rod Ellis' (2005) seminal study.

Gutiérrez (2013) argues that in order to decide whether a sentence is acceptable or unacceptable, participants must engage in semantic processing and noticing, whereas reflection may or may not take place. Semantic processing and noticing can potentially be carried out based on implicit knowledge, while reflection clearly requires the use of explicit knowledge. Two aspects that have been investigated in connection with the question of whether implicit or explicit knowledge is tapped by GJTs are time pressure and task stimulus. Findings to date have been interpreted as suggesting that timed GJTs access implicit knowledge, while untimed GJTs access explicit knowledge. At the same time, it is still unclear whether judging grammatical vs. ungrammatical sentences draws on different types of knowledge. In addition, time pressure and task stimulus may interact, of course.

Accordingly, the researcher set out to investigate whether L2 learners draw on different types of knowledge when judging grammatical and ungrammatical sentences in timed and untimed conditions. The study involved Canadian university learners of L2 Spanish (N = 49) in either the third or the fifth term of instruction, roughly corresponding to CEFR levels A2 and B1 respectively in terms of proficiency. Apart from completing a timed and an untimed GJT, the participants also sat a metalinguistic knowledge test. Each GJT contained the same 64 sentences targeting 16 L2 structures that had been the subject of explicit instruction. Half of the items were grammatical, half ungrammatical. The timed GJT was controlled via an automated Powerpoint slide show, with each sentence visible for 6–9 seconds, depending on length. Participants logged their responses on a separate answer sheet. The metalinguistic knowledge test targeted the same 16 structures. The test included sentences with an underlined error, and participants were asked to provide the pedagogical grammar rules that were violated. Thus, the test was a measure of explicit knowledge.

Results show that the participants obtained higher scores on the untimed than on the timed GJT, and higher scores on grammatical than on ungrammatical sentences on both tests. If divided into sections (timed grammatical, timed ungrammatical, untimed grammatical, untimed ungrammatical), significant positive correlations are in evidence throughout, with the relationships between grammatical and ungrammatical test sections stronger than between timed and untimed test sections. All GJT sections correlate with the metalinguistic knowledge test, with larger effect sizes in evidence for the ungrammatical sections.

An exploratory factor analysis yields two components with an eigenvalue greater than 1 explaining 79% of the total variance. The ungrammatical GJT sections and the metalinguistic knowledge test load on one factor labelled explicit knowledge, while the grammatical GJT sections load on a second factor labelled implicit knowledge. As an exploratory factor analysis does not allow for the testing of competing hypotheses or the falsification of a hypothesis, an additional confirmatory factor analysis is run. The two competing hypotheses referred to whether loadings would depend on the factor of time pressure or the factor of grammaticality/stimulus type. In this analysis, the grammatical/ungrammatical model shows a good fit, but the timed/untimed model does not, thus confirming the result of the exploratory factor analysis.

Repeated-measures ANOVAs show a significant effect of time pressure, indicating that the participants were more accurate on the untimed than the timed GJT. There is also a significant effect of task stimulus, indicating that the learners did better on grammatical than ungrammatical sentences. Furthermore, there is a significant interaction between time pressure and task stimulus. Learners found both grammatical and ungrammatical sentences more challenging in the timed than in the untimed condition. An analysis by targeted L2 structure confirms the overall pattern of results, with the exception of two structures that show no differences in terms of timed vs. untimed condition, and two other structures where learners performed better on ungrammatical than grammatical sentences.

On the basis of these findings it is argued that participants processed grammatical and ungrammatical sentences differently. By way of interpretation, the grammatical test sections in both the timed and the untimed condition may have tested implicit knowledge, whereas the ungrammatical test sections in both the timed and the untimed condition may have tested explicit knowledge. The greater variance on ungrammatical items is regarded as evidence in support of this interpretation, beyond the correlational and factor-analytic results. It is clear from the findings that both time pressure and stimulus type play a role in participants' performance on GJTs, but stimulus type (grammatical vs. ungrammatical) seems to have had a larger effect (Gutiérrez, 2013).

Interestingly, another recent study concerned with GJTs as measures of explicit or implicit knowledge reaches the opposite conclusion, that is, time pressure appeared to be more important than stimulus type. Godfroid et al. (2015) examined which knowledge type(s) – explicit or implicit – L1 and L2 speakers of English draw on when judging the acceptability of English sentences. While the study is a conceptual replication of R. Ellis (2005), it employs eye-tracking as a further method beyond the analysis of accuracy scores. Specifically, the researchers compared participants' eye-movement patterns as they judged timed, untimed, grammatical and ungrammatical sentences. Thus the study makes direct use of processing data to supplement product data.

It is rightly pointed out that tasks can only predispose learners towards the use of a particular type of knowledge; what type of knowledge is actually used not only depends on the characteristics of the task at hand, but also on the knowledge sources available to the individual learner. Researchers who have studied implicit and explicit knowledge have argued that time pressure suppresses reflection and thus makes it difficult for the learner to access explicit knowledge. Moreover, ungrammatical items may invite the use of explicit knowledge because of the fact that they contain an error.

Godfroid et al. (2015) explain that eye-tracking records an individual's eye movements as s/he performs a task. The point of gaze is considered to be an index of overt attention and thus offers a window into the individual's cognitive processing. Readers are thought to have target-like knowledge representations if they show sensitivity to errors by fixating longer on the location of the error or regressing more frequently in their reading of erroneous sentences. Regressions in reading are seen as indicative of controlled processing, i.e. attempts to retrieve explicit knowledge. In order to capture regressions, the researchers use a so-called scan path analysis which tracks a participant's eye-movement patterns in time and space. The research questions ask whether timed vs. untimed GJT items and grammatical vs. ungrammatical GJT items elicit different scan paths in L1 and L2 speakers of English.

Accordingly, the study participants are L1 (N = 20) and L2 speakers (N = 40) of English, all of them university students in the U.S. The L2 speakers are from a range of mostly eastern Asian L1 backgrounds. All participants complete two identical GJTs in a written modality, the first one under time pressure, the second one without time pressure. Their eye-movements are tracked during test performance. Each GJT comprises 68 sentences focusing on 17 English structures that were adapted from R. Ellis (2005); half of the sentences are grammatical, half ungrammatical.

Scan paths are computed only for correctly answered items, which results in 32% of the data set being eliminated. Three scan path categories are identified, that is, single-pass reading without regression, which functioned as the baseline representing automatic processing, unfinished reading with regression, and finished reading with regression, both representing controlled processing. In the unfinished reading category, participants made a judgement without reading to the end of the sentence. In the finished reading category, they did read to the end before making a judgement. The independent variables in the analysis are L1/L2 status, time pressure, and grammaticality. A mixed-effects multinomial logistic regression analysis is performed on the data.

Godfroid et al. (2015) report that L1 speakers performed better in terms of accuracy than L2 speakers, as one might expect. L2 speakers' scores showed more variation, with accuracy ranging from 26% on timed ungrammatical items to 82% on untimed grammatical items. The most frequent reading pattern for all participants under all conditions was finished reading with regression. Again, L2 speakers showed increased variation in reading patterns, however, with much more regression in evidence in the untimed than in the timed condition. More finished reading with regression occurred in the untimed than in the timed condition, with a particularly strong increase for grammatical items. Overall, the L1 speakers' processing was essentially unaffected by the different conditions, whereas the L2 speakers showed drastic changes in processing in the timed condition. The untimed grammatical condition stood out as potentially showing the greatest task effects.

The tendency of L2 speakers to regress less under time pressure is interpreted as a qualitative change in processing which is indicative of implicit knowledge being accessed because the timed nature of the task prevents controlled processing and thus access to explicit knowledge. An effect of grammaticality was observed only in the untimed condition, where all participants demonstrated an increase in reading with regression. This response pattern is seen as an artefact of the task, which is to judge the acceptability of sentences; participants' behaviour is thus seen as a departure from natural reading. It is argued that as a consequence, untimed grammatical sentences may be least valid as measures of linguistic knowledge of any type, explicit or implicit. The researchers conclude that timed and untimed (particularly ungrammatical) GJTs measure different types of knowledge. Specifically, timed GJTs may measure implicit knowledge, whereas ungrammatical items on untimed GJTs may measure explicit knowledge (Godfroid et al., 2015).

In conclusion, it would seem that researchers who wish to measure explicit knowledge by means of tests may be better served by employing a metalinguistic knowledge test than a GJT, since it is less clear exactly what type(s) of knowledge GJTs might tap (see Vafaee, Suzuki, & Kachisnke, 2017, for another recent attempt at validation). While timed and untimed administration of a GJT may predispose a participant to use implicit and explicit knowledge, respectively, the interaction of timing with stimulus type must be taken into account as well. Untimed grammatical sentences appear to be particularly problematic (R. Ellis, 2005; Godfroid et al., 2015) and may have to be excluded from analysis altogether. When using a test of metalinguistic knowledge, researchers should bear in mind that metalinguistic labelling tasks and rule illustration tasks will draw on a participant's knowledge of metalanguage, over and above their analysed linguistic knowledge. In the case of a correction, description and explanation task, a participant's knowledge of metalanguage will be required in order to describe and explain error corrections. Error correction in itself can be performed on the basis of analysed linguistic knowledge. As verbalisation is not required, knowledge of metalanguage is not required. Put differently, when correcting an error, learners may draw on implicit knowledge, explicit knowledge, or both types of knowledge in succession or in combination.

Fortunately, tests are not the only tool available to researchers interested in measuring learners' explicit knowledge. Participant self-report in the form of verbal protocols, source attributions, and confidence or certainty ratings constitute supplementary instruments. As mentioned above, some researchers interested in the measurement of explicit and implicit knowledge have argued that greater variance in performance may be regarded as a hallmark of explicit knowledge in use (Gutiérrez, 2013) – a view that is complementary to the argument that systematicity and certainty should be associated with implicit knowledge in use (R. Ellis, 2004, 2005). Empirical research into this issue casts doubt on the accuracy of these specific hypotheses, however. In his validation study, Rod Ellis (2005) found that the designated tests of implicit knowledge did not lead to more certainty or more systematic responses than the designated tests of explicit knowledge. Moreover, in a qualitative investigation with L1 English university-level learners of L2 German, it was found that use of metalinguistic knowledge co-occurred more frequently with certainty and consistent performance than with uncertainty and inconsistent performance on items targeting adjectival agreement (Roehr, 2006). These findings were based on an analysis of stimulated recall protocols (Gass & Mackey, 2000).

The discrepancy between theoretical argumentation and empirical findings with regard to learner certainty/confidence and consistency/systematicity of learner performance suggests that verbal protocols (Jourdenais, 2001; Young, 2005) may be a useful supplementary tool in establishing whether explicit knowledge is being or has been utilised to complete a task. Studies concerned with the notion of noticing are a case in point for this line of research (Camps,

2003; Leow, 1997, 2000). Work by Camps (2003) is a rare example of a study that makes use of both concurrent and retrospective verbal reports, showing how the two types of protocol can usefully complement each other (see review in Chapter 5).

Leow (1997) investigated L1 English university-level learners' awareness of L2 Spanish preterit forms of regular and irregular verbs. Specifically, he was interested in how different levels of awareness would influence learners' recognition and accurate written production of the targeted structure. In the study in question, participants complete a pre-test before being presented with the regular verb forms during a classroom session. Then, think-aloud protocols are recorded while participants are working through a crossword puzzle based on the hitherto unknown irregular verb forms. This is followed by two immediate post-exposure tasks targeting irregular verbs, that is, a multiple-choice recognition task and a gap-fill production task. In order to participate in all phases of the study, learners were required to score zero on the pre-test and achieve 100% success on the crossword puzzle. The latter was interpreted as evidence of noticing of the target structure. The think-aloud protocols ($N = 28$) recorded during completion of the crossword puzzle are analysed in order to establish learners' awareness of the target structure.

Three levels of awareness are identified in the verbal report data: (1) + cognitive change, + meta-awareness, + morphological rule, (2) + cognitive change, + meta-awareness, − morphological rule, and (3) + cognitive change, − meta-awareness, − morphological rule. Cognitive change is defined as "a show of some behavioural or cognitive change due to the experience" of completing the crossword puzzle, meta-awareness is evidenced through "a report of being aware of the experience" and tends to co-occur with hypothesis testing and rule for-mation, and morphological rule denotes "some form of metalinguistic description of the underlying morphological rule" (Leow, 1997, p. 478), that is, evidence of explicit metalinguistic knowledge.

Based on the qualitative analysis, the participants are divided into two groups comprising (a) learners who displayed the higher levels of awareness (1) or (2), and (b) learners who displayed the lower level of awareness (3) without any evidence of meta-awareness or morphological rule knowledge. Quantitative analyses reveal that differences in levels of awareness had an effect on learners' performance on both post-exposure tasks, with higher levels of awareness contributing favourably to successful recognition and to a somewhat lesser extent also to successful written production of the targeted structure (Leow, 1997). In other words, higher levels of awareness as evidenced by hypothesis testing or explicit references to pedago-gical rules in the learners' think-aloud protocols are associated with better performance.

Subsequent research has resulted in a more refined conceptualisation and operationalisation of levels of awareness. Work within an information processing paradigm (Leow, Johnson, & Zárate-Sández, 2011) has emphasised the

124 Measuring Metalinguistic Awareness

importance of the stage at which awareness comes into play, i.e. either at the stage of online construction or intake stage, or at the stage of offline reconstruction or output stage. In addition, it must be borne in mind that the nature of the experimental task participants are asked to complete (e.g. GJT, gap-fill, etc.) as well as the instructions participants are given for their concurrent and/or retrospective verbal reports (e.g. 'Say out loud whatever you are thinking'; 'Did you notice anything while completing the task?'; 'Did you identify a pattern/rule while reading the sentences?', etc.) will impact on how awareness is articulated. With regard to levels of awareness, data-driven approaches to coding have led to a number of possible categorisations, including the identification of awareness at the levels of noticing and understanding (e.g. Rosa & O'Neill, 1999) or at the levels of noticing, reporting and understanding (e.g. Leow, 1997, summarised above). Furthermore, verbal report data may allow the researcher to specify the cognitive processes taking place within each level of awareness, such as reading, translating, pausing and repeating, for instance (Leow et al., 2011). Within the information processing paradigm put forward by Leow and colleagues, different levels of awareness are conceptualised in terms of depth of processing. Thus, what is processed at the intake stage may be reported by participants as awareness at the level of noticing and may be captured by means of recognition tests. However, it is an open question whether information that has reached the intake stage will be processed further with a view to being integrated into the learner's developing knowledge representations. Only information that is processed at this deeper level will be internalised and may be captured by means of production tests, with the learner's output considered a representative sample of their L2 knowledge. Such knowledge may be reported by participants in terms of hypotheses about the L2 or pedagogical grammar rules, for instance, and would thus be characterised as awareness at the level of understanding (Leow, 2015).

Whereas levels of awareness indicative of noticing, reporting and/or understanding are well suited to describe participants' explicit processing of system-based targets such as grammatical structures, a different approach is required to characterise the explicit processing of item-based targets such as vocabulary. Here differentiating between two types of explicit memory, semantic memory and episodic memory, has proved useful (Godfroid & Schmidtke, 2013). Retrospective verbal report data from participants who encountered pseudo-words in an L2 English reading text and were subsequently tested for incidental recognition of these words suggested a distinction between awareness at the level of noetic consciousness, which refers to knowing that something happened (semantic memory) and thus a feeling of knowing, and awareness at the level of autonoetic consciousness, which refers to the recollection of what happened where and when (episodic memory) and thus the ability to re-experience an event. Applied to the study at hand, a participant remembering that a pseudo-word was somewhere in the text s/he had read was coded as awareness at the level of noetic consciousness, while a participant remembering that s/he had read a pseudo-word in a particular sentence was coded as awareness at the level of autonoetic consciousness. The findings of the study show that the higher level of autonoetic awareness was associated with more successful pseudo-word recognition than noetic awareness (Godfroid & Schmidtke, 2013), thus mirroring the results from studies targeting grammatical structures.

Nearly a decade after R. Ellis' (2004) influential review of definitions and measures of explicit knowledge in L2 learning, an updated review concerned with the measurement of both explicit and implicit knowledge was published (Rebuschat, 2013), showcasing clearly the progress made in the field. The focus of the updated review neatly reflects the issues scrutinized up to now, i.e. the capacity of different types of tests (direct vs. indirect), verbal reports and so-called subjective measures (reported certainty judgements and source attributions) to distinguish between explicit and implicit knowledge in use. Test-based research typically compares performance on different types of test, with direct tests instructing participants to make use of all the knowledge they have and indirect tests having no such instructions. Indeed, participants would ideally not even know that they are being tested when completing an indirect test. In an experimental paradigm, the researcher can assume implicit knowledge if a participant shows evidence of learning on an indirect test but not on a direct one. Nonetheless, one cannot be entirely sure that direct tests measure only what they are meant to measure in that the influence of implicit knowledge in particular may be underestimated.

Retrospective verbal reports typically ask participants to verbalise any patterns or rules they have noticed in the input or during an experimental treatment. If participants show a training effect but are unable to describe their knowledge, it is considered to be implicit. Although retrospective verbal reports have been used in both cognitive psychology and L2 learning research, the method has certain limitations. The dissociation between acquired knowledge and the ability to articulate it may not be as clear-cut as anticipated, with failure to verbalise possibly just indicating that the participant finds it difficult to retrieve large amounts of low-confidence knowledge. In addition, retrospective reports in an experimental set-up typically seek to elicit awareness at the level of understanding, which may make it difficult to differentiate between levels of awareness. In this regard, then, retrospective verbal reports are not as sensitive as one might desire. A second and perhaps even more important caveat is that it is not clear whether the reported knowledge was actually used during task performance or is just a result of participants' attempts to provide a rationale for their performance after the event – not to deliberately mislead the researcher, but simply because it is quite natural to try and rationalise or justify one's actions when one is asked about them.

Rebuschat (2013) suggests that the boundary between conscious and unconscious knowledge may be defined subjectively rather than just objectively. The subjective threshold lies at the point where an individual lacks meta-knowledge in the sense that they do not know that they know something. The

126 Measuring Metalinguistic Awareness

objective threshold is the point at which a person does not know that a stimulus was presented. Anything below the subjective threshold would be considered unconscious. The difference between the two thresholds can be illustrated by means of an individual's performance on a GJT. Knowledge is below the objective threshold of consciousness if a participant performs at chance level, and it is below the subjective threshold of consciousness if a participant performs above chance, but believes to be guessing, i.e. if they lack meta-knowledge. Apart from the guessing criterion, a lack of meta-knowledge may be attributable to a dissociation between confidence and accuracy. Thus, asking participants for certainty or confidence ratings is a possible approach. A strong correlation between confidence and accuracy would suggest more explicit knowledge, while equal confidence in both correct and incorrect decisions would indicate more implicit knowledge (Rebuschat, 2013). It is worth noting here that this most recent interpretation of an association between confidence/certainty and improved performance as a hallmark of explicit knowledge is in line with empirical findings to date (R. Ellis, 2005; Roehr, 2006) and in direct contrast with earlier hypotheses reviewed above (R. Ellis, 2004, 2005; Gutiérrez, 2013).

Rebuschat (2013) considers the potential usefulness of source attributions to distinguish between explicit and implicit knowledge. Put differently, participants can be asked to indicate the basis of their responses as guessing, intuition, memory or rule. It could be argued that reported guessing would imply that a learner believes to have no knowledge, intuition would suggest that a learner has implicit knowledge but no explicit knowledge, memory would indicate reported knowledge of a specific instance, and reported rule use would suggest that the learner believes to have drawn on explicit knowledge. A limitation of such subjective measures is their potential unreliability, however. Participants may claim to be guessing even though they have a small degree of awareness, or participants may attribute their knowledge to rule use because this is seen as desirable and/or because this is what they believe to have happened, although they may in fact have retrieved the rule retrospectively after actually answering an item based on intuitive/implicit knowledge.

Using both confidence ratings and source attributions together in a triangulated approach may counterbalance these caveats somewhat. Moreover, a clear advantage lies in the fact that the use of subjective measures is quite straightforward in practical terms. Participants can be asked to report how confident they are in a decision or answer, and they can then be asked to name the basis of their answer. If a participant scores significantly above chance but has no confidence in his/her decision, this would be indicative of implicit knowledge. There would be no correlation between confidence and accuracy. In other words, the participant does not know that s/he has acquired knowledge, despite evidence to the contrary from his/her performance (Rebuschat, 2013).

To summarise, researchers can employ different kinds of tests as well as different types of self-report including verbal protocols, confidence ratings and source attributions to measure L2 learners' explicit knowledge. Recent developments in the application of physiological measures such as eye-tracking and the logging of brain-based event-related potentials (ERP) to the domain of L2 learning have prompted researchers to ask whether such methods can likewise provide insights into whether individuals use explicit or implicit knowledge during language processing. The current state of research suggests that eye-tracking may be an informative measure if it is used in conjunction with traditional test-based measurement (Godfroid et al., 2015; Godfroid & Winke, 2015), that is, if processing and product data are collected, analysed and interpreted in combination. By contrast, it would appear that ERP-based research has not yet reached a stage were the resulting measurements of voltage polarity, amplitude and latency can be interpreted with any certainty as to what knowledge type they might be associated with. As the method is becoming more widely used and empirical evidence is gradually being accumulated, the use of ERP as a (complementary) measure of explicit and/or implicit knowledge may be a viable avenue in the future (Morgan-Short, Faretta-Stutenberg, & Bartlett-Hsu, 2015; Tokowicz & MacWhinney, 2005).

At this point, a note on test-based measurement of explicit knowledge that links back to a previous chapter is in order. In Chapter 4, it was established that metalinguistic awareness and language learning aptitude can be considered as partially overlapping constructs. Accordingly, test-based measures of metalinguistic awareness and language learning aptitude may likewise be closely related or even overlapping in practice (R. Ellis, 2004). For instance, Ranta (2002, 2005) used an L1 metalinguistic task to assess her French-speaking participants' language-analytic ability, that is, a component of aptitude. The task required the school-age learners to detect and correct errors in written sentences. The researcher argued that correct French spelling requires grammatical analysis of sentences and the application of rules of agreement for number and gender, which reflects language-analytic ability and metalinguistic awareness in equal measure. Along similar lines, Roehr (2008b; see also Roehr & Gánem-Gutiérrez, 2009b) used a simplified L2 version of the words-in-sentences subtest of the MLAT as part of a test of metalinguistic knowledge for university-level learners. The common thread in these otherwise very different studies is the fact that despite the similarities in task type, measures of metalinguistic awareness are typically based on L2, while measures of language-analytic ability as a component of language learning aptitude are typically based on L1. Interestingly, this boundary is blurred somewhat in measures of metalinguistic awareness used with young children as well as with adults who have low levels of literacy and/or education, as we will see in the next section.

6.2 Metalinguistic Awareness in Children and Low-Educated Adults

Measures of metalinguistic awareness which are designed for use with young learners or learners with low levels of literacy and/or education tend to be

128 Measuring Metalinguistic Awareness

informed by Bialystok's framework of analysis and control according to which metalinguistic ability requires both highly analysed linguistic knowledge and high control of linguistic processing (see Chapter 2). Despite this commonality, it is possible to distinguish between measures informed by a cognitive-developmental perspective in the psycholinguistic sense and measures representing an educational perspective. The former type of measure normally relies on individual administration of highly controlled tests by a researcher, whereas the latter type may be group-administered and/or administered by a teacher who does not have specialist knowledge.

Taking a language-educational perspective, Tellier (2013) developed a test of metalinguistic awareness for English-speaking children aged 8 to 11. The test is suitable for group administration in mixed-ability classes and is based on the assumption that English-speaking children typically learn Indo-European L2s at school. The measure comprises eleven tasks that are graded in terms of cognitive complexity, with complexity defined as the number of mental manipulations needed to perform a task (Stankov, 2003). All the tasks require children to demonstrate high levels of analysis and control in order to complete them successfully. The tasks draw on domains relevant to both L1 and L2 learning, such as lexical semantics, morphosyntax, ambiguity and basic metalinguistic terminology, and they address cognates, similarities and differences between languages, and translation.

The test is divided into two sections, with tasks based on European languages presented in the first section (Tasks 1–5). Tasks 1–4 assess children's ability to make comparisons between different languages which may or (more likely) may not be known to them; Task 5 asks children to compare two sentences in L1 English. The tasks in the second section (Tasks 6–11) require the manipulation of a constructed language specifically developed for the purpose of the test; the lexicon of the constructed language is formed from anagrams of Esperanto lexemes. Task 6 investigates children's understanding of metalinguistic terminology – in this instance, labels for parts of speech. Task 8 looks at children's understanding of the relationship words in a sentence have to one another, and Task 9 requires children to spot the common morphological and graphological features in lists of words and create two more words which could belong to the same word class. Tasks 7, 10 and 11 examine a child's ability to handle metalinguistic concepts that are unfamiliar from L1 English but relevant for L2 learning of other European languages, that is, accusative case marking, subject-verb agreement in the plural, and grammatical gender, respectively. The test has been used in a number of studies and has shown very good reliability throughout (Tellier, 2015; Tellier & Roehr-Brackin, 2013a, 2013b, 2017). It can be downloaded from the IRIS digital repository of L2 research instruments.

A measure that can be seen as bridging the conceptual gap between Tellier's (2013) test, which is aimed at measuring metalinguistic awareness in school children who have experienced or are about to experience L2 instruction, and cognitive-developmental measures, which are primarily used in research with bilingual or multilingual children who have been exposed to more than one language in an immersion setting, is a metalinguistic awareness test battery for monolingual speakers developed by Pinto and colleagues (Pinto et al., 1999). The tests are labelled MAT-1, MAT-2 and MAT-3 and are aimed at learners aged 4 to 8, 9 to 13 and 14 years upwards, respectively, based on the argument that metalinguistic skills continue to develop into adulthood. At the onset of adulthood, defined here as roughly coinciding with the end of secondary education, meta-linguistic development is believed to be reflected in an increase of encyclopaedic knowledge, the acquisition of metalanguage for formal linguistic categories, improved comprehension and production of figurative language, the development of metacognition in terms of Piaget's concept of formal-operational thought, that is, a logical approach to problem-solving, and an improved ability to reconstruct speakers' or writers' communicative intentions.

MAT-1 focuses on the child's ability to separate language form and function. Most of the seven sub-tests can be administered orally. The authors point out that MAT-1 is not intended to be predictive of early literacy success. It should however be "predictive of future development in the same area" (Pinto et al., 1999, p. 40), e.g. as measured by MAT-2. The MAT-1 sub-tests assess word order correction, evaluation of word length, lexical segmentation, rhyme, symbol substitution, printed word, letter and number identification, and the morphology and function of written signs.

MAT-2 draws on the measures used in Hakes (1980) (see Chapter 2), which have been adapted by adding requests for explanations of answers to every item. This makes the test unsuitable for very young children, so it has been moved to a higher age range compared with the source study. Explanatory answers are evaluated qualitatively for levels of elaboration and sophistication. Explicit and analytically-based rule knowledge is required. The test has six sub-tests measuring compre-hension, synonymy, acceptability, ambiguity, grammatical function and phonemic segmentation. MAT-3 aims to assess metalinguistic abilities in adolescents and adults. It has an interest in the educational and social relevance of metalinguistic abilities. Part 1 of the test focuses on comprehension and acceptability, while Part 2 assesses figurative language comprehension.

The MAT test battery is not widely used in L2 learning research, possibly because the English-language version summarised here appears to be a direct translation of the Italian original and does not always provide fully idiomatic formulations. What is more, the chosen approach to measurement does not sit easily with either of the main theoretical paradigms informing SLA research, that is, a cognitive-developmental perspective of metalinguistic ability, whether edu-cational or psycholinguistic in nature, or an applied linguistics perspective relying on the distinction between explicit and implicit knowledge.

Researchers taking a cognitive-developmental perspective as defined in this volume tend to rely on a range of tasks which satisfy the criteria of a high level of

130 Measuring Metalinguistic Awareness

analysis of linguistic knowledge, a high level of control of linguistic processing, or both. Unlike measures representing a language-educational perspective where tasks are typically integrated in terms of analysis and control, a psycholinguistic approach is often – though certainly not always – characterised by the use of separate tasks capturing analysis of knowledge and control of processing. Specifically, tasks that require the detection, extraction or articulation of linguistic properties or structures are thought to draw primarily on analysis of linguistic knowledge. Thus, tasks drawing on an awareness of syntax, an awareness of the concept of word, error correction, the provision of definitions as well as tasks requiring participants to paraphrase or make judgements of ambiguity would appear to tap analysed knowledge. Conversely, tasks involving misleading cues and requiring a focus away from meaning are thought to draw primarily on control, i.e. their solution depends on the appropriate selection, inhibition and integration of information. Tasks included in this category are sentence segmentation tasks, symbol substitution tasks, tasks requiring the repetition of deviant sentences, and Piaget's (1929) sun/moon problem (Bialystok, 1988).

The sun/moon problem requires a child to recognise the essential arbitrariness of linguistic form-meaning mappings. The child is asked: "Suppose you were making up names for things, could you call the sun 'the moon' and the moon 'the sun'?" If the child responds in the negative, the researcher persuades the child that this is possible. The child is then asked: "Suppose everybody decided to call the sun 'the moon' and the moon 'the sun'. What would you call the thing in the sky when you go to bed at night? What would the sky look like when you're going to bed?" The correct answers to these questions would be (a) the sun and (b) dark. Variations of this task are possible, e.g. the target words might be 'cat' and 'dog', together with pictures of a cat and a dog (Bialystok, 1988). The principle that is being tested remains the same, of course.

A more integrated measure that has been used to assess metalinguistic awareness in children is a verbal fluency task (Bialystok et al., 2014). In this test, participants are given one minute to generate as many words as possible in accordance with a given criterion, that is, a semantic category such as items of clothing, animals, etc., or an initial letter, such as f, a, s, etc. The category fluency condition assesses the richness of lexical representations and rapid access to lexical items, so it can function as a measure of linguistic ability as well. Unlike the category fluency task, the letter fluency task does not conform to the structure of human memory representations; members of a particular category are associated with each other, but words beginning with a particular letter are not. Moreover, the letter fluency task typically includes restrictions in the sense that morphological variants of the same word, proper names, etc. are excluded. The letter fluency condition thus assesses monitoring, attention and selection (control of processing); it also requires a certain level of analysis. It is thus considered a metalinguistic task.

Children's metalinguistic awareness can also be assessed by means of GJTs, although the conditions that are being contrasted are different from the timed/untimed and grammatical/ungrammatical conditions typically used in measures of explicit knowledge administered to adults. Work by Bialystok and colleagues (Bialystok, 1988; Bialystok & Craik, 2010; Bialystok & Martin, 2004; Bialystok et al., 2014) has made use of sentences in four conditions, that is, (1) grammatically and semantically correct (e.g. *Why is the dog barking so loudly? Apples grow on trees.*), (2) grammatically incorrect and semantically correct (e.g. *Why the dog is barking so loudly? Apples on trees grow.*), (3) grammatically correct but semantically anomalous (e.g. *Why is the cat barking so loudly? Apples grow on noses.*), and (4) grammatically and semantically incorrect (e.g. *Why the cat is barking so loudly? Apples on noses grow.*). The critical conditions requiring high levels of analysis of knowledge and control of processing are (2) and (3), respectively. Correctly judging (2) as ungrammatical is challenging because it requires the child to focus on form and spot the grammatical error. Correctly judging (3) as grammatical is likewise challenging because it requires the child not to be distracted by the semantic anomaly. Like the letter condition in a verbal fluency task, these GJT conditions draw on analysis and control in conjunction.

Research with low-educated adult learners is still in very short supply. If researchers wish to assess the metalinguistic awareness of illiterate adults or adults with low levels of literacy, they clearly cannot rely on the kind of written instruments that would be used with educated and fully literate learners. Indeed, in terms of literacy level, low-educated adults may be comparable to pre-school-age children or children in the early years of schooling who are beginning to learn how to read and write. Accordingly, Kurvers et al. (2006) employed a battery of tests which comprises some of the measures already referred to. Their metalinguistic awareness test battery for adults with very low levels of literacy and education comprised three measures of phonological awareness (rhyme production, rhyme judgement, word segmentation), four measures of lexical/semantic awareness (sentence segmentation, word-referent differentiation, word length judgement, word judgement), and a measure of textual/discourse awareness (syllogisms) (see Chapter 2; repeated here for convenience).

Specifically, rhyme production required participants to respond to a given word with a rhyming word. Rhyme judgement asked them to decide whether two words that were presented to them rhymed or not. A progressive segmentation task asked participants to break sentences and then phrases down into pieces (sentence segmentation), and then to further break down multisyllabic and monosyllabic words into even smaller pieces, i.e. phonemes (word segmentation). The word-referent differentiation task was a take on Piaget's sun/moon problem in that it involved swapping the names of 'cat' and 'dog' for associated pictures and requiring the participants to answer questions about the animals under their new names, e.g. "What noise does the animal make that is called 'dog' now?".

The word length judgement task (see also Yelland et al., 1993) required participants to choose the longer word from a pair of words. The task included congruent, incongruent and neutral pairs. In the case of congruent pairs, word length and real-world size of the referent were matched (e.g. *goat – elephant*), whereas in the case of incongruent pairs, they were mismatched, with small referents having long names and large referents short names. Neutral items were based on words and referents of roughly equal size. The word judgement task required participants to judge whether a given utterance was a word or not. Stimuli included content words, function words, groups of words, and sentences. Finally, syllogisms required participants to solve simple syllogisms and explain their answers, e.g. "All stones on the moon are blue. A man goes to the moon and takes a stone. What colour is that stone?" (Kurvers et al., 2006, p. 76).

6.3 Measures of Executive Function

Executive function is the fundamental general cognitive capacity underlying an individual's control of linguistic processing (see Chapter 2). Unlike measures aimed at assessing analysis of linguistic knowledge and control of linguistic processing, measures of pure executive function are non-linguistic in nature, relying on visual or general conceptual stimuli instead. Executive function tasks are thus designed to tap an individual's ability to select task-relevant information and responses, to inhibit irrelevant information and responses, to resolve conflict, and to manage switching of attention, as required. Executive function measures can be used with both children and adults, although the approach to data analysis which is taken may differ in accordance with the age and cognitive capacities of the learner sample that is being tested. Studies with prime-of-life adults would typically analyse response times, since performance may well be at ceiling in terms of accuracy. Studies with children would analyse either response time data or accuracy data or both; accuracy data would be used in cases of tasks that are easy for cognitively mature individuals, but challenging for young participants.

Widely-used measures of executive function in studies with L2 learners, bilinguals and multilinguals include the Simon task and the Flanker task, and perhaps to a somewhat lesser extent the more complex Attentional Network task and the Dimensional Change Card Sort (DCCS) task (Bialystok & Craik, 2010; Bialystok et al., 2012; Bialystok & Martin, 2004; Poarch & van Hell, 2012) (see Chapter 2). A description of the Simon task will serve to illustrate the key characteristics of a typical executive function measure.

The Simon task is a computer-administered measure in which a series of coloured squares is presented on the screen one at a time. The squares vary in colour, e.g. red and green, and in their location on the screen, i.e. left of a central fixation point, right of fixation, or at fixation. Participants are told to press a left button coloured red with their left index finger or a right button coloured green with their right index finger in accordance with the colour of the square on screen, irrespective of the location of the square. In a congruent trial, the square appears on the same side as the correct response button, e.g. a red square appears on the left. In other words, stimulus and response locations are matched. In an

Measuring Metalinguistic Awareness **133**

incongruent trial, the square appears on the opposite side of the correct response button, e.g. a green square appears on the left. In other words, there is a mismatch between stimulus and response locations. In control trials, the square appears at the central fixation point. The fact that response times are longer on incongruent than on congruent trials is referred to as the so-called Simon effect. The magnitude of this effect is thought to reflect an individual's ability to inhibit the pre-potent response triggered by the location of the stimulus and thus provides a measure of executive function.

As illustrated, executive function tasks typically comprise stimuli representing at least two conditions, that is, a condition in which all cues point in the same direction and thus allow for a fast and accurate response, and a condition in which two or more cues are in conflict and thus require the participant to resolve this conflict by inhibiting an initial pre-potent response, re-focusing their attention and making an appropriate selection. Responses to conflicting stimuli will be slower and may be more error-prone, depending on the exact task demands. There may be more than one conflict condition, there may be a neutral control condition to establish a baseline, and the researcher may wish to measure not only the cost of processing incongruent as opposed to congruent or neutral stimuli, but also the cost of switching between different conditions. A considerable number of analyses is possible, but it is worth bearing in mind that children, low-educated learners and perhaps also elderly individuals may exhibit relatively slow response times that do not lend themselves to meaningful analysis in terms of processing costs, resulting in accuracy data being analysed. Data from prime-of-life adults, however, will typically be analysed in terms of response times, as already indicated, because accuracy data will most likely show a ceiling effect.

7

CONCLUDING REMARKS

7.1 Two Theoretical Perspectives

In the chapters of this volume, the construct of metalinguistic awareness in SLA has been discussed from two theoretical perspectives. The first perspective was labelled the cognitive-developmental approach as applied in psycholinguistic and/ or cognitive-psychological research with bilinguals and multilinguals as well as in language-educational research with child L2 learners in the classroom and low-educated adults. The second perspective distinguishes categorically between explicit and implicit knowledge, memory, learning and teaching and is the pre-dominant paradigm informing applied linguistics research with literate and educated adult learners who typically receive L2 instruction. The two perspectives differ in a number of ways. Specifically, the cognitive-developmental approach conceptualises analysis of knowledge and control of processing as being situated on a continuum, with knowledge gradually becoming more analysed and thus more explicit as the individual matures, acquires and develops literacy skills. By contrast, the explicit/ implicit perspective posits a dichotomy between non-conscious, implicit knowledge and processes on the one hand and conscious, explicit knowledge and processes on the other hand. There is a clear threshold between the two types of knowl-edge and processes, which are either conscious or not. The subjective experience of conscious awareness is conceptualised as the interface between the two types of knowledge and processes.

The theoretical differences sit well with the focus points of the empirical research that is informed by each of the two approaches, of course. In the cognitive-developmental approach, bi- or multilingualism is seen as a predictor, i.e. having more than one language is expected to potentially influence general cognition in a mostly positive manner, bringing about improved metalinguistic awareness and improved executive function, for instance. Conversely, in the explicit/implicit perspective, cognitive abilities such as working memory, language learning aptitude and metalinguistic awareness are regarded as predictors whose potentially facilitative effects on L2 learning are then examined. This contrast neatly reflects the research settings predominantly associated with each approach, that is, immersion or naturalistic learning by young children (cognitive-developmental approach) vs. instructed learning by cognitively mature adults (explicit/implicit approach). Accordingly, the two perspectives also have differing interests with regard to the direction of influence of explicit vs. implicit knowledge and processes, as one might expect. Whereas the cognitive-developmental approach essentially focuses on how and why implicit (or less analysed) knowledge and learning may become more explicit (or more analysed), the applied linguistics approach essentially focuses on whether and how explicit knowledge and learning may facilitate implicit knowledge and learning.

Despite the clear differences between the two theoretical perspectives as outlined in the previous paragraphs, it would appear that they are not incompatible. Indeed, applied linguistics researchers such as Rod Ellis and Xavier Gutiérrez make reference to notions associated with the cognitive-developmental approach in their work with adult L2 learners, for instance, and Robert DeKeyser and colleagues have begun to investigate the difference between implicit knowledge and automatized explicit knowledge – constructs which are indistinguishable in practice because both are characterised by automatic processing, but whose distinctness, if shown to be measurable, would have important theoretical implications by offering a combination of cognitive-developmental and explicit/implicit constructs in a single theoretical framework.

However, even at the level of two distinct theoretical perspectives, it would seem that either approach could gain in sophistication and scope by looking towards the other. The explicit/implicit approach might benefit from drawing on the cognitive-developmental approach because the latter can offer a window on how implicit knowledge and learning may influence explicit knowledge and learning – an issue that is relatively neglected in applied linguistics research, given its emphasis on instructed adult L2 learning. It is accepted that adults do not learn exclusively in an explicit manner, however, so a better understanding of how implicit learning proceeds and potentially interacts with explicit processes is clearly relevant. Along similar lines, even young children aged around 6 or 7 can begin to learn explicitly, so if researchers are interested in instructed child L2 learning, they may wish to go beyond the cognitive-developmental perspective and consider how explicit knowledge and learning might impact on implicit knowledge and learning in young learners. Clearly, the explicit/implicit approach has a theoretical apparatus that is likely to prove useful in this regard.

7.2 Directions for Future Research

Apart from heeding alternative theoretical perspectives, future research will likely seek to address the current gaps in our understanding of metalinguistic awareness in SLA. At this stage, we have robust cumulative findings on fundamental issues such as the potential benefits of bi- or multilingualism in children as well as the overall facilitative effects of explicit teaching and learning in instructed adult SLA. However, the vast majority of research to date has worked with certain learner populations while all but ignoring others. Thus, in the cognitive-developmental perspective, there is ample research with bilingual children, but much less research with multilingual children or instructed child L2 learners. How do language learning experience and individual difference variables interact with metalinguistic awareness in these latter types of learners? In the applied linguistics approach, there is ample research with young adults, typically university students, but much less research with low-educated adults or older adults. How does metalinguistic awareness play out in the L2 learning of older learners who can be expected to have well-honed crystallised abilities, life experience, knowledge of the world and strategic knowledge, but whose fluid abilities may be in gradual decline as a natural consequence of maturation?

Throughout this volume, whenever a broader theoretical framework was required, I have drawn on the usage-based approach to language and language learning. The reason for this is rather straightforward: The usage-based approach has a place for metalinguistic awareness as a part of the theoretical framework itself, unlike a number of other SLA theories where notions such as metalinguistic awareness are acknowledged, but ultimately treated as peripheral and certainly as external to the theory per se. Equally importantly, the usage-based approach both acknowledges and tries to account for the dynamic interplay of a multitude of variables in SLA, that is, characteristics of the language input such as frequency or salience of constructions or learning difficulty, characteristics of the learning setting, such as naturalistic vs. instructed, and characteristics of the learner such as cognitive and affective individual differences. It would appear that the role of these moderating variables would benefit from further empirical investigation. What exactly is the relationship between language learning aptitude and metalinguistic awareness, in terms of both theoretical conceptualisation and empirical operationalisation? How do cognitive/learning style and affective variables interact with metalinguistic awareness in L2 learning? We have as yet relatively little understanding of these issues, both in child and adult SLA. Overall, then, there are still a number of avenues waiting to be explored in future research on metalinguistic awareness and second language acquisition.

REFERENCES

Abrahamsson, N., & Hyltenstam, K. (2008). The robustness of aptitude effects in near-native second language acquisition. *Studies in Second Language Acquisition*, 30, 481–509.

Absi, Z. (2014). *Metalinguistic Knowledge and Speaking Proficiency in Syrian University-Level Learners of English.* Unpublished PhD thesis, University of Essex.

Akakura, M. (2012). Evaluating the effectiveness of explicit instruction on implicit and explicit L2 knowledge. *Language Teaching Research*, 16(1), 9–37.

Alderson, J. C., Clapham, C., & Steel, D. (1997). Metalinguistic knowledge, language aptitude and language proficiency. *Language Teaching Research*, 1, 93–121.

Ammar, A., Lightbown, P. M., & Spada, N. (2010). Awareness of L1/L2 differences: Does it matter? *Language Awareness*, 19(2), 129–146.

Anderson, J. R. (1993). *Rules of the Mind.* Hillsdale, NJ: Erlbaum.

Anderson, J. R. (1995). *Learning and Memory: An Integrated Approach.* New York, NY: John Wiley & Sons.

Anderson, J. R. (1996). *The Architecture of Cognition.* Mahwah, NJ: Erlbaum.

Anderson, J. R. (2000). *Cognitive Psychology and Its Implications* (5th). New York, NY: Worth Publishers.

Anderson, N. J. (2008). Metacognition and good language learners. In C. Griffiths (Ed.), *Lessons from good language learners* (pp. 99–109). Cambridge: Cambridge University Press.

Baddeley, A. D. (1997). *Human Memory: Theory and Practice.* Hove: Psychology Press.

Baker, C. (1993). *Foundations of Bilingual Education and Bilingualism.* Clevedon: Multilingual Matters.

Barton, A., Bragg, J., & Serratrice, L. (2009). 'Discovering Language' in primary school: An evaluation of a language awareness programme. *Language Learning Journal*, 37(2), 145–164.

Baum, S., & Titone, D. (2014). Moving toward a neuroplasticity view of bilingualism, executive control, and aging. *Applied Psycholinguistics*, 35(5), 857–894.

Bayne, T., & Chalmers, D. J. (2003). What is the unity of consciousness? In A. Cleeremans (Ed.), *The unity of consciousness: Binding, integration, and dissociation* (pp. 23–58). Oxford: Oxford University Press.

Berko, J. (1958). The child's learning of English morphology. *Word*, 14, 150–177.

Bialystok, E. (1979). Explicit and implicit judgements of L2 grammaticality. *Language Learning*, 29(1), 81–103.

Bialystok, E. (1988). Levels of bilingualism and levels of linguistic awareness. *Developmental Psychology*, 24(4), 560–567.

Bialystok, E. (1994a). Analysis and control in the development of second language proficiency. *Studies in Second Language Acquisition*, 16, 157–168.

Bialystok, E. (1994b). Representation and ways of knowing: Three issues in second language acquisition. In N. C. Ellis (Ed.), *Implicit and explicit learning of languages* (pp. 549–570). London: Academic Press.

Bialystok, E. (2001). *Bilingualism in Development: Language, Literacy, and Cognition*. Cambridge: Cambridge University Press.

Bialystok, E., & Craik, F. I. M. (2010). Cognitive and linguistic processing in the bilingual mind. *Current Directions in Psychological Science*, 19(1), 19–23.

Bialystok, E., & Martin, M. M. (2004). Attention and inhibition in bilingual children: Evidence from the dimensional change card sort task. *Developmental Science*, 7(3), 325–339.

Bialystok, E., Craik, F. I. M., & Luk, G. (2012). Bilingualism: Consequences for mind and brain. *Trends in Cognitive Sciences*, 16(4), 240–250.

Bialystok, E., & Ryan, E. B. (1985). Toward a definition of metalinguistic skill. *Merrill-Palmer Quarterly*, 31(3), 229–251.

Bialystok, E., Peets, K. F., & Moreno, S. (2014). Producing bilinguals through immersion education: Development of metalinguistic awareness. *Applied Psycholinguistics*, 35, 177–191.

Birdsong, D. (1989). *Metalinguistic Performance and Interlinguistic Competence*. Berlin: Springer.

Birdsong, D. (2006). Age and second language acquisition and processing: A selective overview. *Language Learning*, 56(s1), 9–49.

Block, N. (2005). Two neural correlates of consciousness. *Trends in Cognitive Sciences*, 9(2), 46–52.

Bouffard, L. A., & Sarkar, M. (2008). Training 8-year-old immersion students in metalinguistic analysis: An innovation in form-focused pedagogy . *Language Awareness*, 17(1), 3–24.

Bowles, M. (2011). Measuring implicit and explicit linguistic knowledge: What can heritage language learners contribute? *Studies in Second Language Acquisition*, 33, 247–271.

Brooks, P. J., & Kempe, V. (2013). Individual differences in adult foreign language learning: The mediating effect of metalinguistic awareness. *Memory & Cognition*, 41, 281–296.

Bulté, B., & Housen, A. (2012). Defining and operationalising L2 complexity. In A. Housen, F. Kuiken, & I. Vedder (Eds.), *Dimensions of L2 performance and proficiency: Complexity, accuracy and fluency in SLA* (pp. 21–46). Amsterdam: John Benjamins.

Butler, Y. G. (2002). Second language learners' theories on the use of English articles: An analysis of the metalinguistic knowledge used by Japanese students in acquiring the English article system. *Studies in Second Language Acquisition*, 24(3), 451–480.

Cadierno, T., & Eskildsen, S. W. (Eds.). (2015). *Usage-Based Perspectives on Second Language Learning*. Berlin: de Gruyter.

Camps, J. (2003). Concurrent and retrospective verbal reports as tools to better understand the role of attention in second language tasks. *International Journal of Applied Linguistics*, 13(2), 201–221.

Candelier, M. (Ed.) (2004). *Janua Linguarum: The Gateway to Languages*. Strasbourg: Council of Europe Publishing.

References **139**

Carr, T. H., & Curran, T. (1994). Cognitive factors in learning about structured sequences: Applications to syntax. *Studies in Second Language Acquisition*, 16, 205–230.

Carroll, J. B. (1962). The prediction of success in intensive foreign language training. In R. Glaser (Ed.), *Training research and education* (pp. 87–136). New York: John Wiley & Sons.

Carroll, J. B. (1981). Twenty-five years of research on foreign language aptitude. In K. C. Diller (Ed.), *Individual differences and universals in language learning aptitude* (pp. 83–118). Rowley, MA: Newbury House.

Carroll, J. B. (1990). Cognitive abilities in foreign language aptitude: Then and now. In T. S. Parry & C. W. Stansfield (Eds.), *Language Aptitude Reconsidered* (pp. 11–29). Englewood Cliffs, NJ: Prentice Hall.

Carroll, J. B., & Sapon, S. M. (2002). *Modern Language Aptitude Test: MLAT*. N. Bethesda, MD: Second Language Testing Inc.

Cattell, R. (2006). *An Introduction to Mind, Consciousness and Language*. London: Continuum.

Cenoz, J. (2003). The influence of age on the acquisition of English: General proficiency, attitudes and code-mixing. In M. d. P. Garcia Mayo & M. L. Garcia Lecumberri (Eds.), *Age and the acquisition of English as a foreign language* (pp. 77–93). Clevedon: Multilingual Matters.

Cenoz, J., & Jessner, U. (2009). The study of multilingualism in educational contexts. In L. Aronin & B. Hufeisen (Eds.), *The exploration of multilingualism* (pp. 121–138). Amsterdam: John Benjamins.

Chalker, S. (1994). Pedagogical grammar: Principles and problems. In M. Bygate, A. Tonkyn, & E. Williams (Eds.), *Grammar and the language teacher* (pp. 31–44). New York, NY: Prentice Hall.

Clapham, C. (2001). The assessment of metalinguistic knowledge. In C. Elder, A. Brown, E. Grove, K. Hill, N. Iwashita, T. Lumley, T. Macnamara, & K. O'Loughlin (Eds.), *Experimenting with uncertainty: Essays in honour of Alan Davies* (pp. 31–41). Cambridge: Cambridge University Press.

Collentine, J. (2000). Insights into the construction of grammatical knowledge provided by user-behavior tracking technologies. *Language Learning and Technology*, 3(2), 44–57.

Collins, L., Trofimovich, P., White, J., Cardoso, W., & Horst, M. (2009). Some input on the easy/difficult grammar question: An empirical study. *Modern Language Journal*, 93(3), 336–353.

Cummins, J. (1979). Linguistic interdependence and the educational development of bilingual children. *Review of Educational Research*, 49(2), 222–251.

Cummins, J. (1987). Bilingualism, language proficiency, and metalinguistic development. In P. Homel, M. Palij, & D. Aaronson (Eds.), *Childhood bilingualism: Aspects of linguistic, cognitive, and social development* (pp. 57–73). Hillsdale, NJ: Erlbaum.

Dabrowska, E. (2004). *Language, Mind and Brain: Some Psychological and Neurological Constraints on Theories of Grammar*. Edinburgh: Edinburgh University Press.

de Bot, K., & Larsen-Freeman, D. (2011). Researching second language development from a dynamic systems theory perspective. In M. H. Verspoor, K. de Bot, & W. Lowie (Eds.), *A dynamic approach to second language development: Methods and techniques* (pp. 5–23). Amsterdam: John Benjamins.

de Bot, K., Lowie, W., & Verspoor, M. (2007). A dynamic systems theory approach to second language acquisition. *Bilingualism: Language and Cognition*, 10(1), 7–21.

DeKeyser, R. M. (1994). How implicit can adult second language learning be? *AILA Review*, 11, 83–96.

140 References

DeKeyser, R. M. (2000). The robustness of critical period effects in second language acquisition. *Studies in Second Language Acquisition*, 22, 499–533.

DeKeyser, R. M. (2003). Implicit and explicit learning. In C. J. Doughty & M. H. Long (Eds.), *The handbook of second language acquisition* (pp. 313–348). Malden, MA: Blackwell.

DeKeyser, R. M. (2005). What makes learning second-language grammar difficult? A review of issues. *Language Learning*, 55(s1), 1–25.

DeKeyser, R. M. (2012). Age effects in second language learning. In S. M. Gass & A. Mackey (Eds.), *The Routledge handbook of second language acquisition* (pp. 442–460). London: Routledge.

DeKeyser, R. M. (2016). Of moving targets and chameleons: Why the concept of difficulty is so hard to pin down. *Studies in Second Language Acquisition*, 38(2), 353–363.

DeKeyser, R. M. (Ed.) (2007). *Practice in a Second Language: Perspectives from Applied Linguistics and Cognitive Psychology*. Cambridge: Cambridge University Press.

Dienes, Z., & Perner, J. (2003). Unifying consciousness with explicit knowledge. In A. Cleeremans (Ed.), *The unity of consciousness: Binding, integration, and dissociation* (pp. 214–232). Oxford: Oxford University Press.

Dietz, G. (2002). On rule complexity: A structural approach. *EuroSLA Yearbook*, 2, 263–286.

Doughty, C. J. (2003). Instructed SLA: Constraints, compensation, and enhancement. In C. J. Doughty & M. H. Long (Eds.), *The handbook of second language acquisition* (pp. 256–310). Malden, MA: Blackwell.

Doughty, C. J., & Long, M. H. (Eds.). (2003). *The Handbook of Second Language Acquisition*. Malden, MA: Blackwell.

Dunlosky, J. (1998). Epilogue: Linking metacognitive theory to education. In D. J. Hacker, J. Dunlosky, & A. C. Graesser (Eds.), *Metacognition in educational theory and practice* (pp. 367–381). Mahwah, NJ: Erlbaum.

Dörnyei, Z. (2005). *The Psychology of the Language Learner: Individual Differences in Second Language Acquisition*. Mahwah, NJ: Erlbaum.

Dörnyei, Z. (2009). *The Psychology of Second Language Acquisition*. Oxford: Oxford University Press.

Dörnyei, Z., & Skehan, P. (2003). Individual differences in second language learning. In C. J. Doughty & M. H. Long (Eds.), *The handbook of second language acquisition* (pp. 589–630). Malden, MA: Blackwell.

Elder, C., & Manwaring, D. (2004). The relationship between metalinguistic knowledge and learning outcomes among undergraduate students of Chinese. *Language Awareness*, 13(3), 145–162.

Elder, C., Warren, J., Hajek, J., Manwaring, D., & Davies, A. (1999). Metalinguistic knowledge: How important is it in studying a language at university? *Australian Review of Applied Linguistics*, 22(1), 81–95.

Ellis, N. C. (1994). Consciousness in second language learning: Psychological perspectives on the role of conscious processes in vocabulary acquisition. *AILA Review*, 11, 37–56.

Ellis, N. C. (2001). Memory for language. In P. Robinson (Ed.), *Cognition and second language instruction* (pp. 33–68). Cambridge: Cambridge University Press.

Ellis, N. C. (2002). Reflections on frequency effects in language processing. *Studies in Second Language Acquisition*, 24(2), 297–340.

Ellis, N. C. (2003). Constructions, chunking, and connectionism: The emergence of second language structure. In C. J. Doughty & M. H. Long (Eds.), *The handbook of second language acquisition* (pp. 63–103). Malden, MA: Blackwell.

Ellis, N. C. (2005). At the interface: Dynamic interactions of explicit and implicit language knowledge. *Studies in Second Language Acquisition*, 27(2), 305–352.

Ellis, N. C. (2007). The associative-cognitive CREED. In B. VanPatten & J. Williams (Eds.), *Theories in second language acquisition: An introduction* (pp. 77–95). Mahwah, NJ: Erlbaum.

Ellis, N. C. (2011). Implicit and explicit SLA and their interface. In C. Sanz & R. P. Leow (Eds.), *Implicit and explicit language learning: Conditions, processes, and knowledge in SLA and bilingualism* (pp. 35–47). Washington, DC: Georgetown University Press.

Ellis, N. C. (2015). Implicit AND explicit language learning: Their dynamic interface and complexity. In P. Rebuschat (Ed.), *Implicit and explicit learning of languages* (pp. 3–23). Amsterdam: John Benjamins.

Ellis, N. C. (2016). Salience, cognition, language complexity, and complex adaptive systems. *Studies in Second Language Acquisition*, 38(2), 341–351.

Ellis, N. C., & Larsen-Freeman, D. (2006). Language emergence: Implications for applied linguistics. *Applied Linguistics*, 27(4), 558–589.

Ellis, R. (1997). *SLA Research and Language Teaching*. Oxford: Oxford University Press.

Ellis, R. (2001). Introduction: Investigating form-focused instruction. *Language Learning*, 51(1), 1–46.

Ellis, R. (2004). The definition and measurement of L2 explicit knowledge. *Language Learning*, 54(2), 227–275.

Ellis, R. (2005). Measuring implicit and explicit knowledge of a second language: A psychometric study. *Studies in Second Language Acquisition*, 27(2), 141–172.

Ellis, R. (2006a). Current issues in the teaching of grammar: An SLA perspective. *TESOL Quarterly*, 40(1), 83–107.

Ellis, R. (2006b). Modelling learning difficulty and second language proficiency: The differential contributions of implicit and explicit knowledge. *Applied Linguistics*, 27(3), 431–463.

Ellis, R., Loewen, S., Elder, C., Erlam, R., Philp, J., & Reinders, H. (2009). *Implicit and Explicit Knowledge in Second Language Learning, Testing and Teaching*. Bristol: Multilingual Matters.

Ellis, R., & Shintani, N. (2014). *Exploring Language Pedagogy Through Second Language Acquisition Research*. London: Routledge.

Engel, A. K. (2003). Temporal binding and the neural correlates of consciousness. In A. Cleeremans (Ed.), *The unity of consciousness: Binding, integration, and dissociation* (pp. 132–152). Oxford: Oxford University Press.

Erlam, R. (2006). Elicited imitation as a measure of L2 implicit knowledge: An empirical validation study. *Applied Linguistics*, 27(3), 464–491.

Erlam, R. (2013). Effects of instruction on learners' acquisition of metalinguistic knowledge. In K. Roehr & G. A. Gánem-Gutiérrez (Eds.), *The metalinguistic dimension in instructed second language learning* (pp. 71–94). London: Bloomsbury.

Fettes, M. (1997). Esperanto and language awareness. In L. Van Lier & D. Corson (Eds.), *Encyclopedia of language and education, Vol. 6: Knowledge about language* (pp. 151–159). Dordrecht: Kluwer.

Flavell, J. H. (1979). Metacognition and cognitive monitoring: A new area of cognitive-developmental inquiry. *American Psychologist*, 34, 906–911.

Gánem-Gutiérrez, G. A., & Nogués Meléndez, C. (2013). Mediating the development of L2 oral performance through dynamic assessment: Focusing on the metalinguistic dimension. In K. Roehr & G. A. Gánem-Gutiérrez (Eds.), *The metalinguistic dimension in instructed second language learning* (pp. 195–219). London: Bloomsbury.

142 References

Gánem-Gutiérrez, G. A., & Roehr, K. (2011). Use of L1, metalanguage, and discourse markers: L2 learners' regulation during individual task performance. *International Journal of Applied Linguistics*, 21(3), 297–318.

García Mayo, M. d. P. (2003). Age, length of exposure and grammaticality judgements in the acquisition of English as a foreign language. In M. d. P. García Mayo & M. L. García Lecumberri (Eds.), *Age and the acquisition of English as a foreign language* (pp. 94–114). Clevedon: Multilingual Matters.

Gass, S. M., & Mackey, A. (2000). *Stimulated Recall Methodology in Second Language Research*. Mahwah, NJ: Erlbaum.

Geudens, A. (2006). Phonological awareness and learning to read a first language: Controversies and new perspectives. In I. van de Craats, J. Kurvers, & M. Young-Scholten (Eds.), *Low-educated adult second language and literacy acquisition* (pp. 25–43). Utrecht: LOT.

Godfroid, A., Loewen, S., Jung, S., Park, J.-H., Gass, S., & Ellis, R. (2015). Timed and untimed grammaticality judgments measure distinct types of knowledge: Evidence from eye-movement patterns. *Studies in Second Language Acquisition*, 37, 269–297.

Godfroid, A., & Schmidtke, J. (2013). What do eye movements tell us about awareness? A triangulation of eye-movement data, verbal reports, and vocabulary learning scores. In J. M. Bergsleithner, S. N. Frota, & J. K. Yoshioka (Eds.), *Noticing and second language acquisition: Studies in honor of Richard Schmidt* (pp. 183–205). Honolulu: University of Hawai'i, National Foreign Language Resource Center.

Godfroid, A., & Winke, P. (2015). Investigating implicit and explicit processing using L2 learners' eye-movement data. In P. Rebuschat (Ed.), *Implicit and explicit learning of languages* (pp. 325–348). Amsterdam: John Benjamins.

Golonka, E. M. (2006). Predictors revised: Linguistic knowledge and metalinguistic awareness in second language gain in Russian. *Modern Language Journal*, 90(4), 496–505.

Gombert, J. E. (1992). *Metalinguistic Development*. Hemel Hempstead: Harvester.

Goo, J., Granena, G., Yilmaz, Y., & Novella, M. (2015). Implicit and explicit instruction in L2 learning: Norris & Ortega (2000) revisited and updated. In P. Rebuschat (Ed.), *Implicit and explicit learning of languages* (pp. 443–482). Amsterdam: John Benjamins.

Granena, G. (2013). Individual differences in sequence learning ability and second language acquisition in early childhood and adulthood. *Language Learning*, 63(4), 665–703.

Granena, G. (2016). Cognitive aptitudes for implicit and explicit learning and information-processing styles: An individual differences study. *Applied Psycholinguistics*, 37, 577–600.

Green, P. S., & Hecht, K. (1992). Implicit and explicit grammar: An empirical study. *Applied Linguistics*, 13(2), 168–184.

Gruber, H. E., & Vonèche, J. J. (Eds.). (1977). *The Essential Piaget*. London: Routledge.

Gutiérrez, X. (2013). The construct validity of grammaticality judgment tests as measures of implicit and explicit knowledge. *Studies in Second Language Acquisition*, 35, 423–449.

Gutiérrez, X. (2016). Analyzed knowledge, metalanguage, and second language proficiency. *System*, 60, 42–54.

Hacker, D. J. (1998). Definitions and empirical foundations. In D. J. Hacker, J. Dunlosky, & A. C. Graesser (Eds.), *Metacognition in educational theory and practice* (pp. 1–23). Mahwah, NJ: Erlbaum.

Hakes, D. T. (1980). *The Development of Metalinguistic Abilities in Children*. Berlin: Springer.

Hakuta, K., & Diaz, R. M. (1985). The relationship between degree of bilingualism and cognitive ability: A critical discussion and some new longitudinal data. In K. E. Nelson (Ed.), *Children's language* (Vol. 5, pp. 319–344). Hillsdale, NJ: Lawrence Erlbaum Associates.

References **143**

Hanan, R. E. (2015). *The Effectiveness of Explicit Grammar Instruction for the Young Foreign Language Learner: A Classroom-Based Experimental Study*. Unpublished PhD thesis, University of York.

Harley, B. (1998). The role of focus-on-form tasks in promoting child L2 acquisition. In C. Doughty & J. Williams (Eds.), *Focus on form in classroom second language acquisition* (pp. 156–174). Cambridge: Cambridge University Press.

Harley, B., & Hart, D. (1997). Language aptitude and second language proficiency in classroom learners of different starting ages. *Studies in Second Language Acquisition, 19*, 379–400.

Hawkins, E. (2005). Out of this nettle, drop-out, we pluck this flower, opportunity: Rethinking the school foreign language apprenticeship. *Language Learning Journal, 32*(1), 4–17.

Herdina, P., & Jessner, U. (2002). *A Dynamic Model of Multilingualism: Perspectives of Change in Psycholinguistics*. Clevedon: Multilingual Matters.

Horst, M., White, J., & Bell, P. (2010). First and second language knowledge in the language classroom. *International Journal of Bilingualism, 14*(3), 331–349.

Housen, A., Pierrard, M., & Van Daele, S. (2005). Structure complexity and the efficacy of explicit grammar instruction. In A. Housen & M. Pierrard (Eds.), *Investigations in instructed second language acquisition* (pp. 235–269). Berlin: Mouton de Gruyter.

Housen, A., & Simoens, H. (2016). Introduction: Cognitive perspectives on difficulty and complexity in L2 acquisition. *Studies in Second Language Acquisition, 38*(2), 163–175.

Howe, M. L., & Lewis, M. D. (2005). The importance of dynamic systems approaches for understanding development. *Developmental Review, 25*, 247–251.

Hu, G. (2002). Psychological constraints on the utility of metalinguistic knowledge in second language production. *Studies in Second Language Acquisition, 24*(3), 347–386.

Hu, G. (2011). Metalinguistic knowledge, metalanguage, and their relationship in L2 learners. *System, 39*(1), 63–77. doi:10.1016/j.system.2011.01.011

Hulstijn, J. H. (2005). Theoretical and empirical issues in the study of implicit and explicit second-language learning: Introduction. *Studies in Second Language Acquisition, 27*(2), 129–140.

Hulstijn, J. H. (2015). Explaining phenomena of first and second language acquisition with the constructs of implicit and explicit learning: The virtues and pitfalls of a two-system view. In P. Rebuschat (Ed.), *Implicit and explicit learning of languages* (pp. 25–46). Amsterdam: John Benjamins.

Hulstijn, J. H., & de Graaff, R. (1994). Under what conditions does explicit knowledge of a second language facilitate the acquisition of implicit knowledge? A research proposal. *AILA Review, 11*, 97–112.

Hunt, R. R., & Ellis, H. C. (2004). *Fundamentals of Cognitive Psychology* (7th). New York: McGraw Hill.

Hyltenstam, K., & Abrahamsson, N. (2003). Maturational constraints in SLA. In C. J. Doughty & M. H. Long (Eds.), *The Handbook of Second Language Acquisition* (pp. 539–588). Malden, MA: Blackwell.

James, C., & Garrett, P. (1991). The scope of language awareness. In C. James & P. Garrett (Eds.), *Language awareness in the classroom* (pp. 3–21). London: Longman.

Jessner, U. (1999). Metalinguistic awareness in multilinguals: Cognitive aspects of third language learning. *Language Awareness, 8*(3&4), 201–209.

Jessner, U. (2003). A dynamic approach to language attrition in multilingual systems. In V. J. Cook (Ed.), *Effects of the second language on the first* (pp. 234–246). Clevedon: Multilingual Matters.

144 References

Jessner, U. (2006). *Linguistic Awareness in Multilinguals: English as a Third Language*. Edinburgh: Edinburgh University Press.

Jessner, U. (2008). A DST model of multilingualism and the role of metalinguistic awareness. *Modern Language Journal*, 92(2), 270–283.

Jessner, U. (2014). On multilingual awareness or why the multilingual learner is a specific language learner. In M. Pawlak & L. Aronin (Eds.), *Essential topics in applied linguistics and multilingualism: Studies in honor of David Singleton* (pp. 175–184). Cham: Springer.

Johnson, J. S., & Newport, E. L. (1989). Critical period effects in second language learning: The influence of maturational state on the acquisition of English as a second language. *Cognitive Psychology*, 21, 60–99.

Johnson, K. (1996). *Language Teaching and Skill Learning*. Oxford: Blackwell.

Jones, N., Barnes, A., & Hunt, M. (2005). Thinking through languages: A multi-lingual approach to primary school languages. *Language Learning Journal*, 32(1), 63–67.

Jourdenais, R. (2001). Cognition, instruction, and protocol analysis. In P. Robinson (Ed.), *Cognition and second language instruction* (pp. 354–376). Cambridge: Cambridge University Press.

Karmiloff, K., & Karmiloff-Smith, A. (2002). *Pathways to Language: From Fetus to Adolescent*. Cambridge, MA: Harvard University Press.

Keck, C., & Kim, Y. (2014). *Pedagogical Grammar*. Amsterdam: John Benjamins.

Klapper, J., & Rees, J. (2003). Reviewing the case for explicit grammar instruction in the university foreign language learning context. *Language Teaching Research*, 7(3), 285–314.

Kormos, J. (2013). New conceptualizations of language aptitude in second language attainment. In G. Granena & M. H. Long (Eds.), *Sensitive periods, language aptitude, and ultimate L2 attainment* (pp. 131–152). Amsterdam: John Benjamins.

Krashen, S. D. (1981). *Second language acquisition and second language learning*. Oxford: Pergamon.

Krashen, S. D. (1982). *Principles and Practice in Second Language Acquisition*. Oxford: Pergamon.

Krashen, S. D., & Terrell, T. D. (1983). *The natural approach: Language acquisition in the classroom*. Oxford: Pergamon.

Kurvers, J., van Hout, R., & Vallen, T. (2006). Discovering language: Metalinguistic awareness of adult illiterates. In I. van de Craats, J. Kurvers, & M. Young-Scholten (Eds.), *Low-educated adult second language and literacy acquisition* (pp. 69–88). Utrecht: LOT.

Larsen-Freeman, D. (1997). Chaos/complexity science and second language acquisition. *Applied Linguistics*, 18(2), 141–165.

Larsen-Freeman, D. (2003). *Teaching Language: From Grammar to Grammaring*. Boston, MA: Heinle.

Larsen-Freeman, D., & Cameron, L. (2008). *Complex systems and applied linguistics*. Oxford: Oxford University Press.

Larson-Hall, J. (2008). Weighing the benefits of studying a foreign language at a younger starting age in a minimal input situation. *Second Language Research*, 24(1), 35–63.

Leow, R. P. (1997). Attention, awareness, and foreign language behavior. *Language Learning*, 47, 467–505.

Leow, R. P. (2000). A study of the role of awareness in foreign language behavior: Aware versus unaware learners. *Studies in Second Language Acquisition*, 22(4), 557–584.

Leow, R. P. (2015). *Explicit Learning in the L2 Dlassroom: A Student-Centered Approach*. New York, N.Y.: Routledge.

Leow, R. P., & Bowles, M. A. (2005). Attention and awareness in SLA. In C. Sanz (Ed.), *Mind and context in adult second language acquisition: Methods, theory, and practice* (pp. 179–203). Washington, DC: Georgetown University Press.

Leow, R. P., Johnson, E., & Zárate-Sández, G. (2011). Getting a grip on the slippery construct of awareness: Toward a finer-grained methodological perspective. In C. Sanz & R. P. Leow (Eds.), *Implicit and explicit language learning: Conditions, processes, and knowledge in SLA and bilingualism* (pp. 61–72). Washington, DC: Georgetown University Press.

Lichtman, K. (2013). Developmental comparisons of implicit and explicit language learning. *Language Acquisition, 20*(2), 93–108.

Lichtman, K. (2016). Age and learning environment: Are children implicit second language learners? *Journal of Child Language,* 43, 707–730.

Linck, J. A., Hughes, M. M., Campbell, S. G., Silbert, N. H., Tare, M., Jackson, S. R., ... Doughty, C. (2013). Hi-LAB: A new measure of aptitude for high-level language proficiency. *Language Learning,* 63(3), 530–566.

Loewen, S., Li, S., Fei, F., Thompson, A., Nakatsukasa, K., Ahn, S., & Chen, X. (2009). Second language learners' beliefs about grammar instruction and error correction. *Modern Language Journal,* 93(1), 91–104.

Loschky, L., & Bley-Vroman, R. (1993). Grammar and task-based methodology. In G. Crookes & S. M. Gass (Eds.), *Tasks and language learning: Integrating theory and practice.* Clevedon: Multilingual Matters.

Macaro, E., & Masterman, L. (2006). Does intensive explicit grammar instruction make all the difference? *Language Teaching Research,* 10(3), 297–327.

MacWhinney, B. (2001). The competition model: The input, the context, and the brain. In P. Robinson (Ed.), *Cognition and second language instruction* (pp. 69–90). Cambridge: Cambridge University Press.

Mandell, P. B. (1999). On the reliability of grammaticality judgement tests in second language acquisition research. *Second Language Research,* 15(1), 73–99.

McDonough, S. (2002). *Applied Linguistics in Language Education.* London: Arnold.

Meara, P. (2005). *Llama Language Aptitude Tests.* Swansea: University of Wales.

Milton, J., & Alexiou, T. (2006). Language aptitude development in young learners. In C. Abello-Contesse, R. Chacón-Beltrán, M. D. López-Chiménez, & M. M. Torreblanca-López (Eds.), *Age in L2 acquisition and teaching* (pp. 177–192). Oxford: Peter Lang.

Miyake, A., & Friedman, N. P. (1998). Individual differences in second language proficiency: Working memory as language aptitude. In A. F. Healy & L. E. Bourne (Eds.), *Foreign language learning: Psycholinguistic studies on training and retention* (pp. 339–364). Mahwah, NJ: Erlbaum.

Montemayor, C., & Haladjian, H. H. (2015). *Consciousness, Attention, and Conscious Attention.* Cambridge, MA: MIT Press.

Morgan-Short, K., Faretta-Stutenberg, M., & Bartlett-Hsu, L. (2015). Contributions of event-related potential research to issues of explicit and implicit second language acquisition. In P. Rebuschat (Ed.), *Implicit and explicit learning of languages* (pp. 349–383). Amsterdam: John Benjamins.

Morton, J. B. (2014). Sunny review casts a foreboding shadow over status quo bilingual advantage research. *Applied Psycholinguistics,* 35(5), 929–931.

Morton, J. B., & Harper, S. N. (2007). What did Simon say? Revisiting the bilingual advantage. *Developmental Science,* 10(6), 719–726.

Murphy, V. A., Macaro, E., Alba, S., & Cipolla, C. (2014). The influence of learning a second language in primary school on developing first language literacy skills. *Applied Psycholinguistics,* 36(5), 1133–1153.

Muñoz, C. (2008). Age-related differences in foreign language learning: Revisiting the empirical evidence. *IRAL,* 46, 197–220.

146 References

Muñoz, C. (2009). Input and long-term effects of early learning in a formal setting. In M. Nikolov (Ed.), *The age factor and early language learning* (pp. 141–159). Berlin: Mouton de Gruyter.

Muñoz, C. (2014). The association between aptitude components and language skills in young learners. In M. Pawlak & L. Aronin (Eds.), *Essential topics in applied linguistics and multilingualism: Studies in honour of David Singleton* (pp. 51–68). Cham: Springer.

Muñoz, C. (Ed.) (2006). *Age and the rate of foreign language learning.* Clevedon: Multilingual Matters.

Nicolay, A.-C., & Poncelet, M. (2013). Cognitive advantage in children enrolled in a second-language immersion elementary school program for three years. *Bilingualism: Language and Cognition*, 16(3), 597–607.

Norris, J. M., & Ortega, L. (2001). Does type of instruction make a difference? Substantive findings from a meta-analytic review. *Language Learning*, 51(1), 157–213.

Ortega, L., Tyler, A. E., Park, H. I., & Uno, M. (Eds.). (2016). *The usage-based study of language and multilingualism.* Washington, DC: Georgetown University Press.

Paradis, M. (2004). *A Neurolinguistic Theory of Bilingualism.* Amsterdam: John Benjamins.

Peterson, E. R., & Deary, I. J. (2006). Examining the wholistic-analytic style using preferences in early information processing. *Personality and Individual Differences*, 41, 3–14.

Peterson, E. R., Deary, I. J., & Austin, E. J. (2003). The reliability of Riding's Cognitive Style Analysis test. *Personality and Individual Differences*, 34, 881–891.

Piaget, J. (1929). *The Child's Conception of the World.* London: Routledge.

Pienemann, M. (1999). *Language Processing and Second Language Development: Processability Theory.* Amsterdam: John Benjamins.

Pinto, M. A., Titone, R., & Trusso, F. (1999). *Metalinguistic Awareness.* Pisa: Istituti Editoriali Poligrafici Internazionali.

Poarch, G. J., & van Hell, J. G. (2012). Executive functions and inhibitory control in multilingual children: Evidence from second-language learners, bilinguals, and trilinguals. *Journal of Experimental Child Psychology*, 113, 535–551.

Ranta, L. (2002). The role of learners' language analytic ability in the communicative classroom. In P. Robinson (Ed.), *Individual differences and instructed language learning* (pp. 159–180). Amsterdam: John Benjamins.

Ranta, L. (2005). Language analytic ability and oral production in a second language: Is there a connection? In A. Housen & M. Pierrard (Eds.), *Investigations in instructed second language acquisition* (pp. 99–130). Berlin: Mouton de Gruyter.

Rebuschat, P. (2013). Measuring implicit and explicit knowledge in second language research. *Language Learning*, 63(3), 595–626.

Renou, J. M. (2000). Learner accuracy and learner performance: The quest for a link. *Foreign Language Annals*, 33(2), 168–180.

Robinson, P. (1995). Review article: Attention, memory, and the "noticing" hypothesis. *Language Learning*, 45(2), 283–331.

Robinson, P. (1997). Individual differences and the fundamental similarity of implicit and explicit adult second language learning. *Language Learning*, 47(1), 45–99.

Robinson, P. (2001). Individual differences, cognitive abilities, aptitude complexes and learning conditions in second language acquisition. *Second Language Research*, 17(4), 368–392.

Robinson, P. (2003). Attention and memory during SLA. In C. J. Doughty & M. H. Long (Eds.), *The handbook of second language acquisition* (pp. 631–678). Malden, MA: Blackwell.

Robinson, P. (2005). Aptitude and second language acquisition. *Annual Review of Applied Linguistics*, 25, 46–73.

Robinson, P. (2007). Aptitudes, abilities, contexts, and practice. In R. M. DeKeyser (Ed.), *Practice in a second language: Perspectives from applied linguistics and cognitive psychology* (pp. 256–286). Cambridge: Cambridge University Press.

Robinson, P., & Ellis, N. C. (Eds.). (2008). *Handbook of Cognitive Linguistics and Second Language Acquisition.* New York, NY: Routledge.

Rodríguez Silva, L. H., & Roehr-Brackin, K. (2016a). Language learning aptitude and working memory as predictors of instructed adult L2 learners' explicit and implicit L2 knowledge. Paper presented at the Cognitive Approaches to Language Pedagogy 2 conference, Basel, Switzerland, 10–11 June 2016.

Rodríguez Silva, L. H., & Roehr-Brackin, K. (2016b). Perceived learning difficulty and actual performance: Explicit and implicit knowledge of L2 English grammar points among instructed adult learners. *Studies in Second Language Acquisition*, 38(2), 317–340.

Roehr, K. (2005). *Metalinguistic Knowledge in Second Language Learning: An Emergentist Perspective.* Unpublished PhD thesis, Lancaster University.

Roehr, K. (2006). Metalinguistic knowledge in L2 task performance: A verbal protocol analysis. *Language Awareness*, 15(3), 180–198.

Roehr, K. (2008a). Linguistic and metalinguistic categories in second language learning. *Cognitive Linguistics*, 19(1), 67–106.

Roehr, K. (2008b). Metalinguistic knowledge and language ability in university-level L2 learners. *Applied Linguistics*, 29(2), 173–199.

Roehr, K. (2010). Explicit knowledge and learning in SLA: A cognitive linguistics perspective. *AILA Review*, 23, 7–29.

Roehr, K. (2012). The Springboard to Languages evaluation project: A summary report. In A. Tellier (Ed.), *Esperanto as a starter language for child second-language learners in the primary school* (pp. 23–34). Stoke-on-Trent: Esperanto UK.

Roehr, K., & Gánem-Gutiérrez, G. A. (2009a). Metalinguistic knowledge: A stepping stone towards L2 proficiency? In A. Benati (Ed.), *Issues in second language proficiency* (pp. 79–94). London: Continuum.

Roehr, K., & Gánem-Gutiérrez, G. A. (2009b). The status of metalinguistic knowledge in instructed adult L2 learning. *Language Awareness*, 18(2), 165–181.

Roehr-Brackin, K. (2014). Explicit knowledge and processes from a usage-based perspective: The developmental trajectory of an instructed L2 learner. *Language Learning*, 64(4), 771–808.

Roehr-Brackin, K. (2015). Long-term development in an instructed adult L2 learner: Usage-based and complexity theory applied. In T. Cadierno & S. W. Eskildsen (Eds.), *Usage-based perspectives on second language learning* (pp. 181–206). Berlin: de Gruyter.

Roehr-Brackin, K., & Tellier, A. (2016). *Language Learning Aptitude in Primary-Level L2 Learners.* Paper presented at the EuroSLA 2016 conference, Jyväskylä, Finland, 25–27 August 2016.

Rogers, V., Meara, P., Aspinall, R., Fallon, L., Goss, T., Keey, E., & Thomas, R. (2016). Testing aptitude: Investigating Meara's (2005) LLAMA tests. *EuroSLA Yearbook*, 16, 179–210.

Rosa, E., & O'Neill, M. D. (1999). Explicitness, intake, and the issue of awareness. *Studies in Second Language Acquisition*, 21, 511–556.

Samuel, S. (2015). *An Investigation of a Proposed Bilingual Advantage in Aspects of Executive Function: Evidence From Visual Perspective Taking and Simon Tasks.* Unpublished PhD thesis, University of Essex.

Sanz, C., & Morgan-Short, K. (2005). Explicitness in pedagogical interventions: Input, practice, and feedback. In C. Sanz (Ed.), *Mind and context in adult second language* acquisition: Methods, theory, and practice (pp. 234–263). Washington, DC: Georgetown University Press.

Sawyer, M., & Ranta, L. (2001). Aptitude, individual differences, and instructional design. In P. Robinson (Ed.), *Cognition and second language instruction* (pp. 319–353). Cambridge: Cambridge University Press.

Schachter, J. (1998). Recent research in language learning studies: Promises and problems. *Language Learning*, 48(4), 557–583.

Scheffler, P. (2009). Rule difficulty and the usefulness of instruction. *ELT Journal*, 63(1), 5–12.

Scheffler, P. (2011). Rule difficulty: Teachers' intuitions and learners' performance. *Language Awareness*, 20(3), 221–237.

Scheffler, P. (2013). Learners' perceptions of grammar-translation as consciousness raising. *Language Awareness*, 22(3), 255–269.

Scheffler, P., & Cinciała, M. (2011). Explicit grammar rules and L2 acquisition. *ELT Journal*, 65(1), 13–23.

Schmidt, R. W. (1990). The role of consciousness in SLA learning. *Applied Linguistics*, 11, 129–158.

Schmidt, R. W. (1993). Awareness and second language acquisition. *Annual Review of Applied Linguistics*, 13, 206–226.

Schmidt, R. W. (1994). Deconstructing consciousness in search of useful definitions for applied linguistics. *AILA Review*, 11, 11–26.

Schmidt, R. W. (2001). Attention. In P. Robinson (Ed.), *Cognition and Second Language Instruction* (pp. 3–32). Cambridge: Cambridge University Press.

Schmidt, R. W., & Frota, S. N. (1986). Developing basic conversational ability in a second language: A case study of an adult learner of Portuguese. In R. R. Day (Ed.), *Talking to learn: Conversation in second language acquisition* (pp. 237–326). Cambridge, MA: Newbury House.

Schulz, R. A. (2001). Cultural differences in student and teacher perceptions concerning the role of grammar instruction and corrective feedback: USA-Colombia. *Modern Language Journal*, 85(2), 244–258.

Schütze, C. T. (1996). *The Empirical Base of Linguistics: Grammaticality Judgments and Linguistic Methodology*. Chicago: University of Chicago Press.

Schütze, C. T., & Sprouse, J. (2013). Judgment data. In R. J. Podesva & D. Sharma (Eds.), *Research methods in linguistics* (pp. 27–50). Cambridge: Cambridge University Press.

Segalowitz, N. (2003). Automaticity and second languages. In C. J. Doughty & M. H. Long (Eds.), *The handbook of second language acquisition* (pp. 382–408). Malden, MA: Blackwell.

Serrano, R. (2011). From metalinguistic instruction to metalinguistic knowledge, and from metalinguistic knowledge to performance in error correction and oral production tasks. *Language Awareness*, 20(1), 1–16.

Simard, D., & Wong, W. (2001). Alertness, orientation, and detection: The conceptualization of attentional functions in SLA. *Studies in Second Language Acquisition*, 23, 103–124.

Skehan, P. (1998). *A Cognitive Approach to Language Learning*. Oxford: Oxford University Press.

Skehan, P. (2002). Theorising and updating aptitude. In P. Robinson (Ed.), *Individual differences and instructed language learning* (pp. 69–94). Amsterdam: John Benjamins.

Sorace, A. (1985). Metalinguistic knowledge and language use in acquisition-poor environments. *Applied Linguistics*, 6(3), 239–254.

Spada, N., Shiu, L.-J. J., & Tomita, Y. (2015). Validating an elicited imitation task as a measure of implicit knowledge: Comparisons with other validation studies. *Language Learning*, 65(3), 723–751.

Spada, N., & Tomita, Y. (2010). Interactions between type of instruction and type of language feature: A meta-analysis. *Language Learning*, 60(2), 263–308.

Sparks, R., & Ganschow, L. (2001). Aptitude for learning a foreign language. *Annual Review of Applied Linguistics*, 21, 90–111.

Sparks, R., Ganschow, L., Fluharty, K., & Little, S. (1995–6). An exploratory study on the effects of Latin on the native language skills and foreign language aptitude of students with and without learning disabilities. *The Classic Journal*, 91(2), 165–184.

Stankov, L. (2003). Complexity in human intelligence. In R. J. Sternberg, J. Lautrey, & T. I. Lubart (Eds.), *Models of intelligence: International perspectives* (pp. 27–42). Washington, DC: American Psychological Association.

Sternberg, R. J., Lautrey, J., & Lubart, T. I. (2003). Where are we in the field of intelligence, how did we get here, and where are we going? In R. J. Sternberg, J. Lautrey, & T. I. Lubart (Eds.), *Models of intelligence: International perspectives* (pp. 3–25). Washington, DC: American Psychological Association.

Suzuki, Y., & DeKeyser, R. (2015). Comparing elicited imitation and word monitoring as measures of implicit knowledge. *Language Learning*, 65(4), 860–895.

Suzuki, Y., & DeKeyser, R. (2017). The interface of explicit and implicit knowledge in a second language: Insights from individual differences in cognitive aptitudes. *Language Learning*. doi:10.1111/lang.12241

Svalberg, A. M.-L. (2007). Language awareness and language learning. *Language Teaching*, 40(4), 287–308.

Swain, M. (1998). Focus on form through conscious reflection. In C. J. Doughty & J. Williams (Eds.), *Focus on form in classroom second language acquisition* (pp. 64–81). Cambridge: Cambridge University Press.

Swan, M. (1994). Design criteria for pedagogic language rules. In M. Bygate, A. Tonkyn, & E. Williams (Eds.), *Grammar and the language teacher* (pp. 45–55). New York: Prentice Hall.

Tellier, A. (Ed.) (2012). *Esperanto as a Starter Language for Child Second-Language Learners in the Primary School*. Stoke-on-Trent: Esperanto UK.

Tellier, A. (2013). Developing a measure of metalinguistic awareness for children aged 8–11. In K. Roehr & G. A. Gánem-Gutiérrez (Eds.), *The metalinguistic dimension in instructed second language learning* (pp. 15–43). London: Bloomsbury.

Tellier, A. (2015). *Metalinguistic Awareness and Foreign Language Learning in Primary School: A Classroom Study with Children Aged 8 to 9 Years*. Unpublished PhD thesis, University of Essex.

Tellier, A., & Roehr-Brackin, K. (2013a). Metalinguistic awareness in children with differing language learning experience. *EuroSLA Yearbook*, 13, 81–108.

Tellier, A., & Roehr-Brackin, K. (2013b). The development of language learning aptitude and metalinguistic awareness in primary-school children: A classroom study. *Essex Research Reports in Linguistics*, 62(1), 1–28.

Tellier, A., & Roehr-Brackin, K. (2017). Raising children's metalinguistic awareness to enhance classroom second language learning. In M. d. P. García Mayo (Ed.), *Learning foreign languages in primary school: Research insights* (pp. 22–48). Bristol: Multilingual Matters.

Thepseenu, B., & Roehr, K. (2013). University-level learners' beliefs about metalinguistic knowledge. In K. Roehr & G. A. Gánem-Gutiérrez (Eds.), *The metalinguistic dimension in instructed second language learning* (pp. 95–117). London: Bloomsbury.

Tokowicz, N., & MacWhinney, B. (2005). Implicit and explicit measures of sensitivity to violations in second language grammar: An event-related potential investigation. *Studies in Second Language Acquisition*, 27, 173–204.

Tomasello, M. (2003). *Constructing a Language: A Usage-Based Theory of Language Acquisition.* Cambridge, MA: Harvard University Press.

Tomasello, M. (2005). Beyond formalities: The case of language acquisition. *The Linguistic Review*, 22(2–4), 183–197.

Tomlin, R. S., & Villa, V. (1994). Attention in cognitive science and second language acquisition. *Studies in Second Language Acquisition*, 16, 183–203.

Vafaee, P., Suzuki, Y., & Kachisnke, I. (2017). Validating grammaticality judgment tests: Evidence from two new psycholinguistic measures. *Studies in Second Language Acquisition*, doi:10.1017/S0272263115000455.

van Lier, L. (1995). *Introducing Language Awareness.* London: Penguin.

Wen, Z. (2012). Working memory and second language learning. *International Journal of Applied Linguistics*, 22(1), 1–22.

Westney, P. (1994). Rules and pedagogical grammar. In T. Odlin (Ed.), *Perspectives on pedagogical grammar* (pp. 72–96). Cambridge: Cambridge University Press.

White, J. (2008). Speeding up the acquisition of his and her: Explicit L1/L2 contrasts help. In J. Philp, R. Oliver, & A. Mackey (Eds.), *Second Language Acquisition and the Younger Learner: Child's Play?* (pp. 193–228). Amsterdam: John Benjamins.

White, J., & Ranta, L. (2002). Examining the interface between metalinguistic task performance and oral production in a second language. *Language Awareness*, 11(4), 259–290.

White, L., Spada, N., Lightbown, P. M., & Ranta, L. (1991). Input enhancement and L2 question formation. *Applied Linguistics*, 12(4), 416–432.

Winitz, H. (1996). Grammaticality judgment as a function of explicit and implicit instruction in Spanish. *Modern Language Journal*, 80(1), 32–46.

Yalçın, Ş., & Spada, N. (2016). Language aptitude and grammatical difficulty: An EFL classroom-based study. *Studies in Second Language Acquisition*, 38(2), 239–263.

Yelland, G. W., Pollard, J., & Mercuri, A. (1993). The metalinguistic benefits of limited contact with a second language. *Applied Psycholinguistics*, 14, 423–444.

Young, K. A. (2005). Direct from the source: The value of 'think-aloud' data in understanding learning. *Journal of Educational Enquiry*, 6(1), 19–33.

Zhang, R. (2015). Measuring university-level L2 learners' implicit and explicit linguistic knowledge. *Studies in Second Language Acquisition*, 37, 457–486.

Ziętek, A. A., & Roehr, K. (2011). Metalinguistic knowledge and cognitive style in Polish classroom learners of English. *System*, 39(4), 417–426.

INDEX

Adaptive Control of Thought (ACT)
  model 64
additional languages (L2) 3–5, 10, 17–18,
  20–2, 24, 33–43; and achievement
  100–6; directions for 136; and executive
  function 132; and explicit knowledge
  62–5, 68, 73–80, 85, 87–8; and explicit
  learning 62–99; and implicit knowledge
  62–5, 68, 73–80, 85, 87–8; and implicit
  learning 62–99; and interface positions 4,
  62, 64–5, 68, 134; and language
  awareness 44–50; and language learning
  aptitude 86; and learning difficulty 82–4;
  and measures 114–25, 127–9; and
  primary-school classrooms 53–60; and
  theoretical perspectives 134–5
adjectives 1, 51, 97–8, 122
adolescents 46, 57, 62, 64, 95, 100,
  113, 129
adults 7, 9, 12, 15–19, 23, 31–3; and
  bilingualism 41; and empirical evidence
  92, 95, 100; and future research 135–6;
  and measures 127–33; and
  primary-school classrooms 57; and
  theoretical perspectives 62, 64, 88,
  134–5
adverbs 80, 114
advertising 16, 46
aesthetics 45
age-of-onset studies 56–7, 59
AILA Review 82
alertness 35, 75–6

algorithms 79
allomorphs 83
alphabetic languages 14–15, 18, 39
American English language 11
Ammar, A. 55–6
analysis of knowledge 20–2, 24–7, 31, 128,
  130–2, 134
anaphora 7
applied linguistics 2–4, 110, 118, 129,
  134–6
apprenticeship languages 46–7, 53
aptitude components 86–8
Aristotle 79–81
Asia 121
Association for Language Awareness 45
attention processes 1–2, 4–6, 20–1, 23–4,
  27–8, 30–1; and cognitive
  developmental perspective 34–8; and
  empirical evidence 89–92, 103–4; and
  measures 120, 130, 132–3; and
  primary-school classrooms 57, 60–1; and
  theoretical perspectives 65–7, 69–71,
  73–82, 84
Attentional Network Task (ANT) 34–6,
  38, 132
Australia 39, 101
automatic processing 2, 7–8, 13, 20, 22,
  64–5, 67, 103–4, 114, 121, 135
autonoetic consciousness 124–5

Baddeley, A.D. 64, 68–9
Barton, A. 50

152 Index

Baum, S. 31–3
Bayne, T. 71, 73
Bialystok, E. 1–3, 13–14, 18, 20–2, 24, 27–30, 36–8, 128, 131
bias 12, 66, 92–3, 96
bilingualism 3, 5, 18, 20, 47, 129; and additional languages 33–41; advantages of 22–41; directions for 136; and executive function 132; and multilingualism 42–3; and theoretical perspectives 134
biology 66, 69–71, 73
Bouffard, L.A. 53, 55
brain structure 22, 32, 65–7, 69, 72, 77, 127

Camps, J. 104–6, 123
Canada 33, 37, 53, 55, 59, 117, 119
Canadians 25, 28
Carroll, J.B. 86
categorisation 79–82, 103, 124, 130
Chalmers, D.J. 71, 73
character systems 15
children 3, 5–20, 22–3, 25–40, 46–62, 88, 127–36
Chinese language 28, 30, 69, 101–3, 115
citizenship 46, 48
class 11, 25–6
cognitive change 76, 123
cognitive developmental perspective 3–41, 128–30, 134–6
cognitive reserve 23, 32
cognitive science 10, 64, 68, 70–1, 73, 75, 77
Collins, L. 84
Common European Framework of Reference (CEFR) 117, 119
communicative sensitivity 42–3
complexity theory 44, 84–6, 108, 128
comprehension 11–12, 51, 65, 67, 82, 91, 117, 129
conceptual inhibition 28–31
concrete-operational thought 8–11, 13, 18, 41
confidence intervals 93–4
confidence ratings 115, 126
conflict monitoring 34–8
conflict resolution 34–6, 132–3
congruity effect 39–40
conscious studies 68–9
consciousness 6, 20, 65–76, 91, 103, 117, 124–6
conservation 11–13

control of processing 20–2, 24–7, 31, 128, 130–2, 134
correlational studies 99, 101–2, 120
cortex 65, 71
Craik, F.I.M. 22
cross-linguistic awareness 43, 52
cue validity 103, 130, 133

De Graaff, R. 82
DeKeyser, R.M. 82–3, 135
dementia 32
Descartes, R. 69
detection 75–6
Dimensional Change Card Sort (DCCS) 27–31, 132
Discovering language project 48–50
divergent thinking 42
diversity 47
Dutch language 16–17

early reading stage 14, 18
Elder, C. 101–2
Ellis, N. 64–6, 68
Ellis, R. 85, 114, 118, 120–1, 125, 135
emergent literacy approach 14
empirical studies 4, 10–13, 15–18, 22, 25–36, 38–9; and bilingualism 41; directions for 136; and explicit knowledge/learning 89–113; and implicit/explicit knowledge 62–3, 71, 74–5, 77, 84; and language awareness 44, 48–52; and language learning aptitude 88; and measures 114, 117, 122, 126–7; in primary-school classroom 53–61; and theoretical perspectives 134
Engel, A.K. 70
England 46–8, 56
English language 12, 25–6, 28–30, 34–5, 37–9; and bilingualism 41; and empirical evidence 92, 100–4, 107–11; and language awareness 46–51; and measures 114–16, 120–4, 128–9; and multilingualism 43; and primary-school classrooms 53–6, 58, 60; and theoretical perspectives 67, 80–1, 83
epilinguistic behaviour 6–8, 13
epipragmatics 7
episodic memory 2, 65, 67–70, 124
epitextual behaviour 7
errors/error analysis 21, 24–5, 35, 37, 53–5, 60; and empirical evidence 91, 98–101, 103–4, 107–9, 111; and measures

116–20, 122, 127, 130–1, 133; and theoretical perspectives 68
Esperanto language 50, 52, 57–9, 128
ethnicity 16, 31
Europe 46–7, 57–8, 60, 69
European languages 128
event-related potentials (ERP) 127
EVLANG project 47
evolution 69–70
executive function 23–4, 31–8, 132–3, 135
explicit knowledge 1–4, 56–7, 89–113; definitions 20; explicitness hierarchy 77; as interface 62–73; and L2 achievement 100–6; and self-report as measure 114–27; and testing as measure 114–27; and theoretical perspectives 134–5
explicit learning 3–4, 56–7, 61–113, 135–6
explicit memory 2–3, 62
Extended Cognitive Style Analysis – Wholist/Analytic measure 111
eye-tracking 120–1, 127

falsification 119
fast-track learning 113
feedback 7, 13, 53–4, 65, 68, 90–1, 95–6
figurative language 129
first language (L1) 3, 5, 10, 12, 16–18, 20–1; and bilingualism 37–9, 41; and cognitive developmental perspective 24; and empirical evidence 102–4, 106–12; and explicit learning 99; and implicit/explicit knowledge 68, 79, 83–4, 88; and L2 achievement 100; and language awareness 44–5, 48; and measures 114–15, 120–3, 127–8; and multilingualism 43; in primary school classroom 53–6, 60
Flanker Task 38, 132
fluent reading stage 14, 18
focus on form (FonF) 90–4, 97–8
focus on forms (FonFS) 90–4, 97–9
focus on meaning (FonM) 90–2
form-focused instruction 21, 53, 56, 59–62, 64, 89–91, 99–100, 102–3, 108, 112, 114, 117
formal linguistics 45, 76, 129
formal-operational thought 8–9, 18, 129
French language 25, 29, 37–8, 49–50, 53–6, 59–60, 98, 127
future research 4, 32–3, 44, 91, 94, 97, 106, 111, 113, 127, 135–6

Gánem-Gutiérrez, G.A. 107, 109–10
Garrett, P. 45
gender 54, 60–1, 83, 105, 127–8
German language 34–5, 49, 59, 97, 100, 107–8, 122
Germany 34
global inhibition 23
Godfroid, A. 120–1
Gombert, J.E. 5–8, 13, 15
Goo, J. 95–6
grammar 7, 23, 26–7, 35–7, 51, 53–5; and empirical evidence 90–1, 95, 97–8, 100–3, 108–10, 112; and learning difficulty 82–6; and measures 114–21, 124–5, 127–9, 131; and metalinguistic understanding 77–80; and primary-school classrooms 60–1; and theoretical perspectives 63, 87
grammaticality judgement tasks (GJT) 55–6, 92, 98, 100, 112–13, 115–22, 124, 126, 130–1
graphemes 15, 41, 57, 128
Greek language 69
Gutiérrez, X. 118, 135

Hakes, D.T. 10–13, 129
Harley, B. 60–1
Harper, S.N. 31
Hawkins, E. 46–7
hippocampus 65, 67
horizontal décalage 9
Horst, M. 84
Hu, G. 102–3
Hulstijn, J.H. 82

illiteracy 15–19, 41, 131
immersion education 25, 33, 36–8, 47, 53, 55, 59–60, 97, 129, 135
implicit knowledge 2, 4, 8, 62–73, 110, 112, 114–16, 118–22, 125–7, 134–5
implicit learning 3, 56–7, 62–93, 95–7
implicit memory 2–3
incidental learning 74–5, 124
Indo-European languages 128
information processing paradigm 24, 90, 112, 123–4
information technology 46
inhibition 21, 23–4, 27–32, 34, 38, 75, 130, 132
input variables 106–13
intercultural awareness 48–9
interface positions 4, 62, 64–5, 68, 134
internalisation 8–9, 124

154 Index

internet 47
IRIS 128
Italian language 26–7, 39–40, 59, 83, 129
item-based learning 10, 61, 81, 85, 124

JA-LING project 47
James, C. 45
Japanese language 49
Jessner, U. 42–4, 87
Jones, N. 48

Kachisnke, I. 122
Klapper, J. 97–9
Korean language 83
Krashen, S.D. 64
Kurvers, J. 15–16, 18, 41, 131

labelling tasks 116, 122
language learning 3, 40–61, 81; directions
   for 136; and explicit learning 89–99; and
   implicit/explicit knowledge 79; and
   input variables 106–13; language
   awareness 3, 44–53; language games 60;
   language learning aptitude 4, 59, 86–7,
   102, 106–8, 111–13, 127, 135–6; and
   learner role 106–13; learning
   difficulty 82–6
language-analytic ability 58, 87–8, 106–7,
   112, 127
language-educational perspective 3, 128,
   130, 134
Larsen-Freeman, D. 78
Latin language 49, 58
learner beliefs/role 4, 102, 106–13
learning difficulty 4, 82–6, 106, 108–10,
   112–13, 136
learning style 77, 108, 136
Leow, R.P. 73, 123–4
linguistic processing 4, 8, 23–4, 36, 128,
   130, 132
literacy skills 3, 8, 13–19, 39–41, 46–9, 52,
   88, 127, 129, 134
LLAMA battery 112
local inhibition 23
low-education levels 127–32, 134, 136
Luk, G. 22

M-Factor 42–4
Macaro, E. 99
mammals 66, 70
Manwaring, D. 101–2
Martin, M.M. 27–30
Masterman, L. 99

MAT tests 129
meaning-focused instruction 21, 89–90
memory see working memory
mental representations 20–1, 27–8, 31, 36,
   67, 70–2, 74
Mercuri, A. 38
meta-analysis of studies 91–7
metacognition 5, 51–2, 102, 108, 113, 129
metaknowledge 126
metalanguage 45, 63, 74, 85–6, 100, 114,
   117–18, 122, 129
metalexical behaviour 7, 14, 18
metalinguistic ability 2, 6, 15–16, 18, 21–2,
   41, 43, 87, 106, 128–9
metalinguistic awareness 3–4, 16, 23–4, 34,
   37, 106; and analysis/control framework
   20–2; in children 127–32; definitions 2,
   15; in development 5–13; directions for
   135–6; as explicit knowledge/learning
   62–113; and language awareness 50–2;
   in language education 42–61; and
   language learning aptitude 86–8; and
   literacy 13–19; measurement of 4, 37–8,
   40–1, 58, 60, 113–33; and metalinguistic
   understanding 73–82; and
   multilingualism 42, 44–5; phases of
   7–8, 10; in primary school classroom
   53–61; role of 1; and theoretical
   perspectives 134–5
metalinguistic behaviour 6, 13
metalinguistic capacity 2
metalinguistic development 1
metalinguistic knowledge 5, 24, 37, 79–80,
   101–4, 106–11; definitions 1–2, 21; and
   empirical evidence 113; and explicit
   learning 89–99; and measures 115–19,
   122–3, 125, 127
metalinguistic skill 2
metalinguistic terminology 53–4, 63, 102,
   117, 128
metalinguistic understanding 73–82, 104
metalinguistics 1
metaphonology 6, 18
metaphors 7
metaphysics 69
metapragmatics 7, 18
metasemantics 7, 14, 18
Mexican Spanish language 110
migration 16, 22
Modern Language Aptitude Test (MLAT)
   107, 127
monolingualism 11, 18, 22–3, 25–7, 29–40,
   43–4, 129

Moreno, S. 36
Moroccans 16
morphemes 15, 37, 77, 83
morphology 15, 37, 57, 60, 77, 83, 90, 123, 128–30
Morton, J.B. 31
multicompetence 44
multiculturalism 45
multilingualism 3, 18, 32–4, 42–5, 47, 129, 132, 134, 136
music 46

naturalistic learning 57, 90, 98, 135–6
neocortex 67
Netherlands 15
neural systems 65, 67, 69–71
neurobiology 66
neuroimaging 77
neurophysiology 72
neuroplasticity 22, 33
neuroscience 70
New Zealand 114
noetic consciousness 124–5
Norris, J.M. 91–2, 94–6
noticing hypothesis 73–4, 77, 90, 104–6, 118, 122, 124
nouns 20, 51, 54, 56, 60–1, 80, 83, 116
number 9, 11, 48, 52, 105, 107, 127, 129
numeracy skills 52

orientation 35–6, 75–7
Ortega, L. 91–2, 94–6
orthography 15

Paradis, M. 64
Peabody Picture Vocabulary Test (PPVT) 25–7, 39
Peabody Picture Vocabulary Test-Revised (PPVT-R) 28–9, 37
pedagogy 63, 77–80, 82, 84–5, 90, 97–8; and empirical evidence 100–1, 103–4, 108, 110; and explicit learning 90; and measures 114, 116–17, 119, 124
Peets, K.F. 36
phenomenology 69, 72–3
philosophy 64, 68–71, 73
phonemes 6, 11–18, 41, 57, 87–8, 129, 131
phonics 14
phonological awareness 14–18, 38–40, 131
phonology 15, 53–4, 60, 68, 77, 88, 90
physiology 127
Piaget, J. 8–10, 18, 25, 129–31
Pinto, M.A. 129

Poarch, G.J. 34, 36
poetry 21, 48
Polish language 100, 108, 111
Pollard, J. 38
Portuguese language 74
pre-literacy stage 14–16, 18
preoperational thought 8–9
prepositions 97–8, 109, 116
process orientation 104
pronouns 56, 92, 105
propaganda 46
propositional thought 8–10
prototype theory 103–4, 106
pseudo-words 124–5
psycholinguistics 66, 84, 128–9, 134
psychology 44, 90, 102, 104, 106, 125; and theoretical perspectives 64–5, 68, 70, 75, 79, 81, 84–5, 134
Punjabi language 49

qualia 68, 72–3

Ranta, L. 60, 87, 127
Raven's Coloured Progressive Matrices 28–9, 37
reading see literacy skills
Rebuschat, P. 125–6
Rees, J. 97–9
response inhibition 28, 30, 38
response times 35–7, 132–3
rhyme 16–18, 21, 39, 129, 131
Rodríguez Silva, L.H. 110
Roehr, K. 79, 81, 85, 107, 109–11, 127
Roehr-Brackin, K. 58, 108, 110
Romance languages 57
rule-based processing 6, 79, 81–2, 91, 129
rule-illustration tasks 116, 122

Sarkar, M. 53, 55
scaffolding 68
scan path analysis 120–1
Scheffler, P. 108–10
Schmidt, R.W. 73–5, 77
scrambled-questions tasks 55–6
scripts 15
second language acquisition (SLA) 1–4, 62, 118, 129, 134, 136; and empirical evidence 6, 64, 73–7, 79, 82, 84, 88; and explicit learning 89–91
self-report as measure 114–27
semantic memory 3, 36, 69, 124
semantic processing 118, 128, 130–1
sensorimotor functions 8–9, 66

156 Index

Simon Task 34–6, 132–3
Skehan, P. 112–13
skill acquisition theory 102–3
social construction 67, 80
Somalians 16
song 39, 46, 48
source attributions 126–7
Spada, N. 84, 111
Spanish language 49–50, 83, 105–7, 110, 116–17, 119, 123
special educational needs 48
spelling 107, 127
Springboard to Languages project 50–1, 53
starter languages 53, 56–9
stylistic preferences 108, 111, 113
subjective measures 125–6
subliminal learning 74
sun/moon problem 24–5, 130–1
Suzuki, Y. 122
Swan, M. 78
syllogisms 16–18, 131–2
synonymy 1–3, 7, 11–12, 21, 129
syntax 6, 11, 15, 24–6, 57, 77–8, 83, 90, 97, 128, 130
systems theory 44

task stimuli 28, 118–20
teaching methodology 21, 90
Tellier, A. 58, 128
Test for Attentional Performance in Children 38
testing as measure 114–27
Thai language 109
theoretical premises 62–88, 90, 102–3, 108, 118, 122, 129, 134–6
Thepseenu, B. 109–11
Thinking through Languages project 47–8
time pressure 104, 114, 118–21, 131

Titone, D. 31–3
Tomita, Y. 84
Tomlin, R.S. 75–6
triangulation 126
trilingualism 3, 22, 34–6, 43
Trofimovich, P. 84
Turkish language 111
Turks 16

United Kingdom (UK) 46–7
United States (US) 121
usage-based approach 10, 79–81, 84, 108, 136

Vafaee, P. 122
Van Hell, J.G. 34, 36
verbal fluency tasks 36–8, 130–1
verbal protocols 104–5, 122–6
verbs 54, 80, 83, 98, 101, 114, 116, 123, 128
Villa, V. 75–6
vocabulary 3, 23, 25–8, 36–7, 39, 45, 51, 60, 105, 112, 117, 124

White, J. 60, 84
whole-language approach 14
word awareness 39–41
word judgement 16–17, 131–2
word length 16–17, 129, 131–2
working memory 23, 28–9, 32, 62, 66–8, 70, 77, 87, 107, 113, 135
writing *see* literacy skills
wug test 37

Yalçın, S. 111
Yelland, G.W. 38–41

Zietek, A.A. 111